Y0-BIY-752

OXFORD HISTORICAL SERIES
Editors
V. H. GALBRAITH   J. S. WATSON   R. B. WERNHAM

BRITISH SERIES

NOTE

This series comprises carefully selected studies which have been submitted, or are based upon theses submitted, for higher degrees in this University. In 1948 a new General Series was added to a British Series. The British Series is a collection of works which advance knowledge of the structural development, whether political, ecclesiastical, or economic, of British society. The General Series comprises works on any aspect of non-British history, and also works on British history which lie outside the scope of the British Series.

The works listed below are those still in print

BRITISH SERIES

The Medieval Administration of the Channel Islands, 1199–1399.
By J. H. LE PATOUREL. 1937.

Public Order and Popular Disturbances, 1660–1714.
By M. BELOFF. 1938.

The Corporation of Leicester. By R. W. GREAVES. 1939.

Northamptonshire County Elections and Electioneering, 1695–1832.
By ERIC G. FORRESTER. 1941.

The English Lands of the Abbey of Bec. By M. MORGAN. 1946.

The Economic Development of some Leicestershire Estates.
By R. H. HILTON. 1947.

The Oxfordshire Election of 1754. By R. J. ROBSON. 1949.

Durham Jurisdictional Peculiars. By FRANK BARLOW. 1950.

Medieval Ecclesiastical Courts in the Diocese of Canterbury.
By BRIAN L. WOODCOCK. 1952.

The English Land Tax in the Eighteenth Century.
By W. R. WARD. 1953.

The Shrewsbury Drapers and the Welsh Wool Trade in the XVI and XVII Centuries. By T. C. MENDENHALL. 1953.

English Monasteries and their Patrons in the Thirteenth Century.
By SUSAN WOOD. 1955.

Feudal Military Service in England. By I. J. SANDERS. 1956.

Wellington's Headquarters. By S. G. P. WARD. 1957.

The Embassy of Sir William White at Constantinople, 1886–1891.
By COLIN L. SMITH. 1957.

The Estates of the Percy Family, 1416–1537. By J. M. W. BEAN. 1958.

GENERAL SERIES

Canonization and Authority in the Western Church. By E. W. KEMP. 1948.

Indians Overseas in British Territories, 1834–54.
By J. M. CUMPSTON. 1953.

The Viceroyalty of Lord Ripon, 1880–1884. By S. GOPAL. 1952.

THE INDEPENDENT IRISH PARTY 1850-9

By

J. H. WHYTE

OXFORD UNIVERSITY PRESS

1958

Oxford University Press, Amen House, London E.C.4
GLASGOW NEW YORK TORONTO MELBOURNE WELLINGTON
BOMBAY CALCUTTA MADRAS KARACHI KUALA LUMPUR
CAPE TOWN IBADAN NAIROBI ACCRA

© *Oxford University Press 1958*

PRINTED IN GREAT BRITAIN

PREFACE

THE movement which forms the subject of this book is almost the least-known link in the chain of Irish agitation which spans the 120 years of the union with Great Britain. The sequence into which it falls is well charted: it is preceded by Emmet's rebellion, the agitation for Catholic emancipation, the tithe war, the repeal movement, and the insurrection of 1848; it is followed by the Fenian disturbances, the exploits of the Home Rule party, and the culmination of the whole series in Sinn Fein. Many of these other movements have called forth a substantial literature: there are plenty of books on the Home Rulers and Sinn Fein, and a number on the Fenians and Young Ireland. O'Connell and Parnell have repeatedly formed subjects for study, and even some of their followers are entombed in full-length biographies. The Irish parliamentary party of the eighteen-fifties, however, has been almost totally overlooked.

The main reason for this, probably, is the extreme ineffectiveness which the movement displayed. Formed by a coalition of two distinct bodies, one representing an agrarian and the other a religious cause, it recruited a nominal following of well over forty M.P.s at the first general election which it fought. But the façade of strength was hardly erected before it began to crumble. Within a few months some of the most prominent members of the party had deserted it; within three years it had shrunk to a mere handful; within seven it had finally ceased to exist as a distinct parliamentary group. It left little mark on the parliaments of its day: not one of the reforms for which it agitated reached the statute book until long after it had ceased to exist as a party, and all but the most detailed political histories of the period find it possible to describe events entirely in terms of Conservative, Liberal, and Peelite, without even mentioning the Irish party.

Yet failures can be as interesting as successes. They may throw quite as much light on the history of their times. This is undoubtedly true of the Irish party of the fifties, for it played an important part in the development of Irish national politics, and its history provides the clues for many later developments. The Fenian movement in the sixties, for instance, owed much of its appeal to the widespread disgust with constitutional agitation that followed the collapse of the party of the fifties; so that in elucidating the causes of that collapse light is necessarily thrown on Fenian origins. Again, the leaders of the Home Rule party in the seventies and eighties were consciously trying to avoid the mistakes of their predecessors; and the policies of Butt and Parnell, different though they were, can be only incompletely understood unless the memories which they had of the fate of previous parliamentary movements are borne in mind. Thirdly, the contrast between the success of the early Home Rule party, gaining in numbers and in spirit at each successive general election, and the failure in the fifties to maintain a party of any kind for more than a few years, suggests that the earlier movement must have faced obstacles in the electoral field that had disappeared by the time its successor rose to prominence. It is not the purpose of this study to pursue these comparisons farther, and indeed they cannot be satisfactorily worked out until some scholar studies Fenianism and the early Home Rule party far more thoroughly than has yet been done. But the fact that such parallels can be drawn suggests that a history of the Irish party of 1850–9 should prove useful in fields beyond its immediate subject.

Of the few existing books on this period, the earliest is A. M. Sullivan's *New Ireland*, first published in 1877. This was a survey of Irish history from the forties to the seventies of the nineteenth century, by the editor of the leading Nationalist weekly of his day, and, as its authorship would lead one to expect, it possessed the merits of first-rate journalism. It was vividly written and it had an enormous success in its day, going through six editions in its first year of publication. A particularly agreeable feature of the book was its total lack of bitterness; for although the author had strongly-held and extreme views on Irish politics, he treated opponents of all hues from Fenians to Orangemen with a tolerance and even generosity that inspired confidence in his objectivity. This combination of merits—of readability and apparent lack of bias—has had its natural reward and every subsequent historian of the period, thankful to find so attractive a presentation of it, has relied, at least in part, on A. M. Sullivan.

But this reliance has had unfortunate consequences, for Sullivan's work has its defects as well as its merits. Writing in the intervals of a busy life, the author, it seems, often preferred to rely on his memory rather than check his references, and the result is that his work is marred by serious errors of fact and emphasis. Subsequent writers, in borrowing from him, have all too frequently accepted the errors as well as the truth to be found in his book.

Nine years after *New Ireland* came out, there appeared the only history yet published of the Irish party of the eighteen-fifties: Sir Charles Gavan Duffy's *The League of North and South*. Duffy was well qualified to write a history of the movement, for he was an author of distinction and had himself taken a prominent part in the events which he described. His narrative expands, and in some places tacitly corrects, Sullivan's account, and as it is the only full-scale study of the movement in print it has formed, even more than Sullivan's work, the basis of all subsequent accounts of the period.

But Duffy's work, like Sullivan's, is not without its limitations. He takes for granted points which need explanation for present-day readers, such as the scope and nature of the immense political influence of the Catholic clergy. He ends his account in 1855, at the point when he himself broke off his connexion with the movement, with the result that later writers have assumed, quite incorrectly, that the movement itself came to an end in that year. Although he is apparently free from any conscious attempt to magnify his own importance, the fact that he is telling the story as it appeared to him means that the part which he himself played is overstressed, and some modern writers have in consequence even referred to the movement as 'Duffy's party', although he was at no stage the most important member of it. He is disappointingly reticent on the inner workings of the movement; and only at two points does he give important information not to be found elsewhere: on the negotiations with the Conservatives in December 1852 and on the mission to Rome in 1855. His book seems indeed to have been put together largely from the back numbers of his own old paper, the *Nation*, for most of the information he gives can be traced back to its pages.

Only two other books so far published are of much value for the history of the party, both of them biographies of men prominent in its counsels. *The Life of Frederick Lucas, M.P.*, published in 1886 by his brother Edward Lucas, is for most of its length an uncritical compilation from articles in Frederick Lucas's old paper, the *Tablet*, but it is saved from worthlessness by the fact that it includes the bulk of the lengthy memorandum which he wrote for the Pope in 1855. M. G. Moore's *An Irish Gentleman, George Henry Moore*, which appeared in 1913, is a much better work, based with skill on the papers of the author's father, but, although it makes some shrewd corrections to Duffy's picture of the facts, it deals only incidentally with the movement as a whole. No author, then, has produced an entirely satisfactory account of the party and there appears to be room for a fresh study of it.

There seem to be two main questions which any such study must answer, two main points of interest in the party's history. The first is how it ever came to reach the apparently formidable position which it had attained at the end of 1852, and the second is how it came to lose this position so completely that in seven years it had ceased to exist: or, more briefly, how did the party rise and how did it fall. This book is constructed, therefore, so that the answers to these two questions will clearly emerge, and it is divided consequently into two parts: the first section discusses the reasons for the party's development and the second the causes of its decline.

It is a pleasure to express my thanks to those who have helped me in the writing of this book. Professor N. H. Gibbs was the supervisor of the B.Litt. thesis from which it developed, and initiated me into the ways of research. Professor T. W. Moody, Professor R. Dudley Edwards, Mr. T. P. O'Neill, Mr. W. A. Davidson, and Mr. T. Charles Edwards all read the typescript at one stage or another and offered valuable suggestions. I derived particular profit from a searching critique by Professor Edwards of an earlier draft of this work. Mr. T. P. O'Neill generously lent me his own notes on the period, and Mr. B. A. Kennedy lent me his M.A. thesis on 'The Struggle for Tenant-Right in Ulster, 1829–50'. Most of all, I owe thanks to my mother for constant encouragement and much practical help.

J. H. W.

CONTENTS

ABBREVIATIONS   xiii

Part I
THE RISE OF THE INDEPENDENT IRISH PARTY

I. THE TENANT LEAGUE	1
II. THE IRISH BRIGADE	14
III. THE ALLIANCE BETWEEN THE LEAGUE AND THE BRIGADE	31
IV. THE SEARCH FOR CANDIDATES	39
V. THE FAILURE OF THE CONSERVATIVE OFFENSIVE	54
VI. THE INFLUENCE OF LANDLORDS AND CLERGY	63
VII. THE ZENITH OF THE INDEPENDENT IRISH PARTY	82

Part II
THE DECLINE OF THE INDEPENDENT IRISH PARTY

VIII. THE DEFECTION OF KEOGH AND SADLEIR	93
IX. THE QUARREL WITH THE BISHOPS	110
X. THE FAILURE OF LEADERSHIP	124
XI. THE DISINTEGRATION OF THE PARLIAMENTARY PARTY	142
XII. THE PARTY AND THE COUNTRY	158

APPENDIXES

A. IRISH LIBERAL M.P.S 1851–2	178
B. IRISH LIBERAL M.P.S 1852–7	180
C. IRISH LIBERAL M.P.S 1857–9	182
BIBLIOGRAPHY	184
INDEX	191

ABBREVIATIONS

B.M. Add. MS.	British Museum Additional Manuscript.
Corruption Committee	Report of the 'Corruption Committee', i.e. *Report from the select committee on complaint (7th February), together with the proceedings of the committee, and the minutes of evidence,* House of Commons papers 1854 (314), viii.
D.E.	*Daily Express.*
Digest of Devon Report	Digest of the report of the Devon Commission, i.e. [J. P. Kennedy], *Digest of evidence taken before Her Majesty's commissioners of inquiry into the state of the law and practice in respect to the occupation of land in Ireland.*
Duffy, *League*	Sir C. G. Duffy, *The League of North and South.*
elect. comm.	Report of an election commission.
elect. pet.	Report of the trial of an election petition.
F.J.	*Freeman's Journal.*
N.L.I.	National Library of Ireland.
Parl. Deb.	*Parliamentary Debates.*

PART I

THE RISE OF THE INDEPENDENT IRISH PARTY

I

THE TENANT LEAGUE

IN the early eighteen-forties, hundreds of thousands of the Irish peasantry were on the verge of destitution. In the years before the great famine their utter poverty impressed every observer. A German traveller, who could make the comparison from personal experience, said that they were worse off than the Letts or the Esthonians, the Russians or Serbs or Bosnians.[1] A Frenchman declared that he had found the North American Indians better provided for.[2] An American, describing the people she saw, concluded: 'I had travelled by sea and by land among the savages of my own country, the poor abused slaves on the plantations, the degraded, untutored, native Canadians: but this eclipsed the whole.'[3] And a Royal Commission, though speaking with the moderation becoming to an official body, reported that the labouring classes probably endured greater sufferings than any other people in Europe.[4] Again and again visitors noticed the same things—the wretchedness of the houses:

There are thousands of cabins in which not a trace of a window is to be seen; nothing but a little square hole in front, which doubles the duty of door, window, and chimney; light, smoke, pigs, and children, all must pass in and out of the same aperture;[5]

---

[1] J. G. Kohl, *Ireland, Scotland and England*, pp. 47-48.
[2] Quoted ibid., p. 47.
[3] A. Nicholson, *Ireland's Welcome to the Stranger*, p. 30.
[4] *Digest* of the Devon Report, ii, p. 1116.
[5] J. G. Kohl, op. cit., p. 48.

the complete lack of worldly goods:

Day clothes scanty, bed clothes almost none, and the children seeking warmth by contact with the pig;[1]

and the monotony of the diet:

For ten months in the year their sole, or almost sole, food is potatoes and a little salt; and as the summer approaches and their stock of potatoes becomes nearly exhausted, they are often obliged to content themselves with a single meal a day.[2]

The impression of so many observers is borne out by official statistics. It was calculated that, as a rough average for the country as a whole, the minimum size of holding that would support a family was eight acres.[3] The figures available on the size of holdings are defective and to some extent contradictory, but it seems that out of something like 800,000 occupiers of land in Ireland well over 300,000 held less than this essential minimum. Many of these would be able to supplement the produce of their holdings by hiring out their labour; but as the supply of labour was greater than the demand there must have been many who could barely make ends meet, and even so this figure takes no account of those who had no holdings at all and were entirely dependent on their employment.[4] A more revealing statistic is that for housing, for the Census Commissioners found that in 1841 no less than 43 per cent. of the people in the Irish countryside were living in the very lowest class of accommodation, mud cabins with only one room.[5] It seems safe to conclude that the proportion of the Irish rural population living on the destitution line was certainly greater than one-third and was probably not less than two-fifths.

Much of this distress, of course, was due to circumstances beyond any government's control: the poor quality of the soil in some districts, the overpopulation of many more, and, perhaps, defects in the character of the people as well. But there was one cause which was not beyond the reach of legislation. This was the lack of incentive to im-

[1] John Wiggins, *The Monster Misery of Ireland*, p. 23.
[2] [James Grant], *Impressions of Ireland and the Irish*, ii, p. 143.
[3] *Digest* of Devon Report, i, p. 399.
[4] For a discussion of the figures see ibid., p. 396.
[5] Quoted ibid., p. 126.

prove. It was generally agreed that, small and overcrowded though their holdings often were, the Irish tenants failed to obtain anything like the full benefit from them that they might have done. The reason appeared to be that they had no guarantee that if they made more profit they would be allowed to keep it. The great majority were tenants-at-will, holding for only a year at a time, and if they improved their land there was nothing to stop the landlord raising the rent the following year, or even turning them out and putting in someone else, leaving them with no return for their efforts.[1] How frequently this actually happened was a matter for argument; but the threat was enough to have a psychological effect on the people.[2] It might be objected that the law was the same in other parts of the British Isles, and did not seem to have the same discouraging effect there. But though the law was the same, the custom was different. In England and Scotland, when a landlord let a farm, he let it as a going concern; he first built the farm-buildings and provided the fences and gates, and afterwards held himself responsible for their repair. In Ulster, the tenant had to equip his own holding, but, as we shall see, custom guaranteed him some security even if law did not. Only in the three southern provinces of Ireland did the extraordinary system prevail whereby the tenant had the worst of both worlds, and was neither granted a farm in good order nor given the encouragement to put it in good order himself.

There was widespread agreement on what the remedy should be. It was suggested that a landlord should be legally bound to compensate an outgoing tenant for any improvements he had made in his holding. This was not unjust to the landlord, for he was paying his money in return for a definite benefit; and it did encourage the tenant, for he knew that he would still receive some return for his hard work even if he had to leave his holding. So sensible did the proposal seem that it was supported by people of many different classes; no fewer than 146 of the witnesses before the Devon

---

[1] *Digest* of Devon Report, i, pp. 156–7.
[2] The Devon Commision did not find many such cases of oppression: see ibid., p. 157; but others argued that they were common: see Lucas's speech in *Parl. Deb.*, series 3, cxxiii. 1545–57 (15 Dec. 1852).

Commission suggested it, and the Commissioners themselves reported in its favour.[1] But despite this distinguished advocacy, no government showed much anxiety to put the proposal into effect. Bills were indeed brought in with that purpose in 1845, 1846, 1848, and 1850; but none of them was strongly pressed and in the event none went beyond the committee stage in the House in which it had been introduced. Here, then, was a grievance of the first magnitude: an enormous evil, the want of security; a clear remedy, compulsory compensation for improvements; and yet a complete failure on the part of the Government to do anything about it.

If affairs were serious even before the famine, they grew far worse after it. Two grievances in particular became prominent. The first was the level of rents. Rents had always been high in Ireland, in relation to the ability of the tenants to meet them,[2] but their payment now became often impossible. True, many of the landlords lowered their rents and wiped off part or all of the arrears due.[3] But the landlords themselves were faced with crushing new burdens, such as a poor rate which in places reached the limit of taxable capacity, and were often in no position to be generous even had they wanted to. The result, in only too many places, was a direct collision. The columns of the press in the years following the famine sometimes read as if a civil war were breaking out. In a belt of counties from Kerry to Wexford the peasantry were organizing themselves in bodies and carrying their crops or cattle into hiding to prevent the landlords seizing them for rent.[4] Landlords were retaliating by placing guards on the crops while they were still growing. In places pitched battles occurred between the bailiffs and the peasantry, which more than once resulted in loss of life.[5]

The second fresh grievance was a vast increase in the number of evictions. Many landlords, determined to make their estates solvent once more, were ruthlessly clearing off

[1] *Digest* of Devon Report, i, p. 154; ii, p. 1125.
[2] Ibid., ii, p. 756.
[3] Fifteen instances are reported in a single issue of the strongly anti-landlord *Nation*: 20 Oct. 1849.
[4] e.g. *Dublin Evening Mail*, 1 Oct. 1849, gives eleven cases in a single issue.
[5] e.g. two examples in *Nation*, 15 Sept. 1849.

tenants who could pay no rent, while others were rooting out their smallholders because they believed that larger farms were more economic and would in the long run bring more prosperity to the country. The Earl of Lucan depopulated a great tract of Mayo; Major Mahon evicted 3,000 people in County Roscommon.[1] Whole columns of the newspapers, sometimes, were given up to the names of those turned out of their holdings; and official figures for the number of people evicted within the knowledge of the police reached the enormous totals of 90,000 in 1849 and 104,000 in 1850.[2] In the years after the famine there was beyond question an appalling amount of misery in the three southern provinces of Ireland. Any one of the three grievances—insecurity of tenure, high rents, and the wave of evictions—could have provided the material for a major agitation. Taken together, they made such an agitation almost inevitable.

Attempts had been made to organize the tenants in self-defence as early as 1847. In January a Tenant League was established in County Cork,[3] and during the year other organizations were set up in at least four other counties.[4] One of these—that inaugurated at Holycross, County Tipperary[5]—is worth a passing mention because of the posthumous influence which its founder, James Fintan Lalor, had on the views of a later generation in Ireland. But none proved a success at the time, two or three meetings seems to have been the most that any of them held, and two years later no trace of them is to be found.

The first society to secure a permanent following was formed at Callan, County Kilkenny, on 14 October 1849.[6] The principal local landlord, the Earl of Desart, evicted 442 persons during these years from his Callan estate,[7] and his rents, in the opinion of the local inhabitants, were about

---

[1] S. G. Osborne, *Gleanings in the West of Ireland*, pp. 107–8; *Weekly F. J.*, 29 Apr. 1848.
[2] *Return . . . of cases of evictions which have come to the knowledge of the constabulary in each of the years from 1849 to 1880*, H.C. 1881 (185), lxxvii.
[3] *F.J.*, 31 Jan. 1847.
[4] For Mayo see *F.J.*, 1 Dec. 1847; for Waterford, Wexford, and Tipperary see *F.J.*, 31 Dec. 1847.
[5] *F.J.*, 20 Sept. 1847.   [6] *Nation*, 20 Oct. 1849.
[7] E. Lucas, *Life of Frederick Lucas*, ii, pp. 217–19.

three times what they might reasonably have been expected to pay.[1] Feeling that the only chance of justice was to combine against the oppressor, the curates of the parish—Fathers O'Shea and Keeffe—founded an organization called the Callan Tenant Protection Society. Its avowed aim was to obtain rents fixed by a valuer independent of the landlord, and its members pledged themselves not to take the land of any evicted tenant who had been prepared to pay a rent so valued.[2]

This was, at last, doing something definite, and the idea soon took hold. Ballyhale, County Kilkenny, was the next place to form a Tenant Protection Society, and it was soon followed by places in Tipperary and Wexford. By March the movement had reached Louth and Kildare; during May it gained its first foothold in Connaught. By the middle of the year at least twenty different societies had been founded in ten different counties.[3] Public interest mounted in proportion to the number of societies: tenant meetings were being held in many places even where no organizations had been formed, and the press was devoting more and more of its space to the movement. By the summer of 1850 the tenants' movement was the outstanding feature of public life in the southern provinces.

Meanwhile, a distinct agitation had been growing up among the tenant-farmers of Ulster. The land system in the

---

[1] *Nation*, 15 Dec. 1849.   [2] Ibid., 10 Nov. 1849.
[3] The dates on which the *Nation*, which was following the movement particularly closely, noticed the formation of each new society, are as follows:

Place	County	Date mentioned	Place	County	Date mentioned
Callan	Kilkenny	20 Oct. 1849	Inniskeen	Louth	23 Feb. 1850
Ballyhale	,,	3 Nov.	Cashel	Tipperary	2 Mar.
Mullinahone	Tipperary	10 Nov.	Galmoy	Kilkenny	9 Mar.
Enniscorthy	Wexford	17 Nov.	Baltinglass	Kildare	23 Mar.
Dunamaggin	Kilkenny	1 Dec.	Clonalvey	Meath	13 Apr.
Limerick	Limerick	1 Dec.	Millstreet	Cork	11 May
Windgap	Kilkenny	8 Dec.	Mayglass	Wexford	11 May
Newtownbarry	Wexford	12 Jan. 1850	Castlebar	Mayo	18 May
Ballingarry	Tipperary	26 Jan.	Kanturk	Cork	25 May
Castlecomer	Kilkenny	9 Feb.	Tuam	Galway	15 June

north differed in one important respect from that of the southern provinces. This difference lay in the prevalence of the custom known as tenant-right. In its details the custom varied from estate to estate, but its essential feature was the right of an outgoing tenant to receive from an incoming tenant a goodwill payment for the farm.[1] This payment often reached a considerable figure—£10, £12, or even £20 an acre.[2] The confidence that he would receive it if he were ever to lose his holding gave the northern tenant that encouragement to spend his energies on the farm which the southern tenant lacked; and, at least partly because of this custom, Ulster had become decidedly the most prosperous province in Ireland. Tenant-right was not recognized by law; but it was backed by a public opinion so determined that landlords seldom dared to ignore it.[3]

The Ulster tenantry, then, did not feel the southern grievance of insecurity of tenure, but the very fact that they were better off gave grounds for another grievance of their own, for they suspected that many landlords would be glad to see them reduced to the same status as their southern neighbours. Witnesses before the Devon Commission, for instance, had stressed the disadvantages of the Ulster custom—that idle tenants could obtain the benefit of it as well as industrious ones, and that an incoming tenant might spend so much on buying the goodwill that he had no capital left for improvements.[4] The Commission itself called it an 'anomalous custom' and only grudgingly admitted the benefits it provided.[5] The Government had tried, however half-heartedly, to do something for the southern tenants by introducing the bills of 1845 and 1846, but it had pointedly avoided taking any steps to protect the Ulster custom. In 1847 Sharman Crawford, Radical M.P. for Rochdale and himself an Ulsterman, tried to repair the omission by bringing in a bill to legalize tenant-right, but it was ignominiously defeated by 112 votes to 25.[6] This made the Ulster tenants suddenly aware of the weakness of their position. Opposition to their cherished custom had appeared in the legislature

---

[1] *Digest* of Devon Report, i, p. 290.　　[2] Ibid., p. 290.
[3] Ibid., p. 319.　　[4] Ibid., p. 290.　　[5] Ibid., ii, p. 1120.
[6] *Parl. Deb.*, series 3, xciii. 645 (16 June 1847).

itself, and it became important to obtain some kind of protection stronger than the force of local opinion. The first tenant-right associations were founded soon after to give Crawford the moral support he so clearly needed if he were to gain the sympathy of the Commons.[1]

Then, during 1848 and 1849, the same effects of the famine as were ravaging the south—high rents and a wave of evictions—made themselves felt in Ulster. In Antrim, the Marquis of Hertford's tenants met and resolved that their rents were 30 per cent. higher than the whole value of their farms.[2] In Monaghan, Mr. Shirley of Lough Fea ejected 260 tenants from his estates in peculiarly barbarous circumstances and made himself perhaps the most notorious evictor in the whole of Ireland.[3] In Donegal there was even to be found a landlord who chose 1849, of all years, to carry out a general raising of his rents.[4] Early in 1850 the tenants' societies founded three years before burst into renewed activity, and a chain of meetings was held across the province to demand once again the legalization of tenant-right. The tenants now received reinforcement from an important new quarter, for the Presbyterian ministers took up their demands in force. Four out of five synods of the Presbyterian Church, and then the General Assembly itself, petitioned Parliament in favour of the legal protection of tenant-right, and a strong deputation, composed largely of ministers, went to London to press their views on leading statesmen of the various parties.[5] By the summer of 1850 the tenant-right movement in the north occupied the same important position as the tenant-protection societies in the south.

These parallel movements among the tenant-farmers of north and south reached their climax at a time when there was no other great issue in Irish politics. From 1842 to 1848 the burning question had been the repeal of the legislative union between Ireland and Great Britain. At its height the

---

[1] B. A. Kennedy, 'The Tenant-Right Agitation in Ulster, 1845–50', in *Bulletin of the Irish Committee of Historical Sciences*, no. 34, p. 3.
[2] *Nation*, 12 Jan. 1850.   [3] Ibid., 22 Sept. 1849.
[4] Ibid., 28 Dec. 1850.
[5] B. A. Kennedy, 'The Tenant-Right Agitation in Ulster, 1845–50', in *Bulletin of the Irish Committee of Historical Sciences*, no. 34, p. 5.

repeal movement had been one of the most impressive demonstrations of popular feeling the world had ever seen, with O'Connell addressing crowds hundreds of thousands strong. But in its later years the movement had split in two. O'Connell's own followers had won many seats at the general election of 1847; but he himself had died shortly before and his party did not even bring up the question of repeal in Parliament. John O'Connell, indeed, revived the Repeal Association in 1849;[1] but he had only a shadow of his father's greatness, he drew small audiences and still smaller subscriptions, and by the summer of 1850 he found it necessary to adjourn the meetings for lack of support.[2] Meanwhile the other wing of the movement—the Young Irelanders—had grown by degrees more intransigent, and had ended by attempting, in July 1848, to raise the country in revolt. The attempt had failed, and nearly all their prominent members had been transported or had fled the country. Charles Gavan Duffy, who alone of their leaders escaped both these fates, admitted, when he re-entered public life in 1849, that repeal was no longer a practical objective.[3] In this situation, then, with the leading Young Irelander frankly admitting failure and the leading Old Irelander patently suffering it, it was clear that the repeal movement was moribund.

This left many influential people, who had hitherto been taken up with the movement, free to transfer their attention elsewhere. To men of such opinions the tenants' agitation had an obvious attraction, for if they could no longer gain legislative independence they might at least hope, by taking up the tenants' cause, to win for Ireland important practical reforms.

Foremost in this group were three quite young men, none of them yet forty, editors of influential papers in Dublin. First was Dr. John Gray, part-owner of the *Freeman's Journal*, the only daily paper in Ireland with popular sympathies. His leading articles were turgid and his speeches often commonplace, but he was a man of determined

---

[1] *Weekly F.J.*, 13 Oct. 1849.
[2] *F.J.*, 10 July 1850: the previous week's subscriptions came to £4. 10s.
[3] *Nation*, 1 Sept. 1849.

character who had gone to prison for his repeal convictions in 1844 and was in later life an energetic promoter of improvements on the Dublin Corporation. A Protestant himself, he was anxious to conciliate the Catholic hierarchy—he was later to accomplish the remarkable feat of remaining on good terms with Archbishop Cullen and Archbishop MacHale at the same time—and his influence was generally thrown on the side of moderation.

Second comes Charles Gavan Duffy, owner and editor of the *Nation*. Duffy had in 1848 incited the people of Ireland to revolt, and many regarded him as a wild and dangerous man. But he was very far from being a revolutionary by nature. If he had never gone into politics he would probably still have been widely known as a man of letters, and his friends included men so diverse as Thomas Carlyle, Cardinal Newman, and John Stuart Mill. As a politician he preferred constitutional to violent methods; and during the Young Ireland agitation he had formed definite ideas about how an Irish movement should be run. He placed his reliance on an Irish parliamentary party, authoritative enough to speak in the name of the country and strong enough to hold the balance between the English factions. But it was not to be a party such as O'Connell had allowed to form behind him. O'Connell's followers shouted loudly enough for repeal on the hustings, but once they reached Parliament they had lost no time in soliciting places from the Liberal Government with which O'Connell was temporarily allied. Duffy calculated that of thirty-eight Repealers elected in the thirties no less than ten received office or titles for themselves.[1] There would be no harm in this so long as the Liberal policy was one which Irishmen could conscientiously support; but the danger would come when they were forced to choose between opposing the Government in the interests of Ireland and supporting it in the interest of themselves, for all too many seemed likely to put their own interests first. There seemed only one way to safeguard the purity of intention of Irish members, and that was to pledge them to accept no favours at the hands of any British government until Ireland's demands were won.[2] This idea of Duffy's is crucial

[1] Sir C. G. Duffy, *My Life in Two Hemispheres*, i, p. 193. [2] Ibid., p. 249.

to the subject of this book—for from it springs the whole project of maintaining an independent, pledge-bound, Irish parliamentary party, distinct from all English groupings.

Third in the triumvirate comes Frederick Lucas. Born in 1812, he was older than Gray by three years and Duffy by four; he was an Englishman, a Quaker by upbringing but a convert to Catholicism. He had founded his paper, the *Tablet*, in 1840 to be the organ in England of his new co-religionists; but feeling that he would have a surer following among the more numerous Catholics of Ireland, he transferred it to Dublin at the end of 1849.[1] As a journalist he was marked by passionate loyalty to his Church, deep sympathy with the poor, and quite remarkable powers of vituperation. The *Tablet*, unlike the *Nation* and the *Freeman's Journal*, is still in existence; but those who know and respect it today would find it hard to recognize in its form of a hundred years ago. Lucas's indignation at the sufferings of the Irish poor led him into unrestrained denunciations of government and landlords: so violent was his language and so extreme his opinions that the Lord-Lieutenant could describe his journal as 'one of the most virulent and most offensive newspapers in all Europe . . . the object of which is to abolish the rights of property and to shake to its very foundations everything on which society depends'.[2] But he was absolutely sincere, and was to turn out the strongest personality in the tenants' movement.

By the spring of 1850, then, all the elements were prepared for a national movement on behalf of the tenants. There were flourishing agitations in both north and south, and leaders to organize the movement were available in Dublin. In April provisional secretaries—Lucas, Gray, and a northerner, Greer—came forward to arrange a conference between all the interests,[3] and at the end of that month an invitation went out to 'all existing Tenant Societies, to the popular journalists and to the most active and influential friends of Tenant Right, in localities which have not yet

[1] E. Lucas, *Life of Frederick Lucas*, i, p. 363.
[2] *Tablet*, 26 Apr. 1851.
[3] Named in *Nation*, 11 May 1850.

been organised'.[1] The invitation was signed by the secretaries and, to broaden the appeal, by John O'Connell and Gavan Duffy—representatives of Old and Young Ireland respectively—by the Lord Mayor and Town Clerk of Dublin, by a second prominent northerner, Dr. M'Knight, and by Gray's partner in the ownership of the *Freeman's Journal*, J. M. Cantwell.[2]

The conference met on 6, 7, and 8 August.[3] The published list of persons present gives about 180 names, roughly one-third of them being Catholic or Presbyterian clergy. The attendance was, geographically, decidedly patchy: well over half of it was accounted for by four counties, Meath, Dublin, Wexford, and Kilkenny, while Connaught seems to have had only a single representative. But the encouraging fact about the conference was the presence of a solid contingent from Ulster: about ten Presbyterian ministers, four Catholic clergy, and fourteen laymen. The co-operation of Presbyterians and Catholics for a common object was an event unexampled since the Union, and tenant-right papers in both north and south grew almost lyrical in their praise of the union of hearts which they claimed it demonstrated.[4] The claim was indeed justified by the proceedings of the conference, for the two groups worked together in harmony and reached without difficulty a common programme that would amply cover the complaints of all the tenantry both north and south. Their main demands may be summarized as follows: (1) tenants should be assured of a fair rent, fixed by an impartial valuation; (2) they should have security of tenure as long as they paid their rents; and (3) they should be able to sell their interest in their holdings at the best price they could obtain. In conclusion, the conference set up, as its instrument for attaining these aims, an organization to be known as the Irish Tenant League.

The new League met for the first time on 9 August 1850. In its deliberations Duffy's ideal of an independent parliamentary party emerged once more: for one of the recom-

---

[1] *Nation*, 27 Apr. 1850.
[2] Ibid., 11 May 1850.
[3] *F.J.*, 7, 8, and 9 Aug. 1850.
[4] See, e.g., *Banner of Ulster*, 13 Aug. 1850; *Londonderry Standard*, 15 Aug. 1850; *Nation*, 10 Aug. 1850; *Cork Examiner*, 12 Aug. 1850.

mendations of the conference was that the new League should support only 'representatives, who will give a written pledge that they will support in and out of Parliament a tenant law, based upon, and carrying into effect, the principles adopted by the Irish Tenant League; and that they will withhold all support from any cabinet that will not advance those principles . . . '.[1] This wording was more stringent in intention than anything Young Ireland had proposed, for the latter had wanted a party pledged merely to take no places from English governments, and now the League was to have one pledged to withhold support from them. At the time the resolution does not seem to have been considered particularly important: it was put almost at the end of the list and comparatively insignificant members of the League were selected to propose it. The main emphasis was on the direct influencing of public opinion: on printed propaganda and public meetings, on founding local associations and organizing petitions to Parliament. But the decision to enter the parliamentary field, however little regarded at the time, was to be of crucial importance later on: for it marks the first step in the foundation of an independent Irish party.

[1] *F.J.*, 10 Aug. 1850.

II

THE IRISH BRIGADE

THE Tenant League decided to enter parliamentary politics at a moment when party distinctions in the House of Commons were unusually confused. Four years previously Sir Robert Peel had split the Conservatives asunder by repealing the corn laws, and there were now three parties in the House, Conservatives, Peelites, and Liberals. To complicate matters still further, the Liberals were divided into two wings, Whig and Radical, and there was a large number of members in all parties who showed little respect for discipline and who were quite prepared on occasion to vote against their friends. Accurate figures of party strengths are in these circumstances out of the question, but roughly it may be said that the Liberals mustered a little over half the House, the Conservatives one-third, and the Peelites less than a sixth. A Liberal government was in office under Lord John Russell.

The 105 members for Ireland could be grouped into the same three parties as the members for Great Britain. Sixty-four of them could in 1850 be considered as Liberals, four as Peelites, and thirty-seven as Conservatives, though it must be emphasized that they are just as difficult to classify as those from any other part of the United Kingdom and that several might well have been listed under some other heading than the one to which they have been assigned here. All the Peelites belonged to the Established Church, as did all the Conservatives with the exception of a solitary Presbyterian; while the Liberals included thirty members of the Established Church and thirty-four Catholics.

It is worth glancing at each group in turn to see how much support the Tenant League could expect to receive from among the existing representatives of Ireland.

It would be unfair to describe the Irish Conservatives as totally hostile to the claims of the tenantry. Though they had been unfriendly even to the moderate government measures of 1848 and 1850, their objections had been based on the details of the bill rather than on its principle,[1] and one of their legal members, Joseph Napier, was already preparing the comprehensive scheme of land reform that he was to introduce two years later.[2] But the fact remains that no bill had yet been introduced which the Conservatives had been willing to support; they were suspicious of any measure that even to a limited degree restricted the landlords' rights; and their spokesmen considered the problem avowedly from the landlords' point of view. The demands of the Tenant League certainly went far beyond anything that they could be expected even to contemplate.

The Irish Peelites were a rapidly dwindling band. The English leaders of the party were individually very able men, but they did nothing to keep their following together. They appointed no whips, they set up no club to act as a Peelite counterpart to the Carlton and Reform, and their neglect had its natural effect on the rank and file, who drifted to one or other of the two main parties.[3] This trend was clearly noticeable among their Irish followers. In 1847 they had formed an appreciable portion of the Irish representation—*The Times*'s classification had given them thirteen members—but by 1850 most of them had drifted back to the Conservatives, some were no longer in Parliament, and one, William Keogh, M.P. for Athlone, had gone over to the Liberals. Of the four who could still be classified as Peelites,[4] three were to retire in the next two years and only a single survivor, Sir John Young, was to stay on into the succeeding parliament. The Irish Peelites showed themselves in debate rather more friendly to the tenantry than the Conservatives;[5] but they had not the power, even if they had the will, to give the tenants' cause much aid.

---

[1] See, e.g., speeches of Lord Claude Hamilton and Thomas Conolly, *Parl. Deb.*, series 3, xcix. 979 and 985 (21 June 1848).

[2] J. L. Montrose, 'The Landlord and Tenant Act of 1860', in *Bulletin of the Irish Committee of Historical Sciences*, no. 1.

[3] This process is described in C. H. Stuart, 'The Formation of the Coalition Cabinet of 1852', in *Trans. R. Hist. Soc.* (5th ser.), iv, pp. 48–49.

[4] Viscount Castlereagh (Down), Viscount Northland (Dungannon), Sir H. Seymour (Lisburn), Sir John Young (Cavan).

[5] See, e.g., speech of Viscount Castlereagh, *Parl. Deb.*, series 3, cviii. 1022 (18 Feb. 1850).

The Irish Liberals of 1850 have sometimes been painted as servile hacks of the ministry, anxious only to vote as the whips required. A study of the division lists shows, however, that this is simply untrue. Only about one-third of the Irish Liberal M.P.s could be called consistent followers of the government: the majority had all voted against the ministry at one time or another on an important issue, and scarcely a single ministerial measure in that parliament escaped being opposed by some at least of the Irish Liberal members. The suspension of Habeas Corpus, for instance, was in 1848 opposed by eight Liberals and in 1849 by twenty-one; the rate-in-aid of 1849 by twenty-four, and the proposal in 1850 to abolish the Lord-Lieutenancy by nineteen.[1] Indeed the most extreme members, such as Michael Sullivan, M.P. for Kilkenny borough, or Thomas Meagher, father of the Young Ireland leader and M.P. for Waterford city, voted against the ministry more often than they supported it; and though they ranked nominally as Liberals they were worse than useless to the party whips. The truth was that the Irish Liberals, far from being of one uniform colour, included individuals of widely differing points of view. At one extreme were men such as Sir Henry Winston Barron, whose Liberalism was of so mild a hue that he frequently voted with the Conservatives. In the centre came a group of moderate members, the Irish Whigs, who generally supported the Government's policy of cautious reform but who were capable of staging a revolt when they thought it necessary: it was an Irish Whig, for instance, who moved the most dangerous amendment to the rate-in-aid scheme of 1849.[2] Finally, on the left wing of the party was a miscellaneous group of members with radical views who were inclined to think that the government did not go far enough. Many of these were survivors of O'Connell's Repeal party, and though the collapse of the repeal movement had deprived them of their principle of unity and they no longer acted together as a distinct body, that did not mean that they had lost interest in Irish grievances. Among such members

---

[1] *Parl. Deb.*, series 3, c. 743; cii. 556; ciii. 314 (Blackall's amendment to replace the rate-in-aid by an income tax); cxi. 1464.
[2] Major Blackall: see previous footnote.

as these, at least, the Tenant League might expect to find friends.

The number of M.P.s, however, who were prepared to support the Tenant League proved disappointingly small. Only two—James Fagan, M.P. for Wexford county, and William Keogh—attended its inaugural conference;[1] only four even sent letters of excuse for their absence.[2] When, in the autumn and winter, the League held a series of county demonstrations, the majority of members invited declined to attend, and of those who did appear most avoided committing themselves to the League's principles. Indeed a study of the letters and speeches of M.P.s at these demonstrations shows that only three—Dr. Maurice Power, M.P. for Cork county, Torrens M'Cullagh, M.P. for Dundalk, and Ouseley Higgins, M.P. for Mayo—could be claimed as having committed themselves unequivocally to the League's cause.[3] It soon emerged that most members, even those with radical sympathies, thought the League's demands too extreme to be practicable: Parliament had not yet accepted even the principle of compulsory compensation for improvements, so it was certainly not likely to agree to fixity of tenure and valued rents. Matthew Corbally, M.P. for Meath, replied to an invitation to attend a League meeting by declaring that 'the proceedings of the Tenant Right Conference have materially injured in public opinion a good and just cause';[4] and though most of his fellow-members were more diplomatic than he, he probably voiced the true opinion of many. As long as the majority of Irish Liberal members felt like this, the Tenant League had little immediate hope of building up an independent party in the House of Commons.

A change, however, was to come over many of the Irish members much more quickly than seemed possible at the time the Tenant League was formed. Before we explain how this happened, a word should be said about the religious situation in Ireland at this period.

---

[1] *F.J.*, 7 Aug. 1850.
[2] Higgins: *F.J.*, 7 Aug.; Moore, M'Cullagh, F. Scully: *F.J.*, 9 Aug. 1850.
[3] *Nation*, 23 Nov., 7 Dec., 21 Dec. 1850.   [4] *Nation*, 12 Oct. 1850.

The Catholic Emancipation Act of 1829 had by no means removed all the grievances of the Catholic majority. In particular, the maintenance of a Protestant Established Church in an overwhelmingly Catholic country was a standing source of irritation. The complaint that the Establishment was over-endowed could indeed be challenged—a Protestant archdeacon went so far as to claim that Church revenues were insufficient to meet essential requirements[1]— but even if that point were conceded it remained invidious that the Church of one-ninth of the population should be in a privileged position: that her bishops, for instance, should have precedence over the bishops of the mass of the people. Not much reference to the question was made in the forties, and the Catholics do not seem to have considered the grievance a pressing one; but it remained a potential cause of agitation, always at hand if they should ever become roused on another issue, and it was all the more dangerous a source of friction because many Liberal Protestants considered the Catholics had a good case. The possibilities of an agitation for disestablishment were shown when in 1849 thirty-three Irish Liberal M.P.s, including eleven Protestants, issued a manifesto describing the Established Church as 'a symbol of conquest, a perpetuation of religious inequality, and a potent cause of the social depression of the great body of the people of that kingdom', and declaring that, so long as it remained, there could never be peace or an end to religious feuds.[2]

On the other hand, many Protestants in England and Ireland, and in particular the friends of the Government, felt that they had just cause for complaint in some of the recent activities of the Catholic hierarchy. In 1845 Sir Robert Peel had embarked on a well-meaning attempt to meet the wants of Catholics and Presbyterians in university education by setting up three undenominational university colleges which would provide an alternative to the Established Church's stronghold of Dublin University; and the Russell government, on coming into office, had continued the same scheme. A majority of the Catholic bishops, how-

---

[1] Stopford, *The Income and Requirements of the Irish Church*, p. 59.
[2] *Weekly F.J.*, 28 July 1849; for further signatures see ibid., 25 Aug.

ever, opposed the colleges on the ground that the faith of Catholic students might be endangered, and in 1850 the assembled hierarchy of Ireland renewed the condemnation at the Synod of Thurles. True, the laity were not expressly forbidden to attend the new institutions, but they were certainly discouraged from doing so, and the consequence was that the infant colleges, so expensively endowed by the state, seemed likely to be crippled from the start. To a Catholic mind the bishops' decision might seem like a legitimate exercise of pastoral rights; but in many Protestants it provoked the sharpest resentment, for it meant in effect that a carefully worked out measure for the regeneration of Ireland, fostered by two successive governments and approved by Parliament, had been virtually repealed, and repealed not by any authority known to the constitution but by a small knot of men answerable to no power in the British Isles. It was easy to paint the decrees of the Synod of Thurles as being dictated by clerical ambition, and even as being part of a plot to extend the influence of the clergy over their flocks.[1]

It was in this none too happy atmosphere that an event occurred which was to bring the latent resentments on either side to sparking-point. On 29 September 1850 the Pope erected in England a hierarchy of archbishop and twelve bishops, taking their titles from towns in the dioceses which they were to rule. The change was occasioned simply by the altered circumstances of the Catholic minority in England, who at this time were still governed by vicars apostolic under the terms of an Apostolic Constitution which had been issued as far back as 1753, when the penal laws had been still on the statute-book and Catholics had not been one-tenth as numerous as they were in 1850. The Constitution was now hopelessly out of date, and the simplest way of superseding it was to extend to England the normal system of Church government by a metropolitan and bishops.[2] There was no intention in all this of provoking the British Government, and Bishop Ullathorne was later to show that

---

[1] For expressions of this view see, e.g., *The Times*, 27 Nov. 1850, and Lord John Russell's speech, *Parl. Deb.*, series 3, cxiv. 189–94 (7 Feb. 1851).
[2] Ward, *The Sequel to Catholic Emancipation*, ii, p. 166.

the Roman curia had gone to considerable trouble to avoid causes of conflict.[1]

But Protestants knew nothing of the secret history of the new hierarchy. All they saw was that Rome had taken a step which was without precedent in modern Europe. Every continental country had laws regulating the entry of papal decrees into its territory, and no continental government would have tolerated the erection of dioceses in its dominions without its consent. Again, the new Archbishop of Westminster in his first pastoral used the unfortunate phrase 'we govern, and shall continue to govern, the counties of Middlesex, Hertford and Essex as ordinary thereof'; and though all he meant was that he would be Catholic bishop in those counties, what he was taken to mean was that he would try to assume temporal jurisdiction in them. To most Protestants, the intention of the Pope's act was clear. It was one more encroachment on the rights of the civil authority, one more experiment in the policy of aggrandizement which had been tried successfully at the Synod of Thurles; and they felt it was time to make a stand. A rash of protest meetings broke out across the three kingdoms, the Prime Minister put himself at the head of the agitation by his celebrated letter to the Bishop of Durham, and when Parliament met again in the following February he introduced a bill to make illegal the assumption by Catholic prelates of titles taken from any place in the United Kingdom.

Now it was the turn of the Irish Liberals to feel aggrieved. Many of them were Catholics and nearly all of them represented Catholic constituencies, so they were bound to consider the matter from a Catholic point of view. A handful, indeed, of Liberal Protestants accepted the Government's arguments and voted for the measure, and one Catholic member with anti-clerical views was prepared to support it provided its effect was to limit the powers of Catholic bishops over their flocks.[2] But to the great majority of Irish Liberals the Government's case seemed totally inadequate. They pointed out, for instance, that the argument from the practice in continental countries was fallacious, for in those countries

---

[1] Ullathorne, *History of the Restoration of the Catholic Hierarchy*, pp. 62, 65.
[2] Chisholm Anstey: *Parl. Deb.*, series 3, cxiv. 93–96 (4 Feb. 1851).

the Church was in varying degrees endowed or protected by the state and so the state could legitimately claim some right of interference in return. A more valid parallel would be with the United States of America, where the Pope had all along created and divided dioceses without reference to the civil power. Again, however imprudent and even insulting Wiseman's pastoral might have been, it was quite illogical to punish the whole Catholic body for the indiscretions of one man. To most Irish Liberals of whatever persuasion, the bill was not a vindication of the rights of the Crown: it was an intolerable infringement of religious liberty and a step back towards the penal laws. On the first reading thirty-nine Irish Liberals opposed the bill, thirteen of them Protestants; and only six, all Protestants, voted for it.[1] On the second reading the opposition was even more extensive, for forty-eight Irish Liberals, including seventeen Protestants, voted against it, while only eight, again all Protestants, supported it.[2]

But no amount of voting against the Ecclesiastical Titles Bill was likely to prevent its passing. Most of the Peelites and Radicals joined the Irish Liberals in opposing it, but the Conservative opposition as well as the main body of the English Liberals were in favour of it, and it obtained enormous majorities at every stage. The only possible way of stopping the measure was to strike at the Government on other issues. The Titles Bill was not the only business before Parliament: in the course of the session controversial questions would certainly arise on which the Conservatives would challenge the Government. There was no great difference in strength between the normal supporters of the Government and the opposition, and if even a proportion of those Irish Liberals who usually supported ministers were to transfer their votes to the other side, they might well bring about a government defeat. And if the Government were defeated often enough, or on a sufficiently serious question, they would probably resign, and a Cabinet crisis would ensue with the result that the Titles Bill might be dropped in the confusion.

---

[1] *Parl. Deb.*, series 3, cxiv. 699 (14 Feb. 1851).
[2] Ibid. cxv. 618 (25 Mar. 1851). Two Irish Peelites, Young and Castlereagh, and one Conservative, Herbert, also voted against the bill at this stage.

This policy was first proposed by George Henry Moore, M.P. for Mayo, with the encouragement of Dr. Gray of the *Freeman's Journal*.[1] Shortly after the beginning of the session Disraeli, the Conservative leader in the Commons, introduced a motion calling on the Government to relieve distress among the agricultural classes, and Moore's plan was that the Irish Liberals should vote on this question with the opposition. Most Irish Liberals had voted against the Government before and had no objection in principle to doing so again; but this was a rather unusual occasion for them to adopt such a course. The motion was a concealed plea for protection, while Irish Liberals, like English ones, were staunch free-traders, and many were reluctant to abandon the ministry on this particular issue. The effort to make a whip against the Government proved, however, fairly successful, for when the House divided twenty Irish Liberals went into the same lobby as the Conservatives,[2] and the ministerial majority, which would have been fifty-four if these members had voted as they normally did, dwindled to fourteen. Eight days later, the Government, defeated unexpectedly on a matter of secondary importance, took the opportunity to resign.

The Irish members were jubilant. They believed that Russell's real reason for resignation was to avoid further humiliation at their hands, and Dr. Gray said explicitly that ' "the Irish vote" has done it'.[3] Lord John Russell soon came back into office, as no one else could form a government, and retained a precarious majority to the end of the session. But, undismayed, the Irish members, their numbers strengthened by recruits to their policy, continued to harass him at every opportunity. On 7 April they voted with the Conservatives on the question of retaining the income-tax, and the Government's majority was thirty-eight. Four days later they tried again on a motion blaming the Government for agricultural distress, and the ministerial majority fell to thirteen. In June they opposed the Government on a motion

---

[1] The authorities for this statement are the speeches of Moore and Gray themselves (M. G. Moore, *An Irish Gentleman*, pp. 172–5): but their account appears convincing and no one else ever claimed the honour of having begun the new policy.

[2] *F.J.*, 17 Feb. 1851.

[3] London correspondent of *F.J.*, 24 Feb. 1851.

censuring the conduct of the Governor of Ceylon, though on this occasion, thanks to the defection of many Conservative members, the ministry had the comfortable majority of eighty. Finally, as a dramatic climax to their campaign, the Irish members walked out of the House during the committee stage of the Titles Bill, when the question under discussion was a Conservative attempt to strengthen the bill which the Government was resisting.[1] The ministry, able for once to pose as the defender of Catholic interests against Conservative intolerance, expected the Irish votes as a matter of course; deprived of them, they lost the divisions and found themselves in the embarrassing position of having to administer a stronger measure than they had intended to put on the statute book. The campaign of the Irish members had, it is true, failed in its main aim, for the Government had not fallen for good and the Ecclesiastical Titles Act had become law. But they at least had the satisfaction of knowing that they had compelled the ministry to waste almost the entire session on this one measure, and by the time the act received the royal assent Protestant indignation against the 'Papal aggression' was much less intense than it had been six months earlier.

The body of members who carried out this policy had no obvious principle of unity. They did not include all the Catholic members, for several Catholics, while opposing the bill itself, continued to give the Government a general support on other matters. On the other hand, some of the most ardent advocates of the new policy were Protestants, notably Henry Grattan, M.P. for Meath and son of the great Irish statesman. Nor were the members of the group of uniform political background. They were strongest, naturally, among those who had been elected as Repealers, but they attracted by no means all the former Repeal vote and it is noteworthy that of the three sons of O'Connell who had seats in Parliament, two continued to give the Government a general support. On the other hand, the movement included some who had not been Repealers at all: Moore had been elected against a Repeal candidate, Keogh had originally been a Peelite, and Grace and Corbally Whigs.

[1] *F.J.*, 1 July 1851.

But however diverse their backgrounds, the members who acted together in opposition to the Government soon acquired a common spirit. They sat apart from the rest of the Liberal party on the opposition benches[1] and concerted tactics in meetings of their own.[2] Before long they required a distinguishing name, and though their opponents occasionally taunted them with the epithet of 'the Pope's Brass Band', they themselves preferred a military metaphor, for they looked on themselves as fighting a desperate battle against overwhelming odds. The name adopted linked them with the Irishmen of the eighteenth century who had sought service in foreign armies rather than submit to English domination, and from early in March they were being generally referred to, by both friend and foe, as 'the Irish Brigade'.[3]

Four members in particular stood out among the Brigadiers. Of these the inaugurator of their policy, G. H. Moore, was naturally one. Moore was a man who had achieved distinction in widely differing fields: he had a national reputation as a steeplechaser[4] and at the same time was a forceful debater, though at this period his speeches were sometimes marred by an over-ornate style. A large landowner in his native county of Mayo, he was by no means on the extreme left of Irish politics, and he declined, for instance, to be proposed for the Council of the Tenant League;[5] but, being Catholic by religion and pugnacious by temperament, he felt strongly on religious questions and it was not surprising that he should take the lead in organizing opposition to the Titles Bill. Indeed if he had had his way the Brigade would have opposed it even more fiercely than was actually the case, for, anticipating Parnell by nearly thirty years, he wanted to use all the forms of the House to obstruct it, but the party overruled him[6] and Brigade spokesmen in debate were careful to disclaim any intention of merely factious opposi-

---

[1] This emerges from incidental references in *Hansard*: e.g. *Parl. Deb.*, series 3, cxv. 1193 (7 Apr. 1851) and cxvi. 1444 (26 May 1851).
[2] See, e.g., M. G. Moore, *An Irish Gentleman*, p. 183.
[3] The first use of this title found is in *Tablet*, 1 Mar. 1851.
[4] M. G. Moore, op. cit., p. 89.
[5] Moore to Lucas, July 1851: N.L.I. MS. 892, f. 332.
[6] M. G. Moore, op. cit., p. 186.

tion.[1] Possibly because of this, Moore dropped somewhat into the background in the later part of the session, and some of his recruits soon equalled or even surpassed him as champions of the cause.

The most vocal of these was John Reynolds, a Dublin merchant who had been elected for his home city as a Repealer in 1847. Reynolds was at the beginning a hesitant convert to the new policy;[2] but he soon forgot his doubts and appears to have made a determined effort to secure the leadership of the party for himself. He was on his feet on almost every occasion that the rules of debate allowed: the index of *Hansard* shows that he spoke nearly twice as often in the course of the session as any other Brigadier. However, the quality of his speeches scarcely matched their quantity: they were long, rambling, and full of solecisms that would have been pathetic were it not for the cheerful self-possession with which he met the derisive laughter of the ministerial benches. Reynolds in fact was the stage Irishman. He could always obtain a hearing because the House was willing to listen and laugh at him; but a party leader needs more than the attention of his opponents, he requires their respect, and that Reynolds could scarcely hope to obtain.

A less noisy but perhaps more successful Brigadier was John Sadleir, Liberal M.P. for Carlow borough since 1847. Sadleir was a good example of the rising class of Catholic businessman. The son of a tenant-farmer, he had succeeded an uncle in a solicitor's practice in Dublin, and had steadily acquired interests in an increasing variety of fields. He became owner of considerable estates in Ireland, chairman of a London bank and director of an Irish one, and built up connexions with a number of railway companies at home and abroad.[3] As a politician, he had shown himself fairly independent in the past but, like Reynolds, he was at first reluctant to adopt the new policy of systematic opposition, and Moore's early impression of him was extremely unfavourable: 'Mr. Sadleir', he wrote, 'is an unscrupulous attorney

---

[1] e.g. Reynolds in *Parl. Deb.*, series 3, cxv. 493 (24 Mar. 1851); Moore ibid. cxvii. 373 (2 June 1851).
[2] *Corruption Committee*, pp. 160–1.
[3] For Sadleir's career see *Annual Register*, 1856, pp. 32 ff.; *Dictionary of National Biography*.

looking out for a place.'[1] But in the later stages of the session Sadleir came out into the open and made some of the most effective speeches against the Titles Bill. He was no orator, but his speeches were what might be expected from a capable man of business: clear, straightforward, and appealing to the reason rather than to the emotions.

Reference to Sadleir leads naturally to mention of his intimate friend, William Keogh, M.P. for Athlone since 1847. Keogh's character has been drawn by A. M. Sullivan and by T. P. O'Connor,[2] and though they are fiercely hostile witnesses their portraits agree so largely, and are supported by such circumstantial detail, that they can be accepted as at least an indication of the truth; and besides, on some points, their views can be corroborated from more reliable sources. Keogh was a barrister but not, apparently, a particularly successful one: he was heavily in debt and he once avowed to Moore that 'money is a great object with me and I have only a broken down profession to look to'.[3] He was an emotional, highly-strung man, liable to violent changes of mood; and yet at the same time he possessed a personal charm so remarkable that it won over even those who most distrusted him: Duffy was to say, at a moment when he was in bitter political controversy with Keogh, that 'it was hard to know that gentleman without having a certain kindness for him'.[4] Keogh was a curious person to emerge as champion of an Irish popular cause. In the previous session he had shown himself to be one of the most consistent supporters of the Liberal government, and only two years previously he had published an open letter to the Lord-Lieutenant in which he had poured scorn on the sentiment of nationality.[5] Sullivan and O'Connor, indeed, depict him as a mere adventurer who joined the movement simply to make political capital for himself; and it is true

---

[1] M. G. Moore, *An Irish Gentleman*, p. 183.
[2] A. M. Sullivan, *New Ireland* (7th ed.), pp. 157–8; T. P. O'Connor, *The Parnell Movement*, pp. 131 ff.
[3] Keogh to Moore, 11 Nov. 1851: N.L.I. MS. 892, f. 341. The extent of Keogh's debts is indicated in *Athlone elect. pet.*
[4] *F.J.*, 12 Jan. 1853.
[5] *Ireland Imperialised: a Letter to the Earl of Clarendon*. Published anonymously, but always attributed to Keogh and never disowned by him.

that Moore's first opinion was as unfavourable of him as it was of Sadleir.[1] But it is hard to believe that anyone could have maintained the mask of deception which such a policy would have rendered necessary for so long a period—least of all a person of Keogh's impulsive temperament. It is significant also that Moore, whose own devotion to the cause never wavered, changed his mind entirely about Keogh and came to give him his complete trust.[2] The question can never be finally settled either way, but it seems more probable, and more in keeping with Keogh's warmhearted character, to suppose that the Titles Bill genuinely aroused his indignation, and that his opposition to it reflected his true feelings. Certainly, once he had decided to adopt the Brigade policy he did so wholeheartedly, and he made some of the ablest and most telling attacks on the Government's course of action. When the bill went into committee his legal knowledge stood him in good stead, and he showed a resource in replying to the arguments of his opponents which soon put him head and shoulders above his fellow-Brigadiers. By the end of May the *Freeman's Journal* was describing him as '*facile princeps* of the opposition',[3] and though the Brigade never formally selected a leader, before the end of the session Keogh had through sheer superiority in talent virtually eliminated all competitors for the place.

The Ecclesiastical Titles Bill produced quite as great an effect among the people of Ireland as it did on their representatives in the Commons. A chain of protest meetings was held across Ireland, and scores of petitions were presented to Parliament. Even Catholics of generally moderate opinions came out against the bill: the Catholic members of the Irish bar signed a protest,[4] and the Archbishop of Dublin, who had hitherto been more friendly to the Government than any other prelate, issued a pastoral against it.[5] By the beginning of March the Chief Secretary was writing in alarm to the Prime Minister:

---

[1] 'Mr. Keogh is an expectant of office': M. G. Moore, op. cit., p. 183.
[2] Ibid., pp. 187-8, 193-4.   [3] *F.J.*, 29 May 1851.
[4] *Tablet*, 1 Mar. 1851.
[5] W. Meagher, *Notices of . . . Most Rev. Daniel Murray*, p. 78.

My accounts from Ireland lead me to believe that the agitation against the bill in its present form is only commencing—county meetings are organizing—& they will be attended I believe by the reasonable and moderate members of the Roman Catholic body. I have myself received a requisition to resign my seat—& there are names attached to that document which nothing short of what the parties think a religious obligation, could have detached from my interests.[1]

The movement of protest reached its culmination on 11 May, when simultaneous meetings were planned for all the parishes of Ireland to protest against the bill.[2] The resulting petitions were so numerous that it took the Irish M.P.s nearly two hours to present them all to the House of Commons.[3]

Nor was all this activity directed simply against the bill: it was directed quite as explicitly in favour of the methods which the Brigade was using to oppose it. Nearly every protest meeting passed resolutions expressing gratitude to the Brigadiers and calling on those M.P.s who had not already done so to join them. Members found their votes being closely examined by their constituents: Maurice O'Connell was called on by the electors of Tralee to explain his vote for the Government on Disraeli's motion, and John O'Connell was censured by the Corporation of Limerick.[4] William Fagan, M.P. for Cork city, was so stung by the rebuke implied in a resolution of his constituents that he resigned his seat.[5]

Not surprisingly, the idea soon grew up of channelling all this enthusiasm into a permanent organization. It is not known who first took the initiative in the scheme, but a committee was meeting in Dublin from the middle of May to make arrangements for the foundation of a new Catholic society,[6] and the new body, the Catholic Defence Association of Great Britain and Ireland, was set up at a great inaugural meeting in the Dublin Rotundo on 19 August.[7] The new association drew subscriptions from Catholic clergy and laity all over the British Isles, but it was from the

---

[1] Sir W. Somerville to Lord John Russell, 4 Mar. 1851: P.R.O. 30/22 9.
[2] See resolutions of aggregate meeting of protest, *F.J.*, 30 Apr. 1851.
[3] *F.J.*, 17 May 1851. [4] *Tablet*, 15 Mar. 1851.
[5] *Cork Examiner*, 14 Apr. 1851.
[6] First reference in *F.J.*, 19 May 1851.
[7] *F.J.*, 20 Aug. 1851.

outset largely the mouthpiece of the Brigadiers. The resolutions passed at the inaugural meeting, for instance, were drawn up by a committee consisting entirely of Irish M.P.s.[1] The address of the Association to the Catholics of the United Kingdom was drawn up by a meeting attended by three prelates, one peer, and eight Brigadiers.[2] And the duties of secretary to the Association were performed, until the appointment of a permanent official at the end of the year, by Keogh, Sadleir, and Reynolds.

The pronouncements of the new organization are of interest, then, chiefly as revealing the future intentions of the Irish Brigade: and they show that the Irish members did not intend to permit the enthusiasm which their activities had called forth to subside. The aims of the new body were not, indeed, exclusively political. It proposed, for instance, to use its funds in disseminating religious books among the Catholic poor, and in assisting Catholic schools and other institutions. But its main purpose was to obtain the redress of Catholic grievances by parliamentary action. First in its list of objects was the repeal of the Titles Act and of 'every other statute imposing any religious or civil disability on the Catholics of the British Empire'; and equal prominence was given to the destruction of what was described as 'the intolerable burden' of the Church Establishment.[3] As its instrument in the attainment of these aims, the Association proposed to maintain a distinct parliamentary party in the House of Commons prepared to make these objects its whole purpose of existence. The address to the Catholics of the United Kingdom, for instance, stated:

All our hopes of redress, under Divine Providence, are centred in the creation and sustainment of a parliamentary party, ready to defend at all hazards, with an independent spirit, our civil and religious liberties.[4]

And a resolution passed unanimously at the inaugural meeting expressed the same point perhaps even more clearly:

[1] Keogh, Reynolds, Sadleir, Moore, O'Flaherty, Higgins, and Meagher: *F.J.*, 11 and 14 Aug. 1851.
[2] The Archbishops of Armagh and Tuam, the Bishop of Meath, Lord Gormanstown; Keogh, Reynolds, Sadleir, Moore, O'Flaherty, Higgins, F. Scully, and Blake: *F.J.*, 26 Sept. 1851.
[3] Objects of the Association: *F.J.*, 18 Oct. 1851.
[4] *F.J.*, 27 Sept. 1851.

That as one of the great constitutional and practical means of carrying out the objects of this meeting, we pledge ourselves to make every effort to strengthen the hands and increase the power of those faithful representatives, who, in the last session of Parliament, so energetically devoted themselves to the formation of an independent party in the legislature, having for its object the maintenance of civil and religious liberty in the British Empire.[1]

These declarations are a good deal less precise in their phrasing than the resolution which the Tenant League had adopted in the previous year, requiring its representatives in Parliament to withhold all support from all governments which did not adopt certain stated reforms. They leave the door open for all sorts of compromises and alliances in Parliament. But they do show that the Brigade intended to hold together and continue for the future as a distinct body in the House of Commons, and it is fair to consider the foundation of the Catholic Defence Association as another step forward in the development of an independent Irish party.

[1] *F.J.*, 20 Aug. 1851.

III

THE ALLIANCE BETWEEN THE LEAGUE AND THE BRIGADE

THERE were now two distinct bodies in the country committed to the policy of building up a separate Irish party—the Tenant League on the one hand and the Catholic Defence Association on the other—and in the interests of both some agreement between them seemed desirable. True, their areas of influence were not identical—the Presbyterian tenants of Ulster cared nothing for the Association and the wealthier Catholics in the south were indifferent or hostile to the League—but in large measure they were appealing to the same people and competition between them was quite likely to cripple them both. Events in 1851 indicated that the Tenant League at least was losing heavily from the contest, for the number of meetings in support of the tenants' claims fell off sharply, and by-election results appeared to show that the electorate considered the religious issue more important than the agrarian one.

Curiously enough, however, it was from within the Tenant League that resistance to such a move appeared. The opposition did not come from the Presbyterian members who, though they openly proclaimed their dislike of the Defence Association, seem to have been quite resigned to accepting its existence.[1] It came from Duffy and his friends on the *Nation*. Duffy had always been critical of the Irish representatives in Parliament, whom he accused of undue servility to the ministry, and although he applauded the Brigadiers' campaign against the Titles Act, he still doubted whether they could be altogether trusted for the future.[2] In the face of his opposition no approach could be made to the Brigadiers, and it seems probable that no agreement would ever have been reached had not the Leaguers' hand been forced by Sharman Crawford. Crawford was an Ulster land-

---
[1] See, e.g., *Banner of Ulster*, 22 Aug. 1851; *Londonderry Standard*, 8 Apr. 1852.
[2] Leaders in *Nation*, 1 Mar., 8 Mar. 1851; Duffy, *League*, pp. 153-4.

lord, but he had made himself the champion in Parliament of the Irish tenants and had been trying ever since 1835 to obtain legislation on their behalf. Since the League had as yet no member of its own in Parliament, he was the inevitable person to be entrusted with a bill, but he considered the League's proposals too extreme, and so negotiations became necessary to find a compromise which both he and they could accept. Lucas and Duffy visited him in London,[1] made good progress in thrashing out a settlement, and arranged a final meeting with him for 20 August in Dublin. Now Crawford, although he sat for an English constituency, was on friendly terms with the Brigade, with whom he had acted during the debates on the Titles Bill, and to this meeting he brought the leading Brigadiers.[2] Thus, willy-nilly, the Tenant League found that it had reached agreement not merely with Crawford but with the Brigade as well.

The meeting agreed on a bill rather stronger than Crawford's previous measures but rather weaker than the full demands of the Tenant League. Crawford extended his proposals—which covered two of the League's objects, fair rent and free sale—to protect certain classes of tenants which he had hitherto left unprovided for, and the League suspended its demand for the third of its objects, security of tenure.[3] Crawford agreed to take charge of the compromise measure in Parliament; and it consequently became known as 'Crawford's bill' and under that name was to provide one of the main issues at the next general election.

This agreement did not by any means cover the whole field of Irish politics. The Brigade committed itself to taking up the land question, but the Tenant League made no complementary commitment on any religious issue. Nevertheless the agreement marks an important stage in the development of the independent policy. For it could no longer be so easily damaged by a conflict in aim: the Brigadiers could no longer draw off support from the tenants' agitation because they were now just as deeply pledged to supporting the

[1] Duffy, *League*, p. 158.
[2] *F.J.*, 21 Aug. 1851. Those present were Keogh, Moore, Reynolds, Sadleir, Blake, O'Flaherty, Higgins, F. Scully, Magan, Maher, Devereux, and Sir Timothy O'Brien.
[3] *The Irish Tenant League*, Dec. 1851.

tenants as the League itself. Henceforward there were not two competing bodies recruiting for an independent party—there was a single coalition.

The unity of the two movements, however, was hardly won when it was endangered by a quarrel among the leaders. The source of the conflict was not a matter of policy: if that had been so, it might have been settled by negotiation. It was something much harder to resolve—the doubts felt by some members of the Tenant League about the sincerity of some members of the Brigade. Duffy, as we have seen, suspected the Brigadiers from the beginning, and would rather not have entered into any compact with them at all. Lucas at first gave them his whole-hearted support, but during the autumn a series of incidents occurred to arouse his distrust. First, he found himself excluded from all office in the Catholic Defence Association. As one of the most prominent Catholics in the British Isles he felt himself entitled to some kind of position in the society, and he jumped to the conclusion that the Brigade was trying to monopolize its control.[1] Then, he learnt that Sadleir was putting up the money for a new paper, the *Telegraph*, which was to cost only threepence and so fill the need for a cheap Catholic journal. Lucas was at first ready with advice and help, but he became convinced as preparations advanced that Sadleir's real intention was to compete with and undercut the sixpenny *Tablet*.[2] Finally, at the end of the year, his indignation was fanned by a third incident—the question of the permanent secretaryship of the Catholic Defence Association. The council of the Association, a mixed body of prelates and laymen, appointed to this post an Englishman, one of the Oxford converts, H. W. Wilberforce. This selection was distasteful to Irishmen, who after all provided most of the support for the organization, and several members of the Brigade took the extreme step of issuing an appeal against the appointment to the people of Ireland.[3] Their action was open to heavy criticism, for up till now the

---

[1] *Tablet*, 25 Oct. 1851. [2] B. O'Reilly, *John MacHale*, ii, pp. 305–8.
[3] *F.J.*, 19 Dec. 1851. The signatories were Keogh, Moore, O'Flaherty, F. Scully, Higgins, Maher, and Sir T. O'Brien.

Brigade had been getting its own way in the Association and it might be expected to submit with a good grace when for once its ideas were overridden. To make matters worse, Lucas discovered that some of those who signed this protest had in fact voted for Wilberforce at the council meeting. This made their appeal to Irish national feeling seem merely hypocritical—a cheap device to gain popularity—and in successive issues of the *Tablet* he poured scorn upon them.[1]

These misunderstandings, serious though they seemed to be, were nothing to the storm that blew up at the end of the following February. Two incidents took place, in quick succession, in which the behaviour of the Brigade required explanation. The first was their conduct during the debate on a Conservative motion censuring the conduct of the Lord Lieutenant of Ireland, Lord Clarendon, in hiring a Dublin newspaper to vilify his political opponents. This was just the sort of question on which the Brigade's principles should have caused them to throw themselves whole-heartedly into the attack, but—with the significant exception of G. H. Moore, who never aroused the suspicions which met some of his colleagues—they made no contribution to the debate and contented themselves with a silent vote at the end.[2] The second incident was their attitude to the Kildare by-election a few days later. In the meantime there had been a ministerial crisis, the Government had fallen, the Conservatives had taken office, and Lord Naas, M.P. for Kildare, had been appointed Chief Secretary for Ireland. The Brigade now turned round completely and from showing complaisance to the Whigs became, as it seemed, sycophants of the Tories. For before standing for re-election, Lord Naas sought and obtained a promise of support from Keogh.[3]

To the critics of the Brigade there was one obvious explanation for these political somersaults. The Brigadiers were returning to type. They were drifting back to their old policy of servility towards those English ministers on whom all hopes of patronage depended.[4] Lord Clarendon was one

---

[1] *Tablet*, 20 and 27 Dec. 1851.
[2] *Parl. Deb.*, series 3, cxix. 764–824 (19 Feb. 1852).
[3] *Parl. Deb.*, series 3, cxxviii. 277 (16 June 1853).
[4] *F.J.*, 5 Apr. 1852; *Tablet*, 10 Apr. 1852.

of the coming men of the English Liberal party, a possible future Prime Minister, and therefore a man they would be especially anxious not to offend; while Lord Naas as Chief Secretary was the dispenser of Irish patronage and so was also a man whose friendship was worth gaining.

At this distance in time the truth about these charges can probably never be known. But, to say the least, they are not very likely. It seems hardly credible that any body of men would have tried to curry favour almost simultaneously with a prominent Liberal like Clarendon and a prominent Conservative like Naas: quite apart from the question of honesty, they must have known that it would not have worked. And in fact the Brigadiers had in each case a straightforward justification of their action. In defence of their silence during the Clarendon debate, they argued that if they, the representatives of the Irish Catholics, had taken the lead in an attack on Lord Clarendon, English Protestants would have hung back, for English opinion was still, eighteen months after the 'papal aggression', extremely suspicious of everything Catholic.[1] With regard to the Kildare election, they argued that Lord Naas was the better of the two candidates from their point of view, for the other was a supporter of Lord John Russell and therefore even more odious to Catholics than a Conservative.[2] The subsequent record of Keogh and Sadleir was such that there is a natural tendency to decide against them whenever their honesty is in question, but in these instances they seem to have given a satisfactory defence of their conduct, and there is no need to suppose that they had any other motive than a desire to advance the independent cause.

Their critics, however, did not even wait to hear what they had to say. They plunged straight into the attack without a moment's pause. Lucas in the *Tablet*, Duffy in the *Nation*, and now Dr. Gray in the *Freeman's Journal* joined in the chorus of recrimination while the Brigade counter-attacked in the columns of the newly-founded *Telegraph*. All restraint was thrown to the winds and both sides seemed to concentrate

---

[1] Keogh's letter in *F.J.*, 28 Feb. 1852; O'Flaherty's speech reported in *Galway Vindicator*, 31 Mar. 1852.
[2] *Telegraph*, 1 Mar. 1852.

on being as offensive as they possibly could to the other. Take for instance this outburst from Lucas:

Does anybody believe that Messrs. Sadleir and Keogh are disinterested patriots? that they can be relied on for one yard or one minute without the closest watchfulness? or that if they got a fair opportunity of practising what the Tuam clergy call a 'free trade in political corruption', they would abstain from doing so, we will not say without scruple, but with the same joy and alacrity with which any man turns into cash the nett profits of a legitimate speculation—or, more appositely—with the satisfaction with which a professed gambler sweeps off the spoils of a pigeon whom he has just plucked in a London Hell?[1]

And yet the men whom he described in these terms were men with whom he still had to co-operate. The quarrel was a most unfortunate omen for the future harmony of the party.

Its immediate effect, indeed, proved to be almost negligible. Hardly any echoes could be heard when the constituencies came to select their candidates; and at the general election there was only one constituency, Meath, where candidates supported by the different wings of the party openly opposed each other.[2] Perhaps this is not surprising, for after all the only people directly concerned were the handful of accusers and the handful of accused. Most advocates of a separate Irish party were unaffected by the question of whether Lucas was right about Keogh or not. The principle of independence remained unquestioned: and its supporters, whether on Lucas's side or Keogh's or neutral, could continue to propagate it.

The real importance of the dispute lay in its clarifying effect on the ideas of those concerned. The members under criticism were attacked because their sincerity was questioned: naturally therefore they countered by affirming their principles in ever more outspoken terms. Reynolds declared that any minister who in future violated the principles of civil and religious liberty would be treated in the same way as Lord John Russell had been.[3] Sadleir wrote that Ireland needed 'public men unwilling to play the part of mere

---

[1] *Tablet*, 10 Apr. 1852.
[2] In Meath, Lucas was adopted by the local tenants' societies (*F.J.*, 26 and 27 Apr. 1852); while the parliamentary committee of the Catholic Defence Association recommended Grattan (*Tablet*, 12 June 1852).
[3] Speech at banquet to the Earl of Arundel: *F.J.*, 29 Jan. 1852.

political partisans, or to become the blind followers of Whig or Tory candidates for office', and added that 'a very small band, prepared to reject and resist the blandishments and intrigues of the two great factions in the legislature, may effectually protect, in the House of Commons, the religious and industrial rights of the people'.[1] A still more emphatic declaration came from Keogh, who told his constituents at Athlone:

I will not support any political party which will not make it the first ingredient of their political existence to repeal the Ecclesiastical Titles Bill. . . . I will have nothing to do with any party which, without interfering with the religious belief of the Protestant population, will not consent to remove from off the Catholics of this country the intolerable burden of sustaining a Church Establishment with which they are not in communion. . . . Touching the question of tenant right . . . I will not support any political party which does not make it part of its political creed to do full justice to the tenant in Ireland. . . . I will not support any political party which does not make the enfranchisement of the land of Ireland—the breaking up of that system of entail which I believe to be perfectly unsuited to this country—a portion of its political creed.[2]

This speech did not of course commit anyone but the speaker himself,[3] but, coming from the leader of the Brigade, it carried weight; and it was the most extreme formulation of the policy to be pursued by an independent Irish party that had yet been made on either wing of the movement.

It has sometimes been argued that the campaign against the Titles Bill was disastrous to the cause of an Irish parliamentary party, and that it would have been much better if the Tenant League had been left to fight the next general election on its own. This argument is supported mainly by reference to the later career of some of the Brigadiers, and it cannot be fully discussed at this point; but, whatever the long-term effects of the Brigade's activities may have been, it is only fair to say that in the short run they did the cause

---

[1] Letter to organizers of the Arundel banquet: *F.J.*, 28 Jan. 1852.
[2] *F.J.*, 30 Oct. 1851. Keogh's final point about breaking up entail was an idea personal to him and Sadleir, and no more is heard about it in the party's history.
[3] Though Higgins described it as 'an exposition of policy which meets with my unqualified approval': speech at Ballina, *F.J.*, 27 Nov. 1851.

of an independent party nothing but good. In 1851 the Tenant League was entering its second year of existence, the country was slowly returning to a modest level of prosperity, and the impact of the League's appeal had begun to wear off. It is probable that, if no other issue had arisen, the year would have proved a quiet one in Irish politics, and that by the time the next general election took place much of the League's original support would have evaporated. The religious issue, however, changed all that: it kept public opinion at fever heat, and by bringing about the rise of the Brigade it provided the first illustration of what an independent party could do. It was thanks to the activities of the Brigade, far more than to those of the League, that the building up of an independent Irish party was a live issue at the next general election. The Brigade may or may not have caused the ultimate collapse of the party; but if there had been no Brigade, there might well have been no party to collapse.

IV

THE SEARCH FOR CANDIDATES

By the spring of 1852 the development of an independent Irish party had reached a momentary halt. A number of M.P.s, and two important organizations in the country, were in varying degrees committed to the idea, but so long as the present parliament continued they had no prospect of strengthening their position except by occasional successes at by-elections. All hopes for the party, then, centred on the next general election. This event could in any case not be long delayed, for in the existing House of Commons parties were so evenly balanced that no government could have a stable majority; and it was brought much nearer when on 20 February 1852 Lord John Russell was defeated on a militia bill by a combination of Conservatives and dissident Liberals, and resigned. A Conservative government took office, with Lord Derby as Prime Minister and Disraeli as Leader of the House of Commons; but it did not command a majority, and it promised to dissolve Parliament as soon as the essential business of the session was complete.[1] From this moment the election campaign had fairly begun.

The first task before the advocates of an independent Irish party was to obtain the selection of suitable candidates. Now this did not entail establishing a completely new party organization: it meant working through an existing one. For many years there had been only one fundamental division in Irish politics, that between Conservative and Liberal, and anyone building up a new movement had to take account of the fact. On the one side there were the clergy of the Established Church, the bulk of the peerage and landed gentry, many Protestant farmers, and most of those Protestant working men who voted in boroughs under a freeman franchise. On the other side were a minority of landowners, the Catholic clergy, most of the tenantry where they were not

[1] See Disraeli's statement: *Parl. Deb.*, series 3, cxix. 1301 (19 Mar. 1852).

under the control of their landlords, and many of the trading and professional classes. There were of course anomalous cases on either side and the party allegiance of an elector could never be deduced with certainty from his social status: but though the party classification was not rigid or symmetrical, it was at least inclusive, for virtually every politically conscious Irishman would accept one or other label as his own. The apparent exceptions to the rule only helped to prove its universality: the Peelites were, in Ireland, merely a transient splinter-group of the Conservatives who had almost disappeared by 1852; and the Repealers had, despite the opposition of most English Liberals to their ideal, ranked as a section of the Liberal party. The two great parties had some kind of organization or leadership in practically every constituency, and they formed the framework into which Irishmen were accustomed to fit their political activities.

Once the case was stated in these terms, the course which the independent leaders had to follow was clear. They all themselves belonged to the Liberal party: Gray, Lucas, and even Duffy would have accepted the label, while the Brigade was nothing else than a splinter-group formed from among the Liberal representatives in the House of Commons. Their task, then, was to win over as many as possible of the Liberals of Ireland to their own point of view.

In practice, this would entail winning over the local organizations which selected candidates. In virtually every constituency of Ireland some kind of machinery existed, or could be created, for this purpose, but the forms which it took were almost infinitely various. Some constituencies, such as Westmeath, possessed a permanent political club, with rules, subscriptions, and a roll of membership,[1] and others, such as Louth, founded a club specially to fight this election.[2] In yet others, the local tenants' societies[3] or the local chambers of commerce[4] approved the candidates. In some places the Liberal electors as a whole adopted the

[1] *F.J.*, 28 Apr. 1852.
[2] *Dundalk Democrat*, 10 Apr. 1852.
[3] e.g. Down: *Northern Whig*, 22 Apr. 1852.
[4] e.g. Tralee: letter in *Kerry Examiner*, 6 Apr. 1852.

candidates, either at a mass meeting, as for instance in Tyrone,[1] or at a series of meetings, as in County Galway,[2] or by a signed invitation, as in County Kilkenny.[3] Sometimes the two methods of direct and indirect choice were combined and the election committee, having chosen its candidates, called a meeting of the electors to approve them.[4] But however much the form of organization varied, in practice they all worked in much the same way, for in every constituency there seems to have been a small group of local leaders, or even a single local leader, who dominated the organization. Where the local organization was a club or committee, one or two names seem always to stand out in reports of proceedings. Where the Liberal electors as a whole nominally chose the candidates, at a mass meeting or by requisition, a few influential persons always organized the meeting or the requisition in the first place—indeed, in such cases the electors did not usually have a choice at all, but merely approved the names which the organizers had already selected. It was on these local leaders, who dominated the clubs or organized the mass meetings or collected signatures for the requisitions, that the choice of candidates effectively rested. The progress of an independent Irish party depended largely on the extent to which they proved willing and able to select candidates favourable to the cause.

Before we investigate how far this aim was achieved, it would be well to analyse the assets which the independent cause possessed, and the obstacles which it had to face, in attaining it.

One advantage on the independent side was that the movement possessed in the Tenant League and the Catholic Defence Association the only nation-wide political organizations of any kind active at the time. These two bodies fulfilled, though to a very limited degree, the functions now performed by a political party's central office. They do not seem to have provided funds for electioneering, but they did

---

[1] *F.J.*, 26 June 1852.
[2] *F.J.*, 2 Apr. and 11 June 1852; *Telegraph*, 4 June 1852.
[3] Printed in *F.J.*, 8 Apr. 1852.
[4] e.g. Wexford county: *F.J.*, 29 May 1852.

something to attain uniformity in policy by giving public advice to the constituencies;[1] and they also acted occasionally as agencies for finding candidates. The Defence Association produced the Liberal candidates for Dublin county,[2] and the Tenant League was asked by two or three constituencies to suggest names.[3]

Much more important than these administrative activities, however, was the fact that these two societies were the mouthpieces of two great interests in the country. The Tenant League had been founded to redress the grievances of the most numerous social class in Ireland, and the Catholic Defence Association had been set up to focus the resentment of the largest religious denomination in the country. These two groups—the tenantry and the Catholics—between them included a great majority of the Liberal electorate: and, perhaps even more important than mere numbers, they included the united ranks of the Catholic clergy, whose political influence was enormous. It does not, of course, follow that every tenant and every Catholic would automatically adopt the line taken by the Tenant League and the Catholic Defence Association. But the great bulk of them probably would have no ground for opposing it, and the presumption is that they would give at least a friendly hearing to any policy put forward by the two organizations which claimed to represent them. Through these two bodies the leaders of the independent cause had a strong claim on the attention of the Liberal public.

Finally, the independents had the support of a large section of the Liberal press. The one Liberal daily in Ireland, the *Freeman's Journal*, was an ardent advocate of the cause, and so were the three Dublin Liberal weeklies, the *Tablet*, *Nation*, and *Weekly Telegraph*; while there was only one Liberal paper in the capital, the feeble *Dublin Evening Post*, which opposed them. In the provinces the lines of division were less clear, for most local Liberal papers supported whatever Liberal candidate was standing in the district, regardless

---

[1] e.g. addresses to the Irish people of the Council of the Tenant League, *F.J.*, 7 Feb. 1852; and of the Catholic Defence Association, *F.J.*, 12 June 1852.
[2] *F.J.*, 1 Apr. 1852.
[3] e.g. Leitrim: *F.J.*, 23 June 1852; New Ross: Duffy, *League*, p. 193.

of his shade of politics; but even here a bias in favour of the independents is noticeable, for very few provincial papers anywhere in Ireland were openly hostile to independent candidates, while a number, among them the influential *Cork Examiner*, were definitely friendly. In short, anyone who followed the Liberal press at all was likely to meet repeated statements of the case for an independent Irish party, and that fact was bound to have some effect on public opinion.

On the other side, the independents had to contend with the deliberate opposition of a section of the Liberal party, who openly contested the view that Irish members should sever their links with all English parties, and who argued that their wisest policy was to remain in general co-operation with the English Liberals. This group was described by its opponents and occasionally by its own members as Whig, and as the label is a convenient one it can be adopted here. The Whigs were often as wholehearted in their condemnation of the Titles Act as the most violent members of the Brigade—indeed in the whole of Ireland there can be found only one Liberal who ventured publicly to defend the measure[1]—but they did not believe that one act of folly on the part of the English Liberal leader should lose him all Irish co-operation for good, when in general he had shown himself considerably more friendly to Irish interests than his Conservative opponents. As one Liberal gentleman put it: 'I believe the general principles actuating the late Government to have been far more conducive to the general prosperity of the Empire than those which are supposed to be advocated by the men now in power.'[2] The Whigs were not numerous and they were not vocal—with the exception of the *Dublin Evening Post* and two or three provincial papers they had no friends in the press—but they were of some importance, for they were strong in the landed section of the party, and landlord influence, as we shall see in a later chapter, was an important factor in deciding elections. They were particularly strong among the minority of aristocratic families who were Liberal by tradition, and we find members

[1] Address of J. W. Fitzpatrick, Queen's County: *F.J.*, 20 May 1852.
[2] Letter of H. M. Tuite, *Dublin Evening Post*, 25 May 1852.

of great houses such as Charlemont, Leitrim, Fitzwilliam, Clanricarde, and Kenmare standing as Whig candidates in various parts of the country.

Apart from the avowed opposition of one section of the party, the independents had to contend with another group whose aspirations were, if not incompatible with, at any rate divergent from, the independent ideal. To some of the northern Presbyterians the election presented itself mainly as a golden opportunity to secure the entry of Presbyterian representatives into the House of Commons, and from the independent point of view the alarming thing about this development was that the people who proved most eager for it were just those who might have been expected to concentrate on the tenants' cause to the exclusion of all else. It was the leading tenant-right organ in the north, the *Banner of Ulster*, which took up the Presbyterian cause most vociferously:

Our universal object, as Presbyterians, must now be to multiply our denominational strength in Parliament. It is an outrageous disgrace to our northern Presbyterianism, that, in despite of its numbers, its wealth, and social importance, its members have hitherto been content to play into the hands of cliques and factions both in 'Church and State', keeping their own body without a place in the parliamentary councils of the empire, as if Presbyterians were a colony of aliens, existing in this country only through the sufferance of Prelacy and of feudal power. With moderate exertion, and with any reputable amount of public spirit, the Presbyterians of Ulster might have eight or ten members of their own Church in the House of Commons, instead of none at all.[1]

It is true that the *Banner of Ulster* was not entirely representative of its co-religionists, for it is possible to find individual Presbyterians who explicitly advocated 'a distinct Irish party';[2] but its attitude indicated that in the north the independent cause held second place in the minds of many of its own friends.

Quite apart from the opposition, deliberate or otherwise,

---

[1] *Banner of Ulster*, 27 Apr. 1852. The statement that there were no Ulster Presbyterians in Parliament was now accurate: their solitary representative, Boyd, Conservative M.P. for Coleraine, had just retired.

[2] Letter of T. N. Underwood to the Protestant electors of Ulster: *Nation*, 22 May 1852.

of other Liberal groups, the independents had to contend with difficulties inherent in the nature of mid-Victorian politics. One such difficulty was the distracting power of government patronage. In the days before competitive entrance examinations, government posts were filled directly by the nomination of the minister concerned; and all the energy which now goes into preparing for examinations was then poured into attracting the notice of ministers with appointments to dispense. It was said that 450 places fell vacant every year,[1] but the demand for them seems to have greatly exceeded supply. Ministers were deluged with requests for places, and one once remarked that as a general rule the first notice he had of an impending vacancy in his department was when applications for it began to come in.[2] Nor was it only ministers whose time was taken up with such matters. They could not possibly interview personally all the applicants for the lesser posts, so they tended to accept the recommendations of political friends, and in particular of M.P.s on the Government side of the house. Applicants, realizing this, would pester members for recommendations: a friend of one borough member stated that he personally had helped to deal with roughly a hundred begging letters.[3] Indeed the amount of time and care that Victorian politicians had to spend on matters of patronage is to modern eyes quite startling, and makes one of the greatest contrasts between the political system of a hundred years ago and that of today.

It was not the ordinary citizen alone who displayed this appetite for places: Members of Parliament could be quite as anxious to obtain them as anyone. Of the Irish Liberal M.P.s elected in 1847, two, Somerville and Bellew, had become junior members of the ministry; two, Major Blackall and Dr. Power, had become colonial governors; and another, Sheil, had obtained the legation at Florence which was one of the most coveted appointments in the diplomatic service.

[1] *Edinburgh Review*, Oct. 1853, p. 579. This is an unofficial estimate: the numerous parliamentary papers on the civil service published during the eighteen-fifties have yielded no official figure.
[2] Evidence of the Duke of Newcastle in *Report from the select committee on Henry Stonor*, H.C. 1854 (278), viii, p. 9.
[3] *Corruption Committee*, p. 151.

Others had been more interested in securing appointments for impecunious relatives: the most successful in this line was probably Sir Henry Winston Barron, M.P. for Waterford city, who was reported some years previously to have placed the following relatives in government service:

son	attaché at Turin
brother	Assistant Barrister
cousin	Stipendiary Magistrate, 1st class
cousin	Stipendiary Magistrate, 2nd class
cousin	Assistant Poor Law Commissioner.

This was quite apart from the baronetcy which he had acquired for himself.[1] Other members, again, used their influence over patronage to strengthen their position in their constituency, for by the judicious disposal of a place here and a promise there, they could reward the faithful, rally waverers, and buy over opponents. The member with the highest reputation for skill in this art was John Patrick Somers, who had represented the borough of Sligo, with intervals, since 1837. Even his political opponents were moved to admiration by his achievements, and a local Conservative paper wrote of him:

We speak without exaggeration when we state that with scarcely an exception, there is not a family in the town, which either in itself or in the person of some near friend or connection, is not under the deepest personal obligations to Mr. Somers. Indeed, during the number of years that Mr. Somers has been member for Sligo, we venture to say that he has obtained appointments for, or otherwise substantially benefited, a greater number of individuals than compose the present constituency of Sligo![2]

Somers lost his re-election in 1852. He appears to have been hoist with his own petard, for it was said that an unpopular application of patronage had made him enemies.[3]

Now this desire for place was one of the greatest hindrances to the independent cause, for places could be obtained only in return for loyal support of an English ministry. In the days before political parties had developed

---

[1] Duffy, *Four Years of Irish History*, p. 320, quoting *Cork Examiner* of unstated date.
[2] *Sligo Journal*, 2 Apr. 1852.   [3] *Corruption Committee*, p. 151.

the almost iron discipline which they maintain today, the refusal of patronage was practically the only means a front bench possessed of disciplining an unruly member, and the whips watched each vote like hawks. G. H. Moore declared that he was only once allowed the disposal of an official appointment, and that was immediately after the only occasion on which he had ever voted for the Government on an important motion.[1] True, not all electors grasped the implications of the system: Moore once received a letter from a constituent which congratulated him on his stand against Lord John Russell and almost immediately went on to ask him to obtain a place from the Government.[2] But whether they realized it or not, the fact remained that Liberals had to take their choice: they could either seek patronage or they could build up an independent Irish party, but they could not do both. And as long as any of them proved more anxious to gain patronage, the independent cause would necessarily suffer.

Another difficulty which the independents had to face was a shortage of candidates. To begin with, the number available was limited by the property qualification, for no commoner could be elected unless he possessed property in the United Kingdom yielding a clear annual income of £300 for borough members and £600 for county representatives. Lucas and Duffy were able to enter Parliament because rich friends provided them with the necessary qualifications,[3] but not everyone could hope to evade the rule in this way, and the retirement of one sitting member, Morgan John O'Connell, was apparently due to the fact that he no longer met the requirements of the law.[4]

The number of candidates offering themselves must have been further diminished by the expense of fighting elections. In the first place, the returning officer had the right to reclaim his costs from the candidates, and as he had to hire poll-booths, employ officials, and advertise the arrangements, it is not surprising to find that his charges averaged £30

[1] Ibid., p. 246.
[2] Rev. H. O'Keane to Moore, 6 Mar. 1851, N.L.I. MS. 891, no. 276.
[3] For Lucas, see under list of election petitions in *Telegraph*, 1 Dec. 1852; for Duffy see Duffy, *League*, p. 255.
[4] *D.E.*, 1 July 1852, quoting *Kerry Evening Post*.

a candidate in the boroughs and £65 a candidate in the counties.[1] On top of this, the candidate had to employ agents and legal advisers, hire committee-rooms, print and distribute literature, and provide transport and refreshment for his voters at polling-time. The Liberals of a few constituencies, such as Meath and County Wexford, paid their candidates' expenses for them,[2] and an occasional individual like Keogh received subscriptions from his friends,[3] but such outside support was quite exceptional. In Mayo, for instance, where the Liberal candidates appear to have been highly popular, the Liberal club none the less required them to pay £400 each towards expenses;[4] and in Tipperary a demand from the election committee for £1,000 at short notice drove one of the sitting members, a Brigadier, into retirement.[5] In Galway city M. J. Blake spent over £1,200 and Lord Dunkellin, who was unsuccessful, a clear £2,000.[6] Fagan and Murphy could consider themselves lucky to secure election in Cork city for only £300 apiece,[7] and even in the small borough of Sligo, Towneley spent £600 or £700.[8]

Then, if he won his election, the new member would have to face the expenses of parliamentary life. M.P.s received no salary, and yet for a good half of the year their parliamentary duties prevented them from giving anything like full attention to their other occupations. Their power of earning was accordingly reduced, and at the same time their expenditure probably increased, because if they lived out of town they would have to maintain a second household in London. All things considered, a parliamentary career was an expensive and time-consuming pastime, and few men could afford to undertake it.

It might be objected that this was a difficulty which faced all sections of the Liberals and not only the advocates of an independent Irish party. But in fact it was likely to hit the independents particularly hard, for it meant that such candidates as did present themselves came from those sections of

---

[1] *Abstract of all fees ... charged by any returning officer ... to any candidate*, H.C. 1852–3 (311), lxxxiii.   [2] Duffy, *League*, pp. 209–10.
[3] *Corruption Committee*, p. 184.   [4] *Mayo elect. pet.*, p. 60.
[5] Letter from N. V. Maher: *F.J.*, 11 Oct. 1853.
[6] *Galway elect. comm.*, p. ix.   [7] *Cork elect. pet.*, p. 379.
[8] *Sligo elect. pet.*, p. 77.

the population which were least likely to favour an extreme policy. Of the different social groups in the Liberal party, the one which was most likely to find the independent policy attractive was the tenant-farmers, but only one candidate anywhere in the country was described as a tenant-farmer: and he can hardly have been a typical one because he had been educated at Stonyhurst and held a Commission of the Peace.[1] A clear majority of the Liberal candidates came from the landowning class; and the remainder were about equally divided between professional men on the one hand and bankers, manufacturers, and merchants on the other.[2] The landowning group, then, was by far the most important, and yet it was precisely this section of the party which was likely to find the independent policy least palatable. Many of its members were Whigs, but even if they were not, the aims of the Tenant League struck directly at their personal interests, and the tactics of both sections of the independents, in appealing directly to the people by mass demonstrations, would appear to them as demagogic. True, a sense of public duty—or an eye to the main chance—might lead such candidates to subordinate their own interests to those of their fellow-Liberals, and many landowning candidates did undertake to support the independent policy. But even in these cases their sincerity might be suspect, and the fear remained that they might revert to Whiggery as soon as they conveniently could.

Such considerations would not carry so much weight with the commercial and professional candidates; but these included in their ranks just those candidates who were most likely to be affected by the patronage system. This was particularly true of the lawyers, for legal and judicial appointments were just as much given in return for political services as were any others, and a lawyer who attracted the favourable notice of a government could hope for any one of a whole

---

[1] Michael Dunne in Queen's County: Duffy, *League*, p. 211; Dod, *Parliamentary Companion*.
[2] A rough count of the 120 Liberal candidates who issued addresses gave the following figures: landowning class 64; trade, industry, and banking 15; professions 20; unknown 20. Most of the candidates whose background was unknown were standing for small boroughs and were more likely to come under the heading of trade, industry, and banking than any other.

range of glittering rewards. One at least of the Irish law officers was always in Parliament; and out of twenty-one Irish judges appointed between 1828 and July 1852, fourteen had been M.P.s.[1] On the other hand, a lawyer who built up no claim to reward could expect to remain an ordinary barrister for the rest of his life, and unless he was a particularly successful one he was unlikely to find this an attractive prospect. For the lawyers perhaps more than for any other group in the House of Commons, the independent policy ran directly counter to their personal interests. True, they were not a numerous group, for only about ten practising barristers stood at the election on the Liberal side; but they were an important one because their ability and their experience in public speaking led them to play a part in Parliament out of proportion to their numbers.

The balance of forces, then, in the Liberal party was by no means certainly in favour of the independents. It was a question whether the independent preponderance in the means of propaganda would outweigh the attractions of the Whig policy for a high proportion of the candidates. The record of by-elections since the first enunciation of the independent policy had not been reassuring. In December 1850 a Tenant League candidate had contested County Limerick and in a three-cornered fight had come bottom of the poll.[2] True, this contest did not necessarily indicate what would happen in the future, for it took place before the extension of the Irish franchise granted in 1850 had come into force; but the by-elections of 1851 had proved hardly more promising. At Dungarvan a staunch advocate of an independent party came forward, John Francis Maguire, but he failed to obtain the support of the influential parish priest and was defeated by a Whig.[3] In Longford the Liberal club offered the seat in the first place to a nominee of the Tenant League, Sergeant Shee, but only on condition that he paid all expenses, and when he refused they turned to a wealthy

[1] E. Ball, *The Judges in Ireland*, ii, pp. 345–59.
[2] Goold (Whig) 239, Dickson (Cons.) 199, Ryan 128: *Nation*, 21 Dec. 1850.
[3] The parish priest objected to Maguire as an advocate of the Queen's Colleges: see letter of the Very Rev. J. Hally, *Tablet*, 5 Apr. 1851.

landowner of indeterminate politics, More O'Ferrall.[1] At Cork city the Liberal candidate, Sergeant Murphy, frankly declined to adopt the Brigade policy and yet he was elected unopposed.[2] At Limerick city an English nobleman, the Earl of Arundel and Surrey, was elected unpledged and uncommitted, his sole qualification being that he was a Catholic and had felt it necessary to resign his English seat on account of his opposition to the Titles Bill.[3] The country was in a frenzy over the Titles Bill, Lord John Russell's Government was detested, and yet four members in succession had been returned without any guarantee that they would oppose him in Parliament.

There were signs, however, that these results might not prove typical. The presence among the independent leaders of landowners like Moore, and barristers like Keogh and Shee, showed that neither the social prejudices of candidates nor the demands of their careers need be decisive. And a by-election early in 1852 indicated that the tide might be turning in the constituencies, for when one of the seats for Cork county fell vacant the Liberal adoption meeting selected a candidate recommended by the Brigade, Vincent Scully, in preference to a Whig of local connexions and high personal character, William Fagan.[4]

As the general election drew nearer, the prospects of success for the independent policy grew definitely more encouraging. In particular, the local leaders who controlled the choice of candidates proved to be friendly to the cause. Indeed, wherever a known advocate of an independent Irish party appeared they almost automatically adopted him: Lucas in Meath, Duffy in New Ross, Gray in Monaghan, all found constituencies without difficulty. Almost all the Brigadiers were enthusiastically readopted, and the only two to be rejected by their constituents were in each case replaced by someone of equally independent views.[5] Where a candidate was as yet uncommitted the adoption meeting often took the opportunity of pledging him to the support of an

---

[1] *Tablet*, 26 Apr. 1851.   [2] *Cork Examiner*, 23 Apr. 1851.
[3] *Tablet*, 2 Aug. 1851.   [4] *Cork Examiner*, 8 Mar. 1852.
[5] Grattan in Meath was replaced by Lucas: *F.J.*, 27 Apr. 1852; and Sir Percy Nugent in Westmeath by Urquhart: *F.J.*, 25 June 1852.

independent Irish party: seven such cases can be found in the newspaper reports.

If constituencies proved eager to adopt independents they seemed even more anxious to weed out Whigs. The King's County committee rejected Sir Andrew Armstrong and the electors of Ennis repudiated the O'Gorman Mahon.[1] The Longford club readopted R. M. Fox only after he had forsworn his past and agreed to remain independent of all governments which did not repeal the Ecclesiastical Titles Act and adopt the principles of Crawford's bill.[2] The Louth club repudiated R. M. Bellew, one of the sitting members who, though a Catholic, had retained office while the Government was piloting the Titles Act through Parliament.[3] The Longford club rejected Hughes, another Catholic who had held office during the same period, which was all the more remarkable because Hughes had influential connexions in the county while the man preferred to him, Colonel Greville, was a stranger.[4] In Waterford city the extreme wing of the party even secured the rejection of a candidate because he had accepted a post, long since abolished, from the government of Lord Melbourne.[5] The only former official to secure adoption anywhere was John Ball, an ex-poor-law commissioner, and he had to sound four different constituencies before finally being adopted by County Carlow only three weeks before polling.[6] A provincial newspaper remarked, with rather heavy humour, that he was known as Racket Ball, 'from the rapidity with which he is passed from hand to hand without ever being suffered to touch the ground'.[7]

The results of the independent leaders' campaign to convert the Liberal party, then, were by no means discouraging. Against all the obstacles sufficient sympathetic candidates had come forward to give most constituencies a chance of

[1] *F.J.*, 1 July 1852; *Clare Journal*, 29 Mar. 1852.
[2] *F.J.*, 24 Apr. 1852.   [3] *F.J.*, 29 Apr. 1852.
[4] *F.J.*, 24 Apr. 1852.
[5] *F.J.*, 15 June 1852; *Waterford News*, 25 June 1852.
[6] Waterford city: *Telegraph*, 14 Apr. 1852; Sligo county: *F.J.*, 28 Apr. 1852; Clonmel: *F.J.*, 29 Apr. 1852, quoting *Limerick Reporter*; Tipperary: *F.J.*, 2 July 1852; Carlow county: *Telegraph*, 5 July 1852.
[7] *King's County Chronicle*, 7 July 1852.

supporting the independent policy; and in practically every case where a choice was available the constituency organizations had made the selection most likely to favour the cause. It is true that Whig candidates rejected by the local organizations could still stand independently, and in fact a number did so; but, deprived of the aid which the Liberal clubs could give them, they were not particularly effective competitors, as the election results were to show. Long before polling began, a landslide from the Whig wing of the party towards the independent seemed probable.

V

THE FAILURE OF THE CONSERVATIVE OFFENSIVE

WHILE the Liberals were preparing for the general election, the Conservatives were equally busy. It is, however, much harder to study the Conservatives' activities, for they had a distaste for publicity which contrasts sharply with the openness of their opponents. While the Liberals advertised their adoption meetings beforehand and welcomed the attendance of the press, the Conservatives held theirs behind closed doors: only in a single instance did a press report appear of the proceedings at a meeting to select a Conservative candidate,[1] and even then the account was jejune compared with the frank and detailed narratives that we have in the case of the Liberals. Again, when Liberals disagreed they had no hesitation in conducting their quarrels in the press, at public meetings, and anywhere else they could obtain a hearing; while whatever dissensions the Conservatives may have had were normally smoothed over in private and nothing more than rumour usually reached the papers. There was indeed one striking exception to this rule, when a Conservative candidate in Down quarrelled with the magnate who had put him forward, and sent the whole correspondence to the press:[2] but the widespread interest which the letters produced was an indication of how exceptional such an incident was.

None the less, enough can be discovered about the Conservative machinery to show that it possessed several advantages which were denied to the other party.

First, it had on its side an immense majority of the Irish landlords. With the probable exception of Kerry, where the Lansdowne and Kenmare estates formed the nucleus of a powerful Whig connexion, there was no county in Ireland

---

[1] Dublin city: *D.E.*, 13 and 15 Mar. 1852.
[2] Letters between D. S. Ker and the Marquess of Londonderry: first published in *Northern Whig*, 15 May 1852, and soon copied into all the principal Irish papers.

where the Conservatives did not have a preponderance of landlord influence. The extent and nature of this influence will be discussed in the next chapter, but it can be said straight away that it was an extremely important factor in deciding the result of elections.

Second, the Conservatives found finance rather less of a problem than the Liberals. Supported as they were by the bulk of the landowning class they had no difficulty in finding candidates who could afford a parliamentary career; and they had no difficulty either in raising subscriptions for election purposes. It was reported, for instance, that £1,000 had been collected for the Cork city election, and £1,440 in Kildare.[1] Furthermore, they received financial help from the Carlton Club in London. Just how far this help extended cannot indeed be calculated, but traces of it are to be found in the correspondence of Lord Naas, Chief Secretary in the Derby government. A candidate in Monaghan complains that his colleague has been given £400 and demands something for himself; the Conservative nominee in Mayo states that he had refunded the assistance given him lest the details should come out in the trial of the Mayo election petition, but he now wants it back and claims £900.[2] These were substantial sums, and if added to the personal resources of the candidates suggest that the Conservatives could dispose of considerably larger funds than their opponents.

Another Conservative asset was that their party was comparatively united. There was no question of a powerful body of opinion pulling in one direction while the self-interest of the candidates pulled in another, for both the great bulk of the candidates and nearly all their most influential supporters came from the same landowning class. There was indeed a difference of emphasis between different sections of the party, as can easily be seen by contrasting the addresses of Conservatives standing in Protestant areas with those of candidates in Catholic districts. The former could be expected to denounce attempts to subvert the Established

---

[1] *D.E.*, 16 July 1852; Marquess of Drogheda to Lord Naas, 7 July 1852: N.L.I. MSS., Mayo papers.
[2] C. P. Leslie to Naas, 3 Oct. 1852; Col. M'Alpine to Naas, 18 July 1853: N.L.I. MSS., Mayo papers.

Church, to demand a frankly Protestant form of national education and perhaps to condemn the Maynooth grant, while the latter would say nothing about the Established Church or scriptural education, and might even give the Maynooth grant their approval. But these differences did not amount to anything like a rift within the party: they were largely the result of the contrasting tactical situations in which candidates found themselves.

Another factor in favour of the Conservatives was the obvious anxiety of their Government to conciliate Irish opinion. The motives for this policy are uncertain: Disraeli spoke of himself as advocating it against strong opposition in the Cabinet and it may perhaps be considered as the fruit of his sympathy with Ireland which dated back to his Young England days;[1] but a more likely explanation is that the Conservatives, being a minority in the House of Commons, needed desperately to gain more seats somewhere, and the most promising field for recruiting in the case of a party based on the landed interest was the rural areas of Ireland. Whatever the causes, however, the Conservative leaders were clearly willing to settle some at least of Ireland's grievances. They started well by appointing Lord Naas, a moderate man, to the office of Chief Secretary in place of one whom Disraeli described as 'a gentleman otherwise highly qualified for it, but of extreme Protestant opinions'.[2] Lord Derby readily supported a motion that the House of Lords should set up a committee to consider the grievance of the Consolidated Annuities—the interest which hard-pressed Irish unions were bound to pay on loans made by the Treasury during the famine.[3] Disraeli gave a friendly reception to a deputation which pressed on him the claims of Galway to be made a transatlantic packet station.[4] The Prime Minister received another deputation which asked for more government aid for Irish railways,[5] and a few weeks later the Lord-Lieutenant was able to announce that the interest on government railway loans would be reduced.[6] Napier, the

---
[1] W. F. Monypenny and G. E. Buckle, *Life of Benjamin Disraeli*, iii, p. 400.
[2] Ibid. The reference is probably to G. A. Hamilton.
[3] *Parl. Deb.*, series 3, cxx. 71–73 (25 Mar. 1852).
[4] *Telegraph*, 9 Apr. 1852.   [5] *Telegraph*, 26 Apr. 1852.
[6] See report of the Cork banquet: *F.J.*, 12 June 1852.

Attorney-General for Ireland, was known to be preparing legislation on the land question which, though falling well short of the provisions of Crawford's bill, was more radical than anything a British government had yet attempted. Finally, ministers showed goodwill by refusing, in the face of strong pressure from extremists among their own supporters, to commit themselves against the Maynooth grant. True, they did not oppose a motion for a committee of inquiry, but they allowed the debate on the motion to be spun out by repeated adjournments until it was too late in the session for such a committee to be appointed.

The Conservatives, then, were in a strong position to fight the election. They seized the opportunity to launch a violent onslaught on the seats held by Liberal M.P.s. Candidates sprang up even in Liberal strongholds such as Tipperary and County Cork, and in all Ireland there seem to have been only nine constituencies in which no Conservative candidate ever appeared. Their expectations of success equalled their exertions—the *Daily Express* hoped for up to sixteen gains,[1] and the London *Morning Herald* counted on ten or twelve.[2] It was most unfortunate for the independent party that the Conservatives should have chosen the same general election as themselves to launch a political offensive. Indeed, if the elections had taken place in the middle of June, the independents might well have found their result decidedly disappointing.

The elections, however, did not begin until the second week in July. Before then the Government had, by a single rash act and its consequences, thrown away all the advantage it might have gained.

On 15 June, there appeared in the *London Gazette* a royal proclamation reminding Her Majesty's Roman Catholic subjects that it was illegal for them to exercise the ceremonies of their religion in public, or for their ecclesiastics to wear publicly the habits of their order; and warning them that any future infringements of the law would be prosecuted. The Home Secretary, Walpole, justified the proclamation

---

[1] See survey of Ireland by provinces in *D.E.*, 8, 9, 10, and 15 June 1852.
[2] Quoted in *Sligo Chronicle*, 10 July 1852.

on the ground that it safeguarded the general peace, for if Catholics were to conduct religious services in public, Protestant feeling would certainly be aroused.[1] There is no reason to doubt that this was the Government's genuine intention. As Disraeli's secretary explained to Lord Naas, after the damage had been done: 'the object with which the proclamation was issued has not been correctly understood. It was intended quite as much against one party as the other —in fact more for the Protection (if I may use such a word) of the Roman Catholics, than for any other purpose'.[2] But Irish Catholics, who had been in a sensitive mood ever since the Ecclesiastical Titles Act, were not to be pacified by such an explanation as this. The law to which the proclamation referred had long been a dead letter—the *Tablet* quoted sixteen instances of its infringement during the period when the Conservatives had last been in office[3]—and its revival was taken as a deliberate insult to the Catholic religion, inspired either by bigotry or by a desire to attract the 'no-popery' vote in England. The Liberal press, whose disagreements had hitherto been so conspicuous, united overnight. The *Tablet* and the *Telegraph* vied with each other in their condemnations of the Government; the *Nation* called the proclamation a 'blasphemous ordinance'; and the *Freeman's Journal*, generally the most temperate of the independent papers, declared: 'The race of the rivals is over. Lord Derby stands pre-eminent and alone by the last act of anti-Catholic bigotry with which he has signalised his administration. The Durham letter can bear no comparison with the Derby proclamation.'[4]

The proclamation, in fact, altered the climate of opinion. Hitherto the Conservatives had not been particularly unpopular in Ireland: some of the extreme Liberals definitely preferred them to Lord John Russell. But the election now became an opportunity to inflict a personal vengeance on Lord Derby and his Government. In the words of one paper which four months earlier had accepted the advent of Lord

---

[1] *Parl. Deb.*, series 3, cxxii. 804–6 (16 June 1852).
[2] T. P. Courtenay to Lord Naas, 9 July 1852: N.L.I. MSS., Mayo papers.
[3] *Tablet*, 19 June 1852.
[4] *Tablet*, 19 June; *Telegraph*, 18 June; *Nation*, 19 June; *F.J.*, 18 June 1852.

Derby as a change for the better: 'The brief taste we have had of a Tory administration has sufficed to unite the Irish people into a solid mass of opposition to them and their policy. Whatever comes after, men are convinced that the existing rule is a nuisance which must as speedily as possible be abolished.'[1]

At this moment, when the Irish Catholics had been thoroughly roused by the proclamation, an event occurred which brought them almost to the pitch of frenzy.

The Catholics of Stockport, in Cheshire, used each summer to hold a procession of their schoolchildren. Feeling between Protestants and Catholics had been bad there for some time, and, owing to the proclamation, the latter feared that their ill-wishers, on the pretext that the procession was illegal, might attack them. None the less, they held their procession as usual, on Sunday, 27 June, and it passed off without being molested. The following day, however, there were several fights between English and Irish labourers; and on Tuesday evening rioting began in earnest. The Irish were driven back into their own quarter of the town, twenty-four of their houses were sacked, two Catholic chapels were wrecked, and—to Catholic minds the worst outrage of all—in one of the chapels the tabernacle was broken open and, it is said, the sacred hosts spilt on the ground.[2]

It is not certain that the riots had anything to do with the procession, it is far from certain that the English began them, and it is even less certain that the proclamation was in any way the cause of them. But the Catholics of Ireland were in no mood to argue these questions. They saw that the riots had followed the proclamation, and they jumped to the conclusion that it was the Government's deliberate intention to incite disorder. The *Tablet* put the accusation explicitly:

Lord Derby and Mr. Walpole have drawn their first blood in Stockport. They have thus done what they attempted to do. They issued the proclamation against processions and vestments to encourage, at the hazard of bloodshed, that anti-Catholic bigotry which they hoped

---

[1] *Cork Examiner*, 23 June: cf. ibid., 25 Feb. 1852.
[2] This account is based on *F.J.*, 2 July 1852, quoting *Manchester Examiner*, and *D.E.*, 2 July 1852, quoting *Manchester Guardian*.

would bring them a few more votes at the elections, and the result is what they foresaw and foreknew. It is our belief that never was outrage and murder more deliberately planned than the Stockport outrages and murders—not, of course, in that exact locality—were planned by Lord Derby and Mr. Walpole when they issued their proclamation against the free exercise of the Catholic religion.[1]

This charge—and its corollary, that to vote for a Conservative candidate, no matter how estimable personally, was to vote for a persecuting Government—at once became the main staple of Liberal propaganda. Hardly a single election meeting passed without one at least of the speakers referring to it. The press harped on it; and election placards —of which several specimens have been preserved by the newspapers—seem to have mentioned nothing else. Here is one from County Mayo:

> Massacre and Sacrilege at Stockport!
> *Irish Catholics murdered in their beds*!!
> Twenty-four houses wrecked and plundered.
> The priest's house burnt!
> The Chapel sacked and pillaged!!
> The TABERNACLE *broken open*!!!
> And the HOLY OF HOLIES SPILT ON THE GROUND!!!
> In consequence of Lord Derby's Proclamation.
> Catholics of Ireland! Whoever votes for a supporter of Lord Derby's Government votes for the massacre of his countrymen!
> The violation of the House of GOD; and
> The pollution of the BODY AND BLOOD OF HIS REDEEMER!!!
> Down with Lord DERBY and M'ALPINE![2]

Such a cataract of propaganda could hardly fail to have its effect on the electors. Indeed, if we had no other evidence we could tell that the Government was losing popularity from the readiness of Conservative candidates to dissociate themselves from it. Already, after the proclamation, M'Clintock in Louth had issued an advertisement declaring that he was pledged to no party;[3] and now Daly in County Galway adopted the same course.[4] Barton at Clonmel and Kennedy in Kildare promised to oppose the Government if

---

[1] *Tablet*, 3 July 1852.   [2] *Telegraph*, 16 July 1852.
[3] *Drogheda Argus*, 3 July 1852.
[4] *Galway Vindicator*, 10 July 1852.

it insulted or persecuted the Catholic faith;[1] and M'Alpine in Mayo promised that, if returned, he would press for an inquiry into the 'infamous' occurrences at Stockport.[2]

Even these disclaimers could not save the Conservative cause. After the news of Stockport, Catholics visibly rallied to candidates opposing the Government. In Clare, a Catholic gentleman declared on nomination day that he had earlier opposed the Liberal candidates, but that Stockport made it impossible for him to do so any longer.[3] In Tipperary, Catholics who normally took no part in politics were reported to be 'much excited' by the news of Stockport,[4] and in Cork city, Catholics of the higher classes who had not hitherto voted Liberal voluntarily offered their support.[5] In County Galway, two Catholic candidates of widely differing shades of politics coalesced at the last moment on the ground that the bigotry of the Government made union against it imperative.[6] In Mayo, a Catholic gentleman who had earlier been named as a possible opponent of the Catholic sitting members, changed his mind and actually proposed one of them at the hustings.[7] In Galway city and Limerick city, the cry of Stockport drew support away from even Liberal candidates who happened to be Protestants.[8]

Supposing that the riots caused among the voters a swing to the Liberals of 5 per cent.—which seems by no means an excessive estimate—they lost the Conservatives four seats, in the counties of Carlow, Clare, Sligo, and Waterford. Their influence may have extended even farther than that, for the Conservative candidates in Athlone, Cork city, and King's County all expected, from their canvasses, to have a majority,[9] and were all, in fact, soundly defeated. And in every case the victorious Liberal was a candidate who was either already pledged to the independent cause or at any

---

[1] For Barton see *Telegraph*, 19 July, quoting *Tipperary Free Press*; and for Kennedy see *F.J.*, 21 July 1852.   [2] *F.J.*, 22 July 1852.
[3] *F.J.*, 29 July 1852, quoting *Limerick Reporter*.
[4] *Cork elect. pet.*, p. 279.   [5] *Cork elect. pet.*, p. 387.
[6] *Galway Mercury*, 24 July 1852.
[7] Valentine O'Connor Blake: see *F.J.*, 17 Apr. 1852, quoting *Tyrawley Herald*, and *F.J.*, 22 July 1852.
[8] *Galway elect. comm.*, p. x; *D.E.*, 12 July 1852, quoting *Limerick Chronicle*.
[9] R. B. Lawes to Lord Naas, 10 July 1852: N.L.I. MSS., Mayo papers; *Cork elect. pet.*, p. 198; Nassau Senior, *Essays &c. relating to Ireland*, ii, p. 23.

rate a potential adherent. The outrages at Stockport won over to the independent party several constituencies which they would not otherwise have carried, and fanned the flames of bitterness in many more. It is not too much to count them along with the Ecclesiastical Titles Act and the oppression of the tenants after the famine as one of the main causes of the spectacular shift in opinion which the elections were to reveal.

VI

THE INFLUENCE OF LANDLORDS AND CLERGY

WE have so far omitted all discussion of a most important factor in the election. This was the influence wielded over the electors by the landlords and the Catholic clergy. So important was it that the Conservatives might almost be called the party of the landlords and the Liberals the party of the priests. And never, perhaps, did their influence reach greater heights than in 1852. The Irish Reform Act of 1850 had trebled the county electorate[1] and had reduced the franchise to a level lower than any since 1829. The new voters belonged to the class which was supposed to be most open to pressure, and at the time the bill was going through Parliament there were doleful warnings about its effects—Conservatives prophesying that it would increase the power of the clergy, and Liberals saying the same about the landlords. The election campaign seems to have fulfilled both predictions. The clergy were so prominent that their activities called forth a small literature of protest,[2] and the Government is said to have seriously considered legislating on the subject.[3] The landlords, on the other side, were accused of planning a nation-wide system of intimidation,[4] and during the elections a Liberal paper declared: 'Never did wealth, and rank, and influence, resort to such infamous means to overawe the weak, to terrify the timid, and to oppress the poor, for the purpose of wresting from their grasp that franchise which the legislature bestowed.'[5] The exact nature of an influence which had so

---

[1] It rose from 31,832 in 1849–50 to 135,245 in 1851. The borough electorate on the other hand declined from 40,234 to 28,301. See *Return of no. of parliamentary electors . . . 1848–9 and 1849–50*, H.C. 1850 (345), xlvi, and *Registered electors (Ireland)*, H.C. 1851 (383), l.
[2] See Bibliography, section 5.
[3] *F.J.*, 19 Nov. 1852.
[4] *Morning Chronicle*, quoted in *D.E.*, 11 June 1852.
[5] *Telegraph*, 26 July 1852.

important an effect on the election results clearly requires further investigation.

Most references to the influence of landlords and clergy suggest that it depended on their power to coerce the voters. This power certainly existed: it was rendered possible by the electoral system of the time. The whole election campaign seems to have been conducted on the principle that the voters' opinions were, by right, public property. Canvassing was often carried out quite openly. In the towns, indeed, it tended to be something of a public event: the candidate would go from house to house accompanied by his principal supporters and followed by a crowd who cheered or groaned as each elector in turn promised or refused his vote.[1] At New Ross, Duffy went to the extent of printing and placarding round the town the names of those electors pledged to him.[2] But the publicity to which the electors were exposed during the canvassing was as nothing to the passionate interest which they aroused on polling day. The booths were set up in some large building where there was plenty of room for people to watch the proceedings; and excitement reached a climax as the electors began filing in to declare their votes. As each man stepped up to the table the agents of the two parties would check his name off their lists; the crowd would wait to cheer if it approved his vote or to groan if it did not; and all the time, perhaps, the unfortunate elector would be conscious of the steady stare of his parish priest or landlord's agent. It was this system which made coercion possible. Anyone could find out, with a little trouble, the opinions of any given elector; anyone, therefore, might use this knowledge to reward or punish the elector for his vote.

Landlords and clergy were not the only people to use the opportunities which this system afforded. Bribery was common in some of the boroughs—the newly-elected member for Sligo was unseated for this offence;[3] and in Galway a parliamentary commission of inquiry reported of one of the candidates: 'His agents and friends, for some

---

[1] e.g. see description of Sadleir's canvass in *Telegraph*, 24 May 1852.
[2] *F.J.*, 16 Apr. 1852.
[3] *Sligo elect. pet.*, pp. 96–97.

time before the election, organised and continued an open and undisguised system of treating, and supplied the freemen not only with beer and whiskey in public-houses, but also with provisions for consumption at home.'[1] In Monaghan, a board of guardians taught a Liberal voter a lesson by dismissing his son from the office of rate-collector;[2] at Carlow the Liberals imprisoned on a false charge a man who intended to vote Conservative;[3] and at Enniskillen a general inspecting military pensioners took the extraordinary course of trying to persuade one of them to vote for the government candidate.[4]

The great majority of the charges of undue influence, however, concern either the landlords or the clergy. Let us consider first the charges against the landlords. In one instance, there is the clearest possible proof of intimidation. Here, the landlord himself, obviously pleased with what he had done, sent the whole correspondence to a Conservative paper for publication.

Belcoop, St. Doulough's, Raheny, August 17, 1852.
Sir—Perhaps you may make use of the enclosed correspondence to suit the purposes of the day. John Murphy is a tenant on the lands of Skehorn, county of Monaghan. I asked him for his vote. He voted against me. I directed the sub-agent, Mr. Johnson, to enforce all rent justly due and payable, without pressure or hardship. He wrote the letter No. 1; this morning I received from Murphy the letter No. 2; I wrote my reply No. 3. You may make what editorial use of the subject and letters you please. If the landlords of the country (i.e. the Conservative) would all do likewise, the priests would soon be considered by their flocks as the political vampires they unquestionably are.

Henry de Burgh.

(No. 1)
Snow Hill, Monaghan, 5th August, 1852.
Sir—I have this day received instructions from Mr. De Burgh, to call on you for all rent and arrears of rent to be paid on your holdings up to May, 1852, otherwise to take the necessary proceedings for the recovery of it—Your obedient,

John Johnson.

P.S. This must be settled next week. J. J.

---
[1] *Galway elect. comm.*, p. ix.   [2] *F.J.*, 6 Aug. 1852.
[3] See report of *Crotty* v. *Dowling* in *D.E.*, 24 Aug. 1852.
[4] *Parl. Deb.*, series 3, cxxii. 597–602 (14 June 1852).

(No. 2)

Skeghorn. August 10th, 1852.

Mr. De Burgh—Sir—Enclosed I send you a note I got from Mr. Johnson, which will, I hope bear my excuse for troubling you. I hope, Sir, you will not persevere at this unusual season to press for rent. What I would be able to accomplish in two months without doing me any injury would be a heavy loss to press for now, as I have grass taken for two of my cows. I would consequently lose their benefit for the three best months, as butter is 3*d*. in the pound better now than in summer. I will be able to pay in October all demands. I fondly hope, respected Sir, you will be so kind and indulgent as to grant the time I have requested, and I will pray for your welfare. I have to remark I have all rent paid up to May, 1851—I am your respectful servant

John Murphy.

Sir—If you favour me with a reply, direct 'In care Mr. John Leghorn, Clones.'

(No. 3)

St. Doulough's, Raheny, August 16th, 1852.

Sir—Yours of the 10th was forwarded here. Mr. Johnson has acted strictly according to his instructions.

You refused your landlord the compliment of your vote. Be it so. Let there be no compliments between us. Vote as you please; *but* pay up your rents to the day they are usually payable, or I shall make you. No doubt but your political supporters will grant you the favour that I refuse, and enable you to pay your year's rent due on the 1st of May 1852—your obedient servant—

Henry de Burgh.

Mr. John Murphy, Scarva, Clones.[1]

This is the only instance in which the proof of victimization comes from the Conservatives themselves; but Liberal sources cite several such cases. An Ulster paper published a land-agent's letter to a County Down tenant telling him that he would be punished for voting Liberal by the loss of his 'abatement'—the reduction in rent which many landlords gave their tenants after the famine.[2] In Donegal, the Earl of Erne is reported to have punished his tenants on a scale carefully graded to match their offence. From those who had voted Liberal, he withdrew the whole of their abatements; from those who had split their votes between the Liberal and a Conservative, he withdrew half; and only

---

[1] *D.E.*, 19 Aug. 1852.   [2] *F.J.*, 31 Dec. 1852, quoting *Banner of Ulster*.

those who had obediently voted for both the Conservative candidates were allowed to continue at the reduced rent.[1] From County Carlow, a parish priest reported three cases of withdrawal of abatements, and three of tenants being served with notices to quit.[2] In Mayo, the private papers of G. H. Moore reveal a peculiarly harsh act of victimization. The agent of Sir Roger Palmer, an absentee landlord, served fifteen tenants—none of whom was a farthing in arrears—with notice to quit for having voted Liberal. The tenants appealed to the landlord[3] but he upheld the agent's action.[4] Moore himself, as the M.P. of the tenants and a personal friend of the landlord, then interceded on their behalf, but Sir Roger's reply, though courteous, was a firm refusal to reverse his decision.[5]

Often there would be no need for the landlord to utter any specific threat or to mete out any specific punishment. The tenants could not be sure what would happen if they went against his wishes. Even if the landlord did not evict them or raise their rents, there were countless lesser ways in which he could make his displeasure felt, and the vague fear of losing his goodwill would be enough to determine many votes. This is how a Clare elector, for instance, accounted for his having voted Conservative:

Had you been left to your own choice, who would you have voted for?—If I had been left to my own election I would have voted for the Liberal side.

You were not left to your own election?—No.

What did Mr. Keane say when he was asking you for your vote?—He asked me if I would give him my interest, and if I did not wish to give it to him, I might not; but I did not wish to have him against me.

If you had not done so, he would have been against you?—I would not wish to disoblige my master or my agent.[6]

It is hard to say how far landlords used their powers over the electors. The glee with which the Liberals announced

---

[1] *F.J.*, 6 Nov. 1852, quoting *Londonderry Standard*.
[2] *Telegraph*, 29 Sept. and 6 Oct. 1852, quoting *Dublin Evening Post*.
[3] Copy of tenants' memorial to Sir R. Palmer: N.L.I. MS. 892, no. 398.
[4] Sir R. Palmer's reply: ibid., no. 399.
[5] Moore to Palmer, 23 Feb. 1853; Palmer to Moore, 26 Feb. 1853: ibid., nos. 414, 421.
[6] *Clare elect. pet.*, p. 75.

the names of landlords who promised to leave their tenants free might suggest that most landlords did not do so. But on the other hand, the number of definite cases of intimidation or victimization which the Liberal press reported was remarkably small. Probably not more than a dozen landlords in the whole of Ireland were accused by name. The reports of the trials of election petitions furnish between them only two instances of landlord persecution,[1] one of which is the case of Sir Roger Palmer's tenants that has already been mentioned. Doubtless many cases went unreported; but it is hard to believe that, if landlords at all normally coerced their tenants, so little would have come out about it. From many counties not a single instance of undue influence was reported. One of the Liberal M.P.s for County Kilkenny declared that he knew of no case of oppression in that county.[2] Some even of the most staunchly Conservative landlords are known to have inflicted no punishment on tenants who disobeyed them. Lord Dungannon, for instance, told his tenants after the Down election that he bore no ill will towards those who had voted against his wishes;[3] and Lord Lorton, whose Catholic tenants in Sligo and Roscommon had revolted against his orders, contented himself with addressing them a public remonstrance through the columns of the local paper.[4] Indeed a landlord's self-interest would have kept any penalization within strict limits. His income depended on his tenants' rent, and if he harassed them too much, he would only make it more difficult for them to pay. The evidence suggests that only a minority of landlords tried to coerce their tenants' votes.

The charges against the priests fall under two distinct headings. On the one hand they were accused of physical violence, of organizing their flocks so as to prevent their opponents, by force or the threat of force, from voting. On the other hand they were accused of abusing their spiritual influence, of controlling the electors in political matters on religious pretexts.

---

[1] *Mayo elect. pet.*, p. 30; *Clare elect. pet.*, p. 117.
[2] Speech of Sergeant Shee: *F.J.*, 10 Sept. 1852.
[3] *D.E.*, 16 Aug. 1852.
[4] *Roscommon and Leitrim Gazette*, 7 Aug. 1852.

That physical force was often used against voters is unquestionable; and in the great majority of cases, the blame lay with the Liberals. Only at Kilrush,[1] at Carrickmacross,[2] and in parts of County Down,[3] was the mob reported to be in Conservative hands; while one Conservative pamphleteer, in contrast, could cite instances of Liberal violence in nineteen different constituencies.[4] The accounts from some places almost suggest a reign of terror. A County Sligo correspondent, for instance, wrote to the *Daily Express*:

> Over and over again have I heard men who had at first promised their votes to the Conservative candidates, say they should lose their lives if they did not vote for the priests' nominee. In every part of this county, except where there were gentlemen active in watching and keeping the peace, the houses of voters were visited either by night or day by large parties with fire-arms who threatened death to those who should not vote for Swift, or made them swear to do so. Those who promised Sir R. Booth and Captain Gore declared that they could not keep their promises, unless they were placed in safety some days before the election. Nearly all who were not thus protected, were carried off by mobs, under the priests' command, and forced to vote for Swift. Many hid in the fields, and in holes and corners, until police were sent to protect them while coming in to vote against this tyranny.[5]

At Newry the mob almost reached the status of a military force, for on the morning of polling day an organized body of men marched on the town and would have occupied it in the Liberal cause had not the Stipendiary Magistrate succeeded in dispersing them before they reached the point where bludgeons were to be issued to them.[6] At Sixmilebridge, County Clare, the excitement of the mob had tragic consequences, for the soldiers escorting a convoy of Conservative voters were goaded by volleys of stones into opening fire, and killed six people.[7] In County Carlow the Conservatives claimed to be able to prove that twenty-nine electors had been shut up in a monastery;[8] though it must be added in mitigation that a Liberal paper reported one of

---

[1] *Clare elect. pet.*, pp. 165–204.
[2] *F.J.*, 2 Aug. 1852.　　　　　　　　[3] *F.J.*, 24 July 1852.
[4] A Barrister, *Observations on Intimidation at Elections in Ireland*.
[5] *D.E.*, 4 Aug. 1852.　　　　　　　　[6] *D.E.*, 5 Aug. 1852.
[7] *F.J.*, 24 July; for the verdict at inquest see *F.J.*, 19 Aug. 1852.
[8] *D.E.*, 2 Aug. 1852, quoting *Leinster Express*.

the Conservative candidates to have 150 voters locked up in his house.[1] Nor did the use of physical force cease with the elections. Three months afterwards, occasional reports were still being published of attacks on Conservative supporters.[2]

We do not have to go to Conservative papers alone for evidence of the use of physical force. The evidence given, under judicial conditions, before parliamentary committees is striking enough. Witnesses from Mayo testified that at Swinford no Conservative could have voted in safety without an escort.[3] Three voters from Sligo[4] and three from Cork[5] swore that fear of the mob made them vote against their conscience: one of the Cork voters had barricaded himself in his attic, but the mob broke into his house, searched every room till they found him, and then carried him by main force to the polling-booth.[6] At Galway the accounts of one candidate included the carefully marked item:

For securing a mob £56. 0. 0.[7]

But it does not follow that the responsibility for all this lay with the priests. Certainly those who made the charge produced remarkably little evidence in support of it. The Conservative *Daily Express*, so assiduous in collecting evidence of Liberal misbehaviour, reported only two or three instances in the whole election campaign where clergy were even alleged to be responsible for violence. The reports of election committees show that priests were present at several scenes of disorder in Mayo, Clare, Cork city, and Sligo,[8] but that does not mean that they were necessarily to blame for it, and the evidence even of hostile witnesses shows that on occasion they tried more or less earnestly to restrain it.[9] At Meelick, County Clare, for instance, a Liberal mob seized a party of Conservative voters at the house where they were being kept, took them into Limerick, and locked them up, with a touch of malicious humour, in a temperance

---

[1] *Telegraph*, 19 July 1852.
[2] e.g. *D.E.*, 23 Oct. 1852, quoting *Fermanagh Reporter*.
[3] *Mayo elect. pet.*, pp. 5, 12.   [4] *Sligo elect. pet.*, pp. 47, 56, 60.
[5] *Cork elect. pet.*, pp. 144, 146–8, 159–60.
[6] *Cork elect. pet.*, pp. 146–8.   [7] *Galway elect. comm.*, p. x.
[8] *Mayo elect. pet.*, pp. 12, 21, 37, 40; *Clare elect. pet.*, pp. 15, 41; *Cork elect. pet.*, pp. 80, 90, 115, 153, 158, 183, 193, 286, 300; *Sligo elect. pet.*, pp. 17, 45, 65.
[9] See e.g. *Cork elect. pet.*, pp. 115, 183.

hotel; but when the ringleader told a priest what he had done, the priest told him to let them go again.[1] The evidence suggests that the first charge against the clergy—that of organizing physical violence—is almost totally unjustified.

The second charge—that the clergy abused their spiritual influence—requires more consideration. If everything that was said about them were true it would justify the most extreme conclusions. From Cork and Tipperary came reports that priests had threatened to refuse the rites of the Church to those who voted Conservative.[2] From Westmeath came the story of a priest telling a voter from the altar that he would be turned into an 'amphibious animal'.[3] Police reports stated that the parish priest of Cloghan had threatened to post the names of those who did not vote Liberal on the chapel door, and that the parish priest of Balbriggan had announced 'he would neither christen, marry or bury the children of those persons who voted for Hamilton or Taylor'.[4] A Catholic Conservative wrote to a London paper that:

A gentleman, Mr. William Kenny, who had his face scraped by a fall from his horse, and who, in consequence, was unable to go to the polling-place to vote, was, since the election, held up to the congregation in most blasphemous language, as an instance of the special interposition of the Almighty to mar his intention of voting against his 'God'.[5]

And this is what J. P. Somers, M.P. for Sligo borough and a Catholic, heard the priest say about him in Sligo chapel:

Will you state to the committee, as nearly as you can, what he said?—He addressed the congregation, in very eloquent terms, on the subject of the Stockport riots.

Did he attribute them to anybody?—He depicted the atrocities that were committed there in very glowing terms; and at the conclusion of his speech, he stated that those riots would never have taken place, if it had not been for the base desertion of such men as their representative, alluding to myself.

Did he add anything more?—He did.

---

[1] *Clare elect. pet.*, pp. 66–67.
[2] *Cork Constitution*, 15 July 1852; *D.E.*, 24 July 1852.
[3] *D.E.*, 9 Aug. 1852, quoting *Westmeath Guardian*.
[4] Police reports, 18 and 24 July 1852: N.L.I. MSS., Mayo papers.
[5] *D.E.*, 17 Aug. 1852.

What was it?—He stated that he had alluded to me from that place, the chapel of Sligo, on several occasions; and he further stated that he had told the people, when he met me face to face, he should repeat in my presence what he had stated in my absence.

What did he go on to state?—He stated that he was happy to have the opportunity of finding me in his chapel, and he pointed to the gallery where I was sitting, every eye in the chapel being fixed on me at the time, or every eye that could by any possibility reach me. He stated that I was a traitor to my religion and my country, and that any man who voted for me voted for hell and the devil; and that every man who voted for my opponent, Mr. Towneley, voted for God and for Heaven.[1]

All these reports come, however, from partisan sources whose interest it was, for various reasons, to make out as black a case as possible. And even if true, it does not follow that they were typical. There is no question that politics were often discussed by priests in their chapels, and Liberal papers have preserved what they said on a number of occasions: but they were normally restrained in their comments on political opponents and the most popular topic seems to have been the unexceptionable one that to accept bribes was sinful. Indeed many of the clergy would have thought it immoral to use extreme language. The Bishop of Cork, for instance, told a Liberal candidate that, though he would allow the clergy to preach against bribery, he would not let them say a word about politics,[2] and the professors at Maynooth all agreed that priests might use their spiritual authority for political ends only on the rarest occasions.[3]

But even if the clergy were shown to use their spiritual influence habitually for political ends, the point against them would still not be proved. The decisive issue is whether by so doing they affected the voting. Now in all the mass of evidence relating to the elections of 1852, there is not a single proved instance that they did so. There are cases, as has already been shown, where electors said they would have voted differently but for the mob or the landlord. There are no cases where they said that they would have voted differently but for the intervention of their priest. The proved

---

[1] *Sligo elect. pet.*, pp. 12–13.   [2] *Cork elect. pet.*, p. 410.
[3] *Report of the Royal Commission on Maynooth*, ii, H.C. 1854–5, [1896–I], xxii, pp. 13, 36, 57, 66, 86, 101, 164.

instances are in fact all the other way: they suggest that not even the strongest language from a priest could induce an elector to alter his vote if he had already made up his mind. The words of the priest at Sligo just quoted did not prevent a number of Catholic electors from voting for Somers. A Cork elector heard his priest declare that if anyone voted against him 'he would not prepare him for the day of his death', but he voted for the Conservative candidate all the same.[1] Sometimes indeed if the clergy pressed the voters too hard they aroused only irritation. After mass one Sunday at Kiltimagh, County Mayo, the priest called out to ask one of the congregation if he was going to vote Liberal—to which the man replied that he had intended to do so but he would now vote Conservative.[2]

It is impossible, however, to prove a negative by direct evidence alone. A more profitable line of approach is to study the general relationship between clergy and laity, to see if it is at all consonant with the theory that the former exercised some species of coercion over the latter. To begin with, it may be noted that a clergyman's political influence bore little relation to his ecclesiastical dignity. The most active politicians were to be found scattered indiscriminately through every rank of the Church—from Archbishop MacHale at the top to the Callan curates and many others at the bottom. If anything the priests most important politically tended to be rather undistinguished ecclesiastically, and a Maynooth professor acidly remarked: 'We used to be from time to time astounded in finding clergymen who had barely escaped being excluded from orders on account of incapacity, turning out political celebrities and leaders in their respective districts'.[3] The inference is that if some clerics were influential in politics, it was at least partly for reasons unconnected with their priestly character.

Again, if the laity disagreed with a priest's politics, they never hesitated to say so. Indeed, in some places they were not content with mere words, for at Limerick, in Louth, and in County Kilkenny, priests supporting one Liberal

---

[1] *Cork elect pet.*, pp. 105, 109.
[2] *Mayo elect. pet.*, p. 48.
[3] *Report of the Royal Commission on Maynooth*, ii, H.C. 1854–5, [1896–I], xxii, p. 86.

candidate are reported to have been stoned by mobs supporting another.[1] Nor do the clergy appear to have tried to keep Liberal politics under their exclusive control. At every political meeting reported in the press, laymen as well as clergymen were present. Indeed there is one constituency—Drogheda—where laymen conducted the whole business of the election and no clergyman is reported to have taken any part from beginning to end. Where the Catholic laity were divided between rival candidates, the clergy were always divided too. At New Ross, for instance, the parish priest and some of the laity backed Sir Thomas Redington while the senior curate with most of the laity backed Duffy. The disagreement between the two priests grew so bitter that the parish priest issued a statement complaining that he had 'come in for a share of the foul abuse of Father Doyle'—Father Doyle being his own curate—to which Father Doyle replied by a public letter regretting that 'Father Walsh should allow himself to be duped by designing knaves'.[2] The conduct of the New Ross clergy was certainly open to criticism, but hardly on the grounds of tyrannical exploitation of the laity. The whole relationship between laity and clergy is incompatible with the theory that the former were in any way unwilling tools of the latter, and even Conservatives would sometimes admit that the proposition was absurd. As the *Daily Express* put it:

[There exists] an extensive class of voters who are merely so many counters in the hands of the Roman Catholic clergy, which these use with the single object of bringing the government and laws of the country into subjection to their Church. And be it observed that these men yield themselves with the most perfect good will to the direction of their priests. There is nothing here that can be called coercion.[3]

If all the evidence is taken into consideration, the claim that the political influence of the clergy rested in some way on the misuse of their spiritual authority cannot be sustained.

It seems then, that neither the influence of the landlords nor that of the clergy can be accounted for in terms of

---

[1] *The Times*, 13 July 1852; *F.J.*, 6 July 1852; *D.E.*, 26 July 1852, quoting *Kilkenny Moderator*.
[2] *Wexford Independent*, 14 and 17 July 1852.
[3] *D.E.*, 11 Sept. 1852.

LANDLORDS AND CLERGY

coercion. The cases of undue pressure on either side are insufficiently frequent to implicate the general bulk of either class. We must look elsewhere for the true causes of their influence.

One way in which both landlords and clergy affected the election campaign was in the selection of candidates. Among the Conservatives, the nomination of candidates seems to have rested almost exclusively with the greatest landowners in each constituency. Many small towns were pocket boroughs in an almost eighteenth-century sense. The Earl of Ranfurly was dominant in Dungannon,[1] the Marquess of Hertford in Lisburn,[2] the Earl of Enniskillen in Enniskillen,[3] the Marquess of Downshire in Carrickfergus,[4] the Earl of Portarlington in Portarlington,[5] and Mr. D. S. Ker in Downpatrick.[6] Nor was this system confined to the boroughs—there also existed what might almost be called pocket counties. In Antrim, one member was nominated by the Marquess of Hertford and the other by Lord O'Neill.[7] In Down, one seat had been so long in the gift of the Marquess of Londonderry that he referred to it as the 'family seat'.[8] In Fermanagh three families—the Brookes, Archdalls, and Coles—had taken it in turns ever since the reign of George II to represent the county and were to continue to do so until the tide of Parnellism overwhelmed them in 1885. In the southern counties, repeated defeats at the hands of the Liberals had shaken the dictatorship wielded by the great Conservative landlords over their party, but even here we read of the Marquess of Sligo selecting the Tory candidate in Mayo[9] and Lords Clancarty and Clonbrock vetoing one in Galway.[10] Only in one constituency do the Conservatives

---

[1] *F.J.*, 27 Apr. 1852; Dod, *Electoral Facts*, p. 100.
[2] *Northern Whig*, 6 Jan. 1852; Dod, op. cit., p. 190.
[3] Dod, op. cit., p. 110; see also reference to 'Cole nominee' in *Parl. Deb.*, series 3, cxxii. 597–602 (14 June 1852).
[4] See account of election in *Northern Whig*, 13 July 1852.
[5] Dod, op. cit., p. 253.
[6] *Northern Whig*, 22 May 1852; Dod, op. cit., p. 91.
[7] *F.J.*, 22 May 1852, quoting *Banner of Ulster*; Lord Massereene's letter in *D.E.*, 3 July 1852.
[8] Correspondence published in *Northern Whig*, 15 May 1852.
[9] M. G. Moore, *An Irish Gentleman*, p. 207.
[10] *Galway Vindicator*, 1 May 1852.

seem to have broken away from the tutelage of the landowning class: in the city of Dublin, the most influential single person seems to have been the Reverend Tresham Gregg, a Protestant clergyman who was the idol of the Protestant working men and who had been powerful enough at the previous general election to unseat a Conservative M.P. of whom he disapproved.[1]

The clergy did not dominate the Liberals in the same way as the landlords dominated the Conservatives, for laymen were active members of all Liberal organizations. But it has already been pointed out[2] that whatever the form of Liberal organization in a given constituency, the choice of candidates rested effectively with a small group of local leaders. Now these leaders were nearly always clergymen. The private papers of G. H. Moore contain a number of letters from constituents on local politics, and in practically every case his correspondent was a priest. In the published reports of adoption meetings, the most prominent people are nearly always priests: we find Father Quaid catechizing the candidates in Clare,[3] Father Doyle smoothing out the disagreements of a divided election committee in New Ross,[4] Father Kieran persuading a candidate who was splitting the vote to withdraw at Dundalk.[5] At Waterford, when the election committee proved unable to agree on its choice of candidates, the bishop intervened and enforced a compromise.[6] In Westmeath, two parish priests—Fathers Kearney and Dowling—so dominated the county Liberal club that when they quarrelled, the club collapsed.[7] Very few laymen could compete in influence with such clerical leaders as these. The influence of both landlords and clergy was at least partly due to the fact that they possessed the decisive voice in the selection of candidates.

Choosing candidates, however, was not the only task to be performed in an election. The next stage was to organize the electors—to canvass them, to secure their promises, and to bring them to the poll. It was here, perhaps, that the land-

---

[1] Sir William Gregory, *An Autobiography*, pp. 136–9.   [2] See p. 41.
[3] *Telegraph*, 11 June 1852.   [4] Duffy, *League*, p. 196.
[5] *Newry Examiner*, 10 and 14 July 1852.
[6] *The Times*, 28 June; *Telegraph*, 2 July 1852.   [7] *F.J.*, 25 June 1852.

lords and clergy performed their most important services. The work was unspectacular and not of the kind which was often mentioned in the papers, so it is difficult to collect evidence for it. But every now and again a newspaper did report the progress of a candidate's canvass, or describe the electors being brought up to the poll; and on these occasions there nearly always seems to have been present either a priest or a landlord or land agent. The Liberal candidate for Newry, for instance, disgustedly described the electioneering methods of his Conservative opponent: 'Mr. Hallewell was accompanied on his canvass by the Agent of the Marquess of Downshire, the Agent of Colonel Close, the Agent, the Sub-Agent, and two bailiffs of the Kilmorey Estate. If this is not landlord influence, I don't know what is.'[1] On the other side, a reporter at New Ross described what must have been a most effective canvass on behalf of the independent candidate:

About sixty substantial farmers, the picked men of the several parishes for a circuit of five miles round the town, accompanied by their respective priests, one from each parish, met at Mr. Duffy's Committee Room, and having procured lists of the electors pledged to him, and of the electors not yet pledged to any candidate, they went round the town in a body to thank the one for their support of the League candidate, and to canvass the other.[2]

From County Sligo, a correspondent of the *Tablet* wrote a long description, all the more valuable because it is unique of its kind, of eight days in the campaign of Richard Swift, the Liberal candidate. Nothing can show more vividly the importance of the clergy in electioneering matters than to give an unadorned précis of Swift's time-table as it emerges from this account:

Tuesday, 1 June
    Skreen and Kilmore West—parish priest assembles his electors to pledge their votes to Swift.
    'Next parish'—parish priest does the same.
    Easky—public meeting. Chairman: an archdeacon. Speakers: many of the local clergy. Dinner given by the parish priest.

[1] *Newry Examiner*, 14 July 1852.   [2] *Nation*, 5 June 1852.

Wednesday, 2 June

Ballina—dinner given by the Bishop of Killala, at which Swift met many of the neighbouring clergy.

Thursday, 3 June

Ballina—public meeting. Chairman: an archdeacon. Speakers included Swift himself, three priests, and one layman.

Friday, 4 June

Castlebaldwin fair—public meeting. Chairman: a dean. After the meeting the electors of the neighbouring parishes, headed by their parish priests, promised their votes to Swift. Dinner given by the parish priest of Ballinafad: many clergy and gentry present.

Saturday, 5 June

Boyle—dinner given by the parish priest: the Bishop of Elphin and many clergy and gentlemen present.

Sunday, 6 June

Gurteen—public meeting: nearly every voter in the neighbourhood promised his vote. Dinner given by the parish priest for the clergy and gentlemen at the meeting: those present included an archdeacon and three parish priests.

Monday, 7 June

Bellaghy—public meeting: those present included an archdeacon and three priests.

Tubbercurry—public meeting. Chairman: a dean. Speakers included two priests and two gentlemen. Electors came forward and promised their votes. Dinner given by the parish priest to a large party of clergy and laity.

Tuesday, 8 June

Kilmactigue—public meeting. Speakers included two priests and two gentlemen. Parish priest brought up his electors to promise their votes to Swift.[1]

The reports of election committees give the same picture of systematic activity on the part of both landlords and clergy. Practically every landlord, agent, or priest who gave evidence had canvassed some at least of his voters. One land-agent in Clare was able to boast that he and his relatives, who between them managed a large part of the county, had polled all but about eight of the electors whom they

[1] *Tablet*, 12 June 1852.

controlled.¹ The trial of the Mayo election petition brought to light a highly-developed system whereby the clergy of the county brought electors to the poll.² It was the duty of the country priests to hire transport, to collect their voters, bring them in to the polling-place, see that they voted, and bring them home again. Meanwhile it was the duty of the priests at the polling towns to hire a hotel where the electors could be refreshed, and if necessary boarded for the night, after they had voted. As all this cost money, one priest in each barony was given a share of the election funds and asked to settle all expenses which the clergy of that barony had incurred. By the performance of this unspectacular but important service, the clergy of Mayo may have had more influence on the election results than by any amount of threats and denunciations.

The direct evidence, then, suggests that the influence of both landlords and clergy owed more to their powers of organization than to their powers of intimidation: it was a matter of leadership, not of coercion. This view is rendered the more probable by the fact that it fits in with the general position in society of landlords and clergy. For the influence exercised by these two classes was not confined to electioneering. In the case of the landlords this is obvious enough, for they were the acknowledged leaders of practically every kind of local activity. From their ranks, in great part, were recruited justices of the peace, grand jurors, poor-law guardians, and officers of the militia. Many of them took a personal interest in their tenants, constantly interfering with advice, encouragement, criticism. The Marquess of Londonderry, indeed, used to write letters to his tenantry from time to time, virtually telling them what to think about current politics.³ In these circumstances tenants would not find it extraordinary if their landlord took the lead at election time; if he arranged for them to be canvassed or brought to the poll. This would simply be an extension of his habit of leadership into the political field.

It is perhaps less obvious that the same is true of the

---

¹ *Clare elect. pet.*, p. 29. ² *Mayo elect. pet.*, pp. 57–84.
³ For specimens, see *Weekly F.J.*, 24 March 1849; *F.J.*, 20 Sept. 1850; *F.J.*, 20 Oct. 1851.

clergy. But they, too, were accustomed to influence in every walk of life. Lucas put the point well a few years later:

In Ireland, the priests have a peculiar function to perform. They occupy towards the Catholic people the place of a gentry or local aristocracy. Between them and the people religion is not a gulf of separation, but a bond of the tenderest union. They belong to the same race as the people, and feel for all their sufferings, temporal as well as spiritual. At the same time, the sacerdotal character, the higher views of life, the greater experience of the world, the more cultivated intellect, raise them above the rank in which they were born; and as they form the *only* educated class which truly sympathizes with the people, they necessarily form the only class to whom, in those temporal matters in which the poor Catholic farmer requires an adviser better educated than himself, he can have recourse, and from whom he can receive guidance. It is not merely in the politics of the people that the priest takes a part, but in all their temporal affairs in which they need counsel and advice; politics are not an exception to other temporal business, but stand on precisely the same line with all the rest.[1]

Ireland virtually possessed two aristocracies: landlords and clergy wielded their sway over the same people. Their political influence was not something exceptional—it was the natural consequence of their function in society.

So much for the nature of landlord and clerical influence: it remains to be decided which did more to affect the election results. Contemporaries themselves did not find this an easy judgement to make, and just how sharply their estimates could differ may be shown by some examples:

A large number of Roman Catholic voters would have preferred, if left to themselves, to vote with their landlords.[2]

Ninety-nine Roman Catholics out of every 100, if left to themselves by priest and landlord, would vote for Roman Catholic and Liberal candidates.[3]

In nine cases out of ten the poor £12 voter cares not twopence who is returned.[4]

But a certain amount can be deduced from the probabilities of the case. It seems legitimate to suppose that landlord

[1] E. Lucas, *Life of Frederick Lucas*, ii, pp. 173-4.
[2] *D.E.*, 4 Aug. 1852, referring to Co. Sligo.
[3] *The Times*, 7 Aug. 1852: letter from XX, M.P.
[4] *Mayo Constitution*, 16 Nov. 1852: letter from 'An Independent Voter'.

influence would be strongest when there was no definite issue in the election campaign. The poor Catholic voter would be most ready to respond to his landlord's canvass when it did not matter greatly who won the election. When there was an important issue the natural sympathies of the electors normally put them against the landlords, as the campaigns for Catholic emancipation and repeal had shown.

Conversely, it seems that a definite election issue would strengthen the influence of the clergy. And this influence would be greater still if the issue was a religious one. Many priests, who might consider it improper for them to interfere in a secular matter like repeal, would then come out into the open; and many laymen, who might in normal times feel that a priest had no more claim on their vote than a landlord, would respond to an appeal to their loyalty as Catholics.

If this reasoning is correct, then there can be no doubt which influence was the more powerful in 1852. For not only were the issues definite and the source of strong popular feeling: they were in great measure religious. The Ecclesiastical Titles Act had made it inevitable that the election would take on the character of a religious crusade; and then, as if to make assurance doubly sure, the Conservatives had presented the country with a second religious issue by the proclamation and its unfortunate sequel at Stockport. Never since the Union, probably, had there been a general election in which religious passion was so much aroused—the Catholic Association's triumphs in 1826 had been confined to a few constituencies—and it seems a safe conclusion that the political influence of the clergy reached its height in 1852. Here, then, was another cause for the rise of the independent Irish party: that its emergence coincided with the zenith of the political influence of the clergy.

VII

THE ZENITH OF THE INDEPENDENT IRISH PARTY

THE general election, according to the leisurely practice of the nineteenth century, took place over a period of weeks. The first results were declared on 9 July, when several borough members were elected unopposed; and the last, that for Donegal, did not come in until 30 July.

The Conservatives' great effort in Ireland was not entirely wasted, for they made a net gain of three members. One seat changed hands in each of the following constituencies:

	Cons. gains	*Cons. losses*
Ulster:	Armagh borough	Newry
	Belfast	
	Down	
	Monaghan	
Leinster:	Dublin city	Carlow county
	Wexford county	
	Wicklow	
Munster:	Youghal	Clare
		Cork city
Connaught:	Leitrim	Galway county
		Sligo county

But this was a long way short of what they had hoped for, and moreover six of their nine gains occurred in constituencies which appear to have had Protestant majorities, and where the situation would consequently favour them.[1] Their three gains in the rest of the country were more than counterbalanced by six losses, and can in any case be accounted for as due to exceptional local circumstances. The success in Wicklow can probably be attributed to a private agreement among the landlords of the county: a Whig landowner retired and a Conservative one quietly succeeded him. The

---

[1] Indirect evidence, such as the phraseology of election addresses, suggests that there was a Protestant majority of electors in the four Ulster constituencies where the Conservatives gained seats, as well as in Dublin city. In Youghal, Butt was reported to have been elected on an entirely Protestant vote: *Cork Constitution*, 15 July 1852.

result in Leitrim mainly demonstrated the unpopularity of the Whigs: the county had been represented by two members of that colour, but the Conservatives and independents each put up one candidate against them and both were successful. In Wexford county the Conservative owed his election entirely to division in the enemy's camp: a large majority of the electorate was Liberal but no fewer than four Liberal candidates went to the poll, thus splitting the vote so effectively that they lost one seat. On the whole the results proved that the Conservatives had definitely lost ground in Catholic areas.

If the results were disappointing for the Conservatives, they were humiliating for the Whigs. It is not possible to construct a table of their precise gains and losses, as has been done for the Conservatives, for many of the new Liberal members were uncommitted to either wing of the party and when the election ended no one knew just how many Whigs there were. But a fair picture of their fortunes can be given by analysing what happened to those who had sat in the previous parliament. From a study of the division lists it appears that thirty-six members sitting at the dissolution could be classified as Whig—that is as members who, however strongly they may have opposed the Titles Act, continued to act generally under the leadership of Lord John Russell. Of these thirty-six, twenty-three were not re-elected. Seven were replaced by Conservatives, thirteen by Liberals of a distinctly more radical type, and only three by members who seemed likely to be of the same political complexion as themselves. Of the thirteen who returned to Parliament, one, R. M. Fox, had before being readopted declared his adhesion to the independent policy;[1] three others, Caulfeild, Heard, and Sir Robert Ferguson, depended heavily on Conservative support;[2] one, Maurice O'Connell, escaped displacement largely on the strength of being the great O'Connell's son;[3] and the remainder had

---

[1] *F.J.*, 24 Apr. 1852.
[2] Heard was originally returned as the joint candidate of both parties: *Cork Examiner*, 13 Feb. 1852; for Caulfeild see *D.E.*, 15 July 1852, and for Ferguson see *Londonderry Sentinel*, 30 Apr. 1852.
[3] J. D. Fitzgerald refused an opportunity to stand against him because of this: *Clare Journal*, 6 May 1852.

a family influence in the constituencies for which they sat. They were, on the whole, elected in spite of being Whigs rather than because of it.

The independents suffered one severe setback: the complete failure of their efforts in Ulster. They did not indeed lose seats there because they had none in their possession: but they had been hoping to reap the fruits of the tenants' agitation of 1847–50 and to be swept to victory on the votes of Catholic and Presbyterian tenant-farmers. Candidates of a radical hue appeared in seven out of the nine counties of Ulster, only Fermanagh and Armagh being left undisturbed. Those chosen were all Protestants, so that there was no danger of the Conservatives using a no-popery cry against them; and they included men personally distinguished in Dr. Gray of the *Freeman's Journal*, who contested Monaghan, and Sharman Crawford, who abandoned his English seat to stand for Down. But the voters failed to turn out as expected. In Tyrone and Monaghan there were complaints of widespread desertions among the Presbyterians;[1] and in Down, though the voters turned out well in the one area where there was an active tenants' organization, in the rest of the county they were usually content to follow their landlords.[2] The only Liberal gain in the entire province was at Newry, and there the new member soon showed himself hostile rather than sympathetic to the independent cause.[3]

Yet this disappointment for the independents was hardly surprising. For one thing, the balance between landlord and clerical influence in the north was quite different from that in the rest of Ireland. The landlords were all the stronger because their power had never yet been successfully challenged: and the Catholic clergy were comparatively helpless, for only a minority of the electors belonged to their flocks. True, many Presbyterian ministers were supporters of the League and some of these took a prominent part in the election: but they were not fathers of their flocks in the same

---

[1] For Tyrone see *Telegraph*, 30 July 1852; for Monaghan *F.J.*, 26 July 1852.
[2] Newtownards, the one polling place where they had a majority, boasted a strong tenants' society: see *Northern Whig*, 8 Apr. 1852.
[3] See his letter to the Tenant League : *F.J.*, 15 Oct. 1852.

way as the Catholic priests and they had no tradition of electoral activity. Furthermore, the issues were different in the north. For the Catholic provinces the two years before the election had contained one political excitement after another—the foundation of the Tenant League in 1850, the Ecclesiastical Titles Bill in 1851, the Stockport riots in 1852. But there had been nothing to arouse the Ulster Presbyterians since the founding of the Tenant League, and returning prosperity had made even the League's ideas seem less important. Elsewhere political activity had been working up to a climax; in Ulster it was running down. Finally, even supposing Liberal candidates had won every seat they contested, it is by no means certain that the independent party would have greatly benefited. As has already been pointed out, the issue of independence versus Whiggery had not been so clearly presented in Ulster as elsewhere, for a portion of the northern Leaguers saw the contest mainly as one to increase Presbyterian representation in Parliament, and candidates under their influence might not, even if elected, have subscribed to the independent policy.

In the south, where the strength of the independent movement lay, the results were very different. For most of the Brigade the election was a personal triumph. Twenty-eight of the sitting members at the dissolution can be classified as Brigadiers, and of these twenty were re-elected. Moore came back again for Mayo, Keogh for Athlone, Sadleir for Carlow. Of the eight who did not re-enter Parliament, seven were succeeded by candidates who were likely to be of equally independent views, and only one, Reynolds, was replaced by a political opponent. He, however, had owed his seat in the Tory constituency of Dublin city to a split in the Conservative camp at the previous general election, and he could hardly have hoped to retain it against a reunited opposition.[1] The only other Brigadier to be defeated at the polls, Grattan, was replaced not because he was too extreme but because he was not extreme enough, for his constituents considered him lukewarm on the land question and had adopted Lucas in his stead.[2]

[1] Sir William Gregory, *An Autobiography*, pp. 136–9.
[2] Report of the Navan meeting: *F.J.*, 27 Apr. 1852.

Among the Liberals entering Parliament for the first time were some of the most influential advocates of an independent Irish party. Not only did Lucas come in for Meath, but Duffy was returned for New Ross, Sergeant Shee was elected for County Kilkenny, and John Francis Maguire, proprietor of the *Cork Examiner*, was successful at his third attempt to open the close borough of Dungarvan. Altogether seventeen of the new members had specifically pledged themselves, in their election addresses or at their adoption meetings, to remain independent of all English parties, and several more had given grounds for supposing that they were favourable. The southern elections had resulted in a sweeping victory for the principle of an independent Irish party.

The next task of the independent leaders was to make certain of their gains. They wanted to pledge those members who were favourable but as yet uncommitted, and to bind still more closely those who had already promised their support. The Tenant League, therefore, with Lucas apparently as its guiding spirit, planned a great conference to be held in Dublin on 8 and 9 September at which the future course of members friendly to its cause could be decided, and from early August a preparatory committee was busy sending out invitations and planning the agenda.[1] Every Liberal M.P. not definitely identified with the Whig wing of the party was invited, and so were hundreds of supporters of the League from all parts of the country.

The conference must have been an imposing sight when it met in the City Assembly House. Out of forty-eight M.P.s invited,[2] forty-one attended,[3] and in addition the room was filled with supporters, clerical and lay, Presbyterian and Catholic, from each province of Ireland. But it went off to a stormy start, for though the M.P.s had attended in force, many of them were in an unfriendly mood. They resented the appearance of being dictated to by a non-parliamentary body, and their feelings were further roused by the fact that

---

[1] The progress of the arrangements is regularly reported in *F.J.*, from 3 Aug. 1852 on.
[2] List in *F.J.*, 28 Aug. 1852.
[3] The only complete list is in *F.J.*, 5 Oct. 1853.

the organizers failed, whether by policy or through incompetence, to circulate the agenda in time for them to study it. And so at the outset of the conference, before any resolutions had been moved, G. H. Moore rose and, claiming to speak on behalf of the majority of M.P.s, declared that 'they did not consider themselves parties to the propositions which might emanate from that meeting, and considered themselves bound by those propositions only so far as their duty to their respective constituents would permit'. This bland declaration struck the organizers of the conference with dismay, for it would, if adhered to, stultify the whole purpose of the meeting, and Gray, Lucas, Shee, and Crawford all asked that at least members should make it clear where they dissented from the resolutions. Moore gave this plea a qualified acceptance: for himself he would 'express the opinions he entertained as fully, as clearly, and as undisguisedly as he had always done', though he did not think it necessary that every one of the members present should make a speech on every resolution from which he dissented. J. M. Cantwell, a member of the League's council, expressed his satisfaction at this, and trusted that M.P.s would at least signify their attitude by voting for or against each resolution as it came up.

The conference then proceeded, and by the first resolution Sharman Crawford was called to the chair. The next five resolutions reaffirmed the principles of Crawford's bill and proved less contentious. The crucial resolution, however, was the seventh, for it contained the pledge to remain independent of all English governments; and here another crisis occurred. Moore, once again, led the opposition: he approved of the principle behind the resolution as strongly as anyone, but he complained that as it stood it would bind them to oppose every government that did not accept the League bill down to its last provision, which would absurdly limit their freedom of action. Two other M.P.s, E. B. Roche and J. D. Fitzgerald, supported him, a priest from County Clare accused the Members of Parliament of being lukewarm in the cause, and an open row seemed likely when Keogh stepped in and poured oil on troubled waters by suggesting a compromise resolution slightly less stringent than the one originally proposed. Moore and Fitzgerald declared themselves satisfied with the amendment, and when it was put to the conference Roche was the only dissentient. Its terms were:

> That in the unanimous opinion of this conference it is essential to the proper management of this cause that the Members of Parliament who have been returned on tenant-right principles should hold themselves perfectly independent of, and in opposition to, all governments which do not make it a part of their policy and a cabinet question to give to the tenantry of Ireland a measure fully embodying the principles of Mr. Sharman Crawford's bill.

The organizers of the conference had won their point. In the face of unexpected opposition they had kept the conference to its purpose.[1]

On 28 October a parallel conference was held to decide on a line of action with regard to religious grievances. The obvious convening body for such a meeting would have been the Catholic Defence Association, but, for reasons which are quite obscure, it had done nothing since the election and had by now practically faded out of existence.[2] The vacuum was filled by a new organization, the Friends of Religious Freedom and Equality, which was founded at a meeting held on the day after the Tenant League conference, under the inspiration apparently of G. H. Moore,[3] who for all his truculence at the League conference remained a staunch upholder of the principle of an independent Irish party. Naturally the new body was less influential than the Tenant League and it attracted a smaller attendance, but none the less twenty-six M.P.s, three of them Protestants, and some scores of sympathizers attended the conference.

The proceedings passed off considerably more smoothly than at the Tenant League's meeting, possibly because Moore, who had started all the arguments at the previous assembly, was himself in the chair at this one. A strong resolution described the Church Establishment as 'a badge of conquest and a legalized robbery', but the next one disclaimed

---

[1] The conference is reported in *F.J.*, 9 Sept. 1852.
[2] *F.J.*, 18 Oct. 1852, denied a report that it had been dissolved, but no subsequent reference to it has been found.
[3] Duffy, *League*, p. 220 n. 2.

all desire to obtain a share in its wealth for Catholics, and declared that 'we shall be content with any secular application of the church revenues which shall be at once just and reasonable and for the common good of all classes of the community'. Another resolution demanded the repeal of 'all laws which impose penalties on the ecclesiastics of any Church, or prohibit the performance of spiritual functions, or the exercise of ecclesiastical rights, order, or jurisdiction', or which 'require peculiar oaths or tests from the members of any religious persuasion', and the next one condemned 'the exclusion from public offices of any subject of the Crown because of his religious faith'. Other resolutions called on Moore and Keogh to bring up these matters in Parliament, and the final and crucial one stated:

That in the opinion of this Conference all Members of Parliament returned by Liberal Irish constituencies should continue independent of, and in opposition to, every government which will not make the concession of perfect religious equality as explained in the foregoing resolutions a part of its policy.[1]

Statistically, the results of these conferences were most encouraging for their promoters. True, three of the old Brigadiers, Monsell, Goold, and Vincent Scully, had avoided committing themselves afresh to the policy which they had previously pursued; but their loss was offset by the adherence of four members who in the previous parliament had ranked as Whigs: French, Murphy, Nicholas Power, and Sir Thomas Burke. Altogether forty-two M.P.s had accepted the pledge of independence at the conferences: twenty-four at both, sixteen at the Tenant League's, and two at that of the Friends of Religious Freedom; and to their numbers may be added Loftus Bland, M.P. for King's County, who was too ill to attend but who, judging by his later conduct, would probably have subscribed to the pledges if he had been present. A still higher total can be reached if to these figures are added those of members who had committed themselves to the same policy either in election addresses or at adoption meetings or both, and in all, if we include Bland, no fewer than forty-eight members appear to have pledged themselves in some way or other to

[1] The conference is reported in *F.J.*, 29 Oct. 1852.

the policy of remaining independent of all English governments until Irish grievances were redressed.

It is worth pausing for a moment to analyse the social background of these forty-eight members. There is a danger in giving precise statistics, for they may produce the impression that Members of Parliament were sharply divided into social groups when the very opposite was the case. Indeed the more one discovers about them the more widely ramified their interests appear to be, and the more difficult in consequence becomes any classification. Kennedy, a land agent, appears also to have had property of his own; M'Mahon, a solicitor, was also a journalist; Cornelius O'Brien, a substantial landowner, was or had been a solicitor; while John Sadleir had good claims to be considered either a landowner, or a professional man, or a financier, though for the present purpose he has been counted in the last category. It is particularly difficult to decide who should or should not be considered a lawyer: a list published after the election showed that no fewer than twenty-three of the Irish members of all parties had been called to the bar,[1] but some of these did not practise while others had ceased to make the law their main interest. With this warning, however, the following figures may be offered as a rough guide to the composition of the independent Irish party:

Landowning class	24
Professions	15
Trade, industry, and finance	9

The professional men include eight barristers, three journalists, a solicitor, a land agent, a doctor, and a former civil servant. These figures may be compared with those for other political groups:

	Whigs	Peelite	Cons.
Landowning class	11	1	32
Professions[2]	2	..	8
Trade, industry, and finance	2	..	1

The figures show from what a limited section of the community Irish politicians were drawn; but they show also that

---

[1] *The Times*, 30 July 1852, quoting *Dublin Evening Mail*.
[2] Whigs: 2 barristers. Conservatives: 6 barristers, 1 solicitor, 1 former civil servant.

this had a less depressing effect on the development of an independent party than might have been expected. A large proportion of the members drawn from the landed gentry, as well as nearly all the Liberal lawyers, were prepared to accept the independent principle. The new policy had made headway even among social groups which might have been expected to prove poor recruiting-grounds.

It is now possible to state in tabular form the changes in the representation of Ireland which had occurred as a result of the election. Once again, a warning must be entered against the value of exact figures, for the term 'independent' covered members with very varying degrees of enthusiasm for the cause. None the less, the numbers do show a striking shift in the balance of political power:

	At dissolution	*After conferences*
Independents	28	48
Uncertain	1	..
Whigs	36	15
Total Liberal	65	63
Peelite	2	1
Conservatives	38	41

The advocates of independence had made a clear gain of almost one-fifth of the seats in Ireland.

The movement to form an independent Irish party had made astonishing progress since its inception at the first conference of the Tenant League little over two years before, and it is worth summarizing the causes. The period had been one of mounting political excitement in Ireland: first there were the tenants' grievances, then the Ecclesiastical Titles Bill, then the Stockport riots. None of these by itself might have been sufficient to alter the balance of political power, but coming as they did one after the other they combined to raise public feeling to a rarely-equalled height; and the last two issues, being religious, had the additional effect of bringing out the Catholic clergy in their full strength and so giving the movement a further immense advantage in three of the four provinces of Ireland. This situation was skilfully exploited by the group of men, originally quite small in number, who advocated an Irish party independent of all English connexions. By their organization of the Tenant League and later of the Catholic Defence Association they channelled public indignation in the direction they wanted it to go; their persistent propaganda persuaded many constituencies to select candidates favourable to their cause; and finally they clinched their success by the conferences of September and October 1852. The spectacular development of an independent Irish party was the result of the able manipulation of a momentarily favourable situation.

The circumstances of its growth, however, had its dangers for the party. It had gained recruits with an ease that was suspicious. It remained to be seen whether the M.P.s who adopted the cause or the electors who chose them would remain faithful if circumstances changed.

PART II

THE DECLINE OF THE INDEPENDENT IRISH PARTY

VIII

THE DEFECTION OF KEOGH AND SADLEIR

THE new parliament assembled on 4 November 1852. Though the Conservatives had increased their strength in the general election they still did not possess a majority in the House of Commons; and the various sections of the Opposition—Liberals and Peelites—did not possess a majority either. The situation was ideal for the Irish party, for it held the balance of power and no party could remain in office without its support. And the party itself appeared, at the beginning of the session, to be more united than ever before. It was some time since Lucas had last delivered a broadside at his colleagues through the columns of the *Tablet*, and a few weeks later he was to pay public tribute to the encouragement which Keogh gave him on the occasion of his maiden speech.[1] All the leaders of the party—Keogh and Sadleir, Moore and Shee, Lucas and Duffy—had been at the Tenant League's conference in September, and they had all taken the same pledge. If only this unity could be maintained, the party might find itself on the highway to victory.

Its unity was first tested within three weeks of the assembly of Parliament. C. P. Villiers, the veteran champion of free trade, introduced a motion praising in strong terms the repeal of the corn laws, which the members of the Government had all opposed in 1846. It was intended as a motion of censure, and its wording was negotiated among the

[1] *Tablet*, 18 Dec. 1852.

different sections of the Opposition so as to bring the largest possible number of votes to bear.[1] This was just the kind of occasion to which the pledges of the Irish party applied; the only question was how they should be interpreted. They were committed to opposing any government which refused to adopt a measure fully embodying the principles of Crawford's bill; but there had as yet been no debate on the Irish land question and it was open to argument whether the Government had yet had a chance of declaring its intentions. At a meeting of the party there was open disagreement on this point: Lucas argued for sounding the Government's attitude before reaching a decision, Keogh scorned the notion that it would ever accept Crawford's bill, and the meeting finally came down on the side of Keogh.[2]

In the event the Government was saved by intervention from another quarter. An adroit amendment by Palmerston, who had reasons of his own for not wanting the Government to fall just yet, detached enough Peelite and Whig votes from the Opposition to ensure the Conservatives a majority.[3] But though this saved the Government for the time being, it did not solve the disagreement among the Irish members. They still differed on the extent to which the Government should be given a fair trial; and in the next few weeks their dissensions were taken an important stage further.

For the Government was showing itself surprisingly friendly to the tenants' cause. On 22 November Joseph Napier, Attorney-General for Ireland, introduced four bills into the House of Commons dealing with the Irish land question.[4] Three of these were largely irrelevant to the Tenant League's demands—a land-improvement bill giving tenants for life more power to improve their estates; a leasing-powers bill, enabling landlords to encourage improvements even when their powers of leasing were restricted; and a consolidation bill to tidy up various anomalies in the law. But the fourth, the Tenants' Improvements Compensation Bill, dealt, as its name implies, directly with one of the greatest grievances of the Irish peasantry, and it dealt with

---

[1] H. C. F. Bell, *Lord Palmerston*, ii, p. 68.
[2] *F.J.*, 22 Nov. 1852.
[3] H. C. F. Bell, op. cit., p. 68.
[4] *Parl. Deb.*, series 3, cxxiii. 305–41 (22 Nov. 1852).

it in terms decidedly more generous than any previous government bill, for while the abortive measures of 1845, 1846, 1848, and 1850 had proposed compulsory compensation for future improvements, Napier extended his measure to cover improvements already existing. The Government made yet another concession when these bills came up for second reading on 7 December, for it allowed the Tenant League's bill to be sent to the same committee that would consider the government measures.[1] In a matter of weeks the claims of the tenants had made more headway in Parliament than they had ever done before. Some at least of the Irish members were beginning to feel that they had more hope of sympathetic treatment from the existing Government than from any likely alternative.

At this stage the administration put out a feeler. It expected to be hard pressed on its forthcoming budget, and the Home Secretary, Walpole, approached Sergeant Shee, who was in charge of the League's bill now that Crawford was no longer in Parliament, to find out on what conditions his friends would be prepared to vote with the Government. Shee called Lucas and Duffy into consultation, and in Duffy's words:

We set down in writing the concessions which would justify our support, of which the chief was that a land bill providing compensation for past improvements should be made a measure on which the Government would stake its existence. Others related to a Catholic University, and Catholic chaplains in the army and navy, prisons, and workhouses. We received back our paper after a day or two with the propositions noted. Some were rejected, others postponed for future consideration: but enough was conceded on the main question to justify us in taking the responsibility of advising our friends to vote against the Whig amendment.[2]

They hoped to bring twenty Irish members into the lobby on the Conservative side.[3]

But the Government had already offended its own supporters by allowing Shee's bill even to go into committee. Lord Derby was badgered by M.P.s;[4] it was said that the

[1] Ibid. 1139 (7 Dec. 1852).
[2] Duffy, *League*, p. 233. The minister concerned is identified as Walpole in Duffy, *My Life in Two Hemispheres*, ii, p. 60.   [3] Duffy, *League*, p. 233.
[4] *Parl. Deb.*, series 3, cxxiii. 1207 (10 Dec. 1852).

Irish officials of the Government threatened resignation;[1] and on 10 December Lord Roden, an Irish Conservative peer, brought matters into the open by asking in the House of Lords if the Government would support Shee's bill in the event of the committee reporting favourably upon it. Lord Derby's reply was emphatic: the Government, he said, had allowed the bill to go to committee purely to remove a possible source of obstruction to their own legislation; they had not by doing so shown any approval of the principle of the bill; on the contrary they were 'decidedly opposed' to it, and were confident that it would never pass.[2] This declaration made it impossible for members of the Irish party to consider any longer supporting the Government. They were pledged to oppose any ministry which did not make a measure equivalent to Shee's bill a Cabinet measure, and here was the Prime Minister condemning Shee's bill in the most decided terms. When the party met, therefore, to decide its attitude on the impending division, it had no difficulty in reaching a unanimous decision to vote against the budget.[3] All sections of the opposition combined—Whigs, Radicals, Peelites, and Irish—and in the early hours of 17 December the ministry was defeated by 305 votes to 286. It forthwith resigned.[4]

This was for the Irish party a tactical triumph. They could claim that the result was due entirely to them. Without their votes all the rest of the Opposition combined would have been insufficient to defeat the Government; and by bringing down the administration they had shown their ability to punish anyone, however exalted, who refused to accede to their demands. But it must also be emphasized how near the party itself was to meeting disaster. If Lord Derby had returned an evasive answer to the Earl of Roden,

[1] Reeve, *The Greville Memoirs*, vii, p. 33.
[2] *Parl. Deb.*, series 3, cxxiii. 1207–10 (10 Dec. 1852).
[3] *Telegraph*, 15 Dec. 1852.
[4] This account of the events of December 1852 is based on Duffy, *League*, pp. 232–5. Another account is given in Reeve, *The Greville Memoirs*, vii, pp. 32–34, which differs from Duffy's in some important details. In particular it states that the Leaguers approached the Government, and not vice versa, and that negotiations began before and not after Shee's bill was sent to committee. But Greville's information came from Delane of *The Times* who had it from Disraeli, and so was only third-hand; Duffy's account seems therefore more likely to have been correct.

twenty Irish Liberals would probably have voted for his government on the budget; and in that case the party would have been split in two. Lucas and Shee and Duffy and their friends, who were prepared to bargain with Lord Derby, would have gone into one lobby; and Keogh and Moore and Sadleir and their friends, who were not, would have gone into the other—and this not on a minor issue but on a division of the utmost importance. Nor would it have been at all clear which side was in the right. The party was pledged to oppose every government which did not accept their full demands both on the land question and on the religious issues as well. Lucas and Shee could argue that the Government had not yet definitely rejected their demands on any of these questions; but Keogh and Sadleir could argue that it had certainly not accepted them, and, if party tradition was any guide at all, was unlikely ever to do so. One can imagine the bitterness that would have ensued if the party had in fact split on this issue—with all the animosities so painfully masked during the past few months pouring themselves on to paper, and neither side with a case strong enough really to win the argument. From all this the party was saved, not by any statesmanship among its own members, but by the refusal of Lord Derby to apply a little diplomacy in the House of Lords.

As events proved, however, the party was not saved for long. The Derby government was replaced by a coalition of Liberals and Peelites. Lord Aberdeen, a Peelite, became Prime Minister and among his party colleagues in the Cabinet were Gladstone and Sir James Graham. Lord John Russell, Lord Clarendon, and Lord Palmerston were the most prominent of the Whigs. The junior ministers included William Monsell, M.P. for County Limerick, as Clerk of the Ordnance, and Sir John Young, M.P. for County Cavan, as Chief Secretary for Ireland. But Irish interest was focused on two of the minor appointments, for among the office-holders were to be found William Keogh as Solicitor-General for Ireland, and John Sadleir as a Lord of the Treasury.

These appointments raised such a storm at the time, and

have remained so notorious ever since, that their merits deserve discussion in detail.

It can be at once agreed that the new Government was, in Irish and Catholic eyes, a decided improvement on the old. From their point of view, indeed, it was the best government that could have been formed in the circumstances of the time. True, it contained the author of the Ecclesiastical Titles Act; but it also included the leaders of the one party in England which had on the whole opposed it. The Peelite leaders had opposed the act in defiance of English opinion and regardless of their own popularity, simply because they thought it the right thing to do; and their presence in the cabinet was the best guarantee that Catholics would not be open to further insults. Again, it is true that the Cabinet contained no one who had committed himself to a radical solution of the Irish land question; but at least it was not handicapped, as Lord Derby had been, by having forty representatives of the Irish landlords sitting on its backbenches in the House of Commons: it was on the face of it in a better position to legislate generously than its predecessor. The policy of opposition had seemed admirable when used to punish Lord John Russell for the Ecclesiastical Titles Act or Lord Derby for the proclamation; it was harder to justify when used against a man like Lord Aberdeen. There was good reason for arguing that the wisest policy for the Irish party was to keep so comparatively favourable a government in office.

Once this was conceded, it might be claimed that the leaders of the Irish party could do more for their cause inside the Government than out of it. This was in fact proved on two separate occasions. The first was at the time the Government was actually being formed. It is clear, from the Aberdeen papers, that fear of offending the Irish members determined the choice for more than one appointment. The Peelites were anxious to retain the ultra-Protestant Blackburne as Chancellor of Ireland; but 'the Brigade would consider Blackburne a declaration of war', and Blackburne was dropped.[1] Again, Lord John Russell pressed strongly

[1] Bessborough to Russell, 23 Dec. 1852: B.M. Add. MS. 43066, f. 140; Clarendon to Aberdeen, 23 Dec. 1852: B.M. Add. MS. 43188, f. 1.

and repeatedly that Sir Thomas Redington, Under-Secretary for Ireland in the previous Liberal government, should return to his old post—indeed there was perhaps no office, senior or junior, that the Whig leader made a more determined effort to carry. But Redington was unpopular in Ireland because, though himself a Catholic, he had remained in office at the time of the Titles Bill; and Lord Aberdeen on that ground resisted all the pressure brought to bear and absolutely refused to appoint him to his old position.[1]

The second occasion on which the influence of the Irish members within the Government made itself felt occurred a few months after the new administration had taken office. On 31 May 1853 G. H. Moore initiated a debate on the Established Church in Ireland. Lord John Russell replied for the Government, and spoke on the whole moderately and reasonably, but in explaining his unwillingness to see any alteration in the Church he allowed himself to say:

It has been but too evident of late years, that the Roman Catholic Church—looking to its proceedings in foreign countries—looking to its proceedings in this country—looking to that Church, acting under the direction of its head, himself a foreign Sovereign, has aimed at political power; and, having aimed at political power, it appears to me to be at variance with a due attachment to the Crown of this country—with a due attachment to the general cause of liberty—with a due attachment to the duties that a subject of the State should perform towards the State.[2]

This was tantamount to saying that no devout Catholic could be a loyal subject. Naturally it caused great offence to the Government's Irish supporters: one of them, J. D. Fitzgerald, denounced the minister there and then;[3] another, Bland, got up and crossed to the opposition benches.[4] But the effective reply came from elsewhere. On 2 June Monsell, Keogh, and Sadleir—the three Catholic office-holders—tendered their resignations, and the Cabinet was startled into action. Russell wrote privately to Lord Aberdeen to offer

---

[1] Aberdeen to Russell, 29 Dec. 1852, Russell to Aberdeen, 18 Jan. 1853, Aberdeen to Russell, 18 Jan. 1853: B.M. Add. MS. 43066, ff. 169, 218–19, 220; Graham to Aberdeen, 25 Dec. 1852: B.M. Add. MS. 43190, f. 384.
[2] *Parl. Deb.*, series 3, cxxvii. 945 (31 May 1853).
[3] Ibid. 951–3.
[4] *F.J.*, 6 June 1853.

his own resignation;[1] Lord Aberdeen asked the Duke of Newcastle, who was the member of the Cabinet most in contact with the Irish vote, to find out on what terms, if any, they would remain in the Government;[2] and they were finally mollified by a disavowal from the Prime Minister:

> I have to inform you that, while the vote on that occasion had the sanction of the Government, the reasons for that vote given by Ld. John Russell & the sentiments of which you complain, are not shared by me, nor by many of my colleagues. I wish this to be distinctly understood, as I might otherwise be justly charged with a departure from those feelings which, both in & out of office I have held & still hold with regard to the Roman Catholic Body, and the open avowal of which had appeared to several Roman Catholic gentlemen to justify them in accepting office under the government.[3]

This disclaimer seemed even stronger when published in the press, for by a misprint the phrase 'many of my colleagues' appeared as 'any of my colleagues'. In either form it was nothing less than a resounding snub to one of the most influential statesmen of the day. Many Irish M.P.s would have given much to have humiliated the author of the Ecclesiastical Titles Act: but the three office-holders alone had done so. And they had been able to do so precisely because they were office-holders, because they could use the weapon of resignation to force the Prime Minister to disavow his chief lieutenant.

There was, then, much to be said for the wisdom of taking office under the new Government. But the wisdom or otherwise of the policy was hardly in question. The accusation against Keogh and Sadleir was not that they were foolish—Monsell, who took office at the same time, almost escaped condemnation. It was that they were dishonest. It was claimed that they had pledged themselves so deeply to remaining independent of the Government that they could not accept office and still be considered honourable men.

Both Keogh and Sadleir had been at the Tenant League conference in September, and had there promised to 'hold themselves perfectly independent of and in opposition to

---

[1] Russell to Aberdeen, 2 June 1853: B.M. Add. MS. 43067, f. 36.
[2] Aberdeen to Russell, 2 June 1853: ibid., f. 38.
[3] Aberdeen to Monsell, 3 June 1853: B.M. Add. MS. 43250, f. 141.

all governments which do not make it a part of their policy and a cabinet question to give to the tenantry of Ireland a measure fully embodying the principles of Mr. Sharman Crawford's bill'. Keogh indeed had committed himself much further. He had agreed to the similar resolution of the Friends of Religious Equality in October; and on two earlier occasions, at Athlone in November 1851 and at Cork in March 1852, he had pledged himself in the most ringing terms to the independent policy. His Athlone speech has already been quoted, and its terms were sweeping enough;[1] but his words at Cork were perhaps even more emphatic: 'So help me God, no matter who the minister may be, no matter who the party in power may be, I will never support that minister or that party unless he comes into power prepared to carry the measures which universal, popular Ireland demands.'[2]

It could hardly be denied, then, that Sadleir and, still more, Keogh, had some strong words to explain away. Keogh never dared to deny the fact: he was more than once challenged to his face in the House of Commons to explain his acceptance of office, but he merely took refuge in silence.[3] Sadleir had less to disavow and made some attempt to do so:

I consented to attend the conference in September last on condition that a declaration would be publicly made, before any resolution was proposed at the conference, whereby other Members of Parliament and myself should be considered as bound by the resolutions of the conference so far as we may deem such resolutions in accordance with our conscientious opinions as representatives of the popular cause; and I have never regarded the seventh resolution as a declaration by which I was to be considered as pledged to act otherwise than in strict accordance with my own convictions.[4]

This was not an argument that could be dismissed out of hand, and if Sadleir had stuck to it he might have made out a tenable case—but he himself deprived it of all value as a defence by his own very next sentence:

Holding the opinions which I have ever held, I need not say I

---

[1] See p. 37.   [2] *Cork Examiner*, 8 Mar. 1852.
[3] *Parl. Deb.*, series 3, cxxviii. 299 (speech of Sir John Pakington, 16 June 1853); ibid. cxxxviii, 162 (Duffy's speech, 4 May 1855) and 2324 (Maguire's speech, 21 June 1855).   [4] *F.J.*, 11 Jan. 1853.

cordially assent to the substance and the spirit of the seventh resolution.

In other words, he did in fact accept the pledge as representing his views.

In that case there was only one way in which Keogh and Sadleir could justify their action. That was to show that they had in fact kept their pledges, that the Government would make 'part of their policy and a Cabinet question' measures meeting the demands of the Tenant League and Religious Equality conferences. Some contemporaries—and not only their allies, but men whose own independence was unquestionable, such as Thomas Meagher, M.P. for Waterford city[1]—considered it unjust to condemn them until the new Government had had an opportunity to make clear its policy. But their opponents considered that delay was unnecessary: that it was clear from the beginning that the Government had no intention of legislating as the Irish party required. The new Chief Secretary, Sir John Young, was a Peelite whose views on the land question as expressed in his address at the general election fell well short of those of the Tenant League, and yet he was able to claim that his opinions as given in that address were in entire accordance with those of Lord Aberdeen.[2] Moreover, if the new officials had obtained assurances from the Government there would have been nothing to prevent them saying so; indeed both were exposed to such relentless attack that they would presumably have been only too glad to prove the charges false. But the most that Keogh ever claimed, in a private letter to Moore, was time for the Government to justify itself:

My dear Moore,

I am Solicitor-General, and I ask you to believe until you see the contrary, that I would not be so if I were not satisfied that full justice would be done to Ireland and Irishmen. I am satisfied that you will see good reason, not only not to oppose, but to support this government. Time and trial is all they want. But this has nothing to do with the subject of your letter. Whether you oppose or support I hope your friendship will remain unbroken, and as far as I can you will always find me ready to carry out your views.[3]

[1] See his letter to organizers of Meath banquet in *F.J.*, 3 Feb. 1853.
[2] See his address in *F.J.*, 4 Jan. 1853.
[3] M. G. Moore, *An Irish Gentleman*, p. 223.

THE DEFECTION OF KEOGH AND SADLEIR 103

The most that the Brigade organ, the *Telegraph*, claimed for him was:

Twelve hours had not elapsed, from the time that Mr. Keogh received his appointment as Law Adviser of the Crown, before he brought under the notice of those with whom he stands more immediately connected in the administration, the urgent necessity of legislating for the tenant-farmers of Ireland, in a spirit of liberality and justice.[1]

Sadleir, in his explanation to his constituents on standing for re-election, went hardly any further. He promised that if the Government tried to trifle with Shee's bill, he would resign;[2] and he also, according to some reports, claimed that Lord John Russell had offered a 'political refutation' of his course on the Ecclesiastical Titles Bill. But when Parliament reassembled, Lord John Russell declared that this statement was completely false and that so far as he knew no conditions had been given to the Irish members of the Government and none had been asked.[3]

Even at the time, then, the arguments seemed heavily weighted against the new officials. It was hardly possible to deny either that they had taken the most solemn pledges or that they had broken them. It is worth noting that fresh evidence, now available, goes even further to support the same conclusion. To begin with, there are some curious facts about Keogh's election in 1852. A House of Commons committee in 1854 discovered that among those who subscribed to his election fund was a Peelite leader, Sidney Herbert;[4] and it also received in evidence a letter written by one of Keogh's supporters during the campaign which stated that Keogh would be in office before six months were out.[5] Among the papers of Lord Naas there survives a letter from an Athlone magistrate, describing an altercation which he had had with Keogh during the election in which the latter had threatened him: 'I'll be Attorney General in three months and have you dismissed.'[6] There may be an innocent explanation for all this: the claims that Keogh would soon

---

[1] *Telegraph*, 31 Dec. 1852. [2] *Weekly Telegraph*, 15 Jan. 1853.
[3] *Parl. Deb.*, series 3, cxxiv. 355 (21 Feb. 1853).
[4] *Corruption Committee*, p. 184.   [5] Ibid., pp. 279–86.
[6] John Willcox to John Wynne, 11 Nov. 1852: N.L.I. MSS., Mayo papers.

be in office may have been mere bombast and Sidney Herbert may have helped him out of disinterested admiration for his conduct. But a more sinister interpretation is also possible. Keogh had a history of close relations with the Peelites—he had originally entered Parliament as one of their number, and during the session of 1851 he would have been thrown in contact with their leaders when they were among the few politicians apart from the Brigade to oppose the Ecclesiastical Titles Bill; so it is possible that he had obtained some kind of assurance from the Peelite leaders that he would receive office in the next Government of which they formed a part and that they already looked on him as an ally. In that case his pose of remaining independent of all English parties was sheer hypocrisy.

The evidence on Keogh's intentions is certainly not conclusive; but as far as Sadleir is concerned ampler and more authoritative material is to be found in the Aberdeen papers now in the British Museum. These contain the correspondence which passed when Sadleir took office, and as they treat the matter more fully than anything which has hitherto been published, they are worth quoting at length.

On accepting office Sadleir wrote:

> 11 Gloucester Square
> Hyde Park.
> 27th Decr. 1852.
>
> My Lord,
> I beg again to thank you for the kind manner in which you have given me the opportunity of consulting some of my friends in the House of Commons before I accepted or declined the office which your Lordship has been good enough to offer me. With their assent I now accept the office.
>
> I believe it is unusual for the person filling the office assigned to me to take any part in debate.
>
> If circumstances should arise which I thought compelled me to speak on particular questions I presume you will not object to my resigning my office in order that I may be at perfect liberty to speak on certain questions.
>
> I have the honour to be, My Lord, your Lordship's faithful servant,
> John Sadleir

There is no hint here that Sadleir expected guarantees on

the Irish policy of the Government. Nor is there in Lord Aberdeen's reply:

Private
Argyll House,
Decr. 27th 1852.

Dear Sir,

 I apprehend that a sense of propriety would prevent any gentleman from speaking against a government of which he was a member; but I am not otherwise aware of any reason for silence on the part of those taking office. At the same time, it must be obvious that any person who contemplates the probability of his being obliged to oppose the government, had better not take office, as the occurrence must be painful to himself, and injurious to them.

 I will not anticipate anything of this kind in your case; and unless you should signify any wish to the contrary, I will request Mr. Hayter to move your writ tomorrow.

I am Dear Sir,
Yours truly
Aberdeen

Four weeks later Sadleir wrote again. He had in the meantime lost his seat on standing for re-election, and he felt it necessary to explain why. At the very end of a letter largely devoted to describing the perfidy of the Carlow electors he ventured for the first time to make a suggestion on policy:

 As I am very anxious to see the government obtaining a large and steady support from this country, you will I trust forgive me for mentioning that there are a number of small measures required to put an end to acknowledged evils which in my opinion have more influence than is generally supposed in repressing improvement and prosperity in Ireland—those measures, if the government can find time to introduce them, would pass without difficulty and viewed afterwards as a whole they would at the close of session furnish cogent proofs why the Irish Liberals ought to support the government. I am rather ashamed to have written so much and I must not transgress further.

This is the nearest that Sadleir ever came to asking for specific assurances; but Lord Aberdeen was not responsive:

London
January 24th 1853.

Dear Sir,

 I regret that the only defeat we have sustained in the late elections should have been in your person; but the account you give of the nature of the proceedings you have had to contend against renders such a result by no means wonderful.

I hope that the arrangements which you anticipate for providing you with a seat may be carried into effect as soon as Parliament meets, and that we shall have the advantage of your assistance.

It has given me pleasure to learn the view which you take of publick feeling in Ireland; and I trust that a reaction will shortly take place in that portion of the Liberal party which is now hostile to the government.

There is certainly no reason to suppose that measures for the improvement of Ireland will be neglected.

I have the honour to be,
Dear Sir,
Very truly yours,
Aberdeen[1]

It seems not too much to say that this last paragraph was as near a snub as the Prime Minister's gentle and courteous nature would allow him to go. Sadleir's attempt to influence policy, belated and half-hearted as it was, had completely failed.

It is clear beyond all question, then, that Keogh and Sadleir had scandalously violated their pledges. The only question on which there can be any doubt, indeed, is at what stage in their career they decided to apostatize: in other words, for how long they had been secret traitors to the movement which they had helped to build up. In Sadleir's case it is quite possible that he had intended to abandon it all along at the first favourable opportunity. The only occasion on which he formally pledged himself to it was at the September conference of the Tenant League: with that exception his public speeches are remarkable rather for the way in which he avoided committing himself to the independent policy than for any eagerness to endorse it, and in a letter to the October conference of the Friends of Religious Equality he openly called for an alliance between English and Irish Liberals.[2] The case of Keogh is harder to judge. He had committed himself far more definitely than Sadleir to the policy of independence, and reason has already been given for supposing that at one time he had been sincere.[3]

[1] B.M. Add. MS. 43248, ff. 108, 109, 326, 334.
[2] *F.J.*, 29 Oct. 1852.   [3] See p. 27.

But if it is true that he was claiming as early as the general election that he would soon be in office, he must presumably have changed his mind before then. The biographer of G. H. Moore suggests that the failure of the Brigadiers' attempt to have their own nominee appointed as permanent secretary of the Catholic Defence Association, in December 1851,[1] had a depressing effect on Keogh's mercurial nature, and that after this disappointment he may have decided to return to the pursuit of his personal interests.[2] No final proof is possible either way, but this theory provides quite a satisfactory explanation of Keogh's behaviour.

The desertion of Keogh and Sadleir naturally aroused the most furious resentment. Sadleir's own paper, the *Telegraph*, of course defended them; and a few individuals—including, as we shall see, some of the northern tenant-righters—approved their course. But on the whole they were met with a blast of condemnation from their late colleagues that would have withered anyone less brazen: the *Freeman's Journal*, the *Tablet*, and the *Nation* assailed them; and the Tenant League and the Friends of Religious Equality passed by overwhelming majorities resolutions of censure.[3] The execration which they then incurred has indeed coloured the views of historians ever since. But the very indignation which their action has provoked can lead to a loss of balance; to heap opprobrium upon them can result in an exaggeration of their importance. Some writers have even implied that their defection was the main cause of the party's failure.[4] This is by no means necessarily so.

Indeed, to claim that they could have had such a catastrophic effect on their party is to misconceive the extent of their influence. No doubt the fact that they had deserted the cause made it easier for others to do so, but if others decided to follow their example, the choice was made independently. Keogh and Sadleir had no control over the average Irish

---
[1] See p. 33.
[2] M. G. Moore, *An Irish Gentleman*, p. 194.
[3] London correspondent, *F.J.*, 30 Dec. 1852; *Tablet*, 1 Jan. 1853; *Nation*, 1 Jan. 1853; *F.J.*, 12 Jan. 1853; *F.J.*, 13 Jan. 1853.
[4] T. P. O'Connor, *The Parnell Movement*, 1st ed., p. 129; cf. A. M. Sullivan, *New Ireland*, 7th ed., p. 168.

member or Irish elector. They did not have the immense personal prestige of an O'Connell or of a Parnell which might have led people unthinkingly to follow their example. They had no control even over the Brigadiers of whom they had previously been leaders, and by no means all the old members of the Brigade followed them on to the ministerial benches.[1] There is only one group of any importance whose defection can be considered as caused by theirs.

This was their immediate connexion in Parliament. Sadleir had built up a small family group in the House of Commons: his brother James sat for Tipperary, his cousins Vincent and Francis Scully for Cork county and Tipperary respectively, and another cousin, Robert Keating, for the city of Waterford. In addition there may have been one or two personal friends who normally followed their lead—perhaps Ouseley Higgins, M.P. for Mayo, and Anthony O'Flaherty, M.P. for the town of Galway. Sadleir was said at the time to be good for seven votes.[2] The loss of seven members was annoying, and it weakened the party both in numbers and prestige; but it could hardly be decisive.

Certainly those who remained loyal to the party saw no need for alarm. They were indignant at so barefaced a betrayal; but they did not despond. Rather their feeling was one of relief. For over a year relations between the leaders of the movement had been poisoned by the suspicions which Keogh and Sadleir aroused in their colleagues. Those suspicions had now been confirmed in the most decided possible manner, but at least the long uncertainty was over, the party knew where it stood and could go forward without further fear of internal enemies. As one writer put it in the *Nation*:

> The schism has established it [the party]. It has winnowed the chaff from the wheat. It has separated what is true, capable, and trustworthy from what is corrupt, impotent, and dangerous.[3]

Another writer was almost exultant:

> I firmly believe that Ireland is stronger in her influence upon England this moment than she has been at any hour since the Union; stronger

---

[1] For details of the course followed by the different M.P.s see Appendix B.
[2] *F.J.*, 31 Dec. 1852.   [3] *Nation*, 12 Mar. 1853.

in her narrowed but incorruptible opposition; and stronger *because* Mr. Keogh and Mr. Sadleir have been bought.[1]

And Lucas in the *Tablet*, though he realized more clearly the difficulties ahead, declared of the Irish party:

I think its prospects are as good as, or better than, they ever were.[2]

About this time the party adopted a distinctive name. The term 'Brigade' had applied originally to those Members of Parliament who had gone into opposition at the time of the Ecclesiastical Titles Bill; it was hardly appropriate to the host of new members returned at the general election, and it became still more unsuitable when two of the most prominent members of the original Brigade had flagrantly abandoned its principles. The new name was a more expressive one. We have seen how at the Tenant League and Religious Equality conferences of 1852 those present pledged themselves to remain 'independent of and in opposition to' all governments which did not adopt certain stated measures. From this it was a short step to name the principle involved that of 'independent opposition', and from that it was but another short step to call the party that professed it the 'Independent Opposition'. This name was used for the first time in the spring of 1853.[3] It summed up the policy of the party so aptly that it rapidly passed into general use and was employed by the Tenant League at its conference in October of that year.[4] Its adoption is perhaps a symbol of the greater *esprit de corps* of the surviving members of the party: the possession of a common label is an indication of the existence of a common feeling, and the adoption at this time of a new title suggests that the common feeling was growing. This was not the characteristic of a movement in decline. Sadleir and Keogh might have taken from the party some of its numerical strength, but they did not seem to have done much harm to its spirit. It is not with them that the main cause of the party's failure must be sought.

[1] *Nation*, 12 Feb. 1853.   [2] *Tablet*, 19 Mar. 1853.
[3] The first instance found is in the resolutions of the Tipperary clergy, dated 5 Apr. 1853, quoted in James Sadleir's letter: *Weekly Telegraph*, 16 Apr. 1853.
[4] *F.J.*, 5 Oct. 1853.

IX

THE QUARREL WITH THE BISHOPS

THE catastrophic effect which has been attributed to the defection of Keogh and Sadleir was not, then, noticed by anyone at the time. The principal historian of the party has, for his part, put forward a different reason for its lack of success. Duffy laid the blame squarely on a section of the Catholic hierarchy: 'We failed at that time and place', he said, 'because we were betrayed by prelates in whom the people had a blind confidence.'[1]

There is nothing at all improbable in such an explanation. It has already been shown what immense influence the Catholic clergy possessed in politics—how they provided almost the whole local leadership of the Liberal party. If the bishops were to interfere with this influence, if they were to forbid the clergy to take part in politics, or to order them to support only a particular section of the Liberal party, the effect on the balance of political power might easily be revolutionary. The bishops had it well within their capacity to wreck the Independent Opposition: the only question was whether they had the will.

During the general election the advocates of an independent party had met with no opposition from within the hierarchy. Some prelates, indeed, remained aloof from public affairs and others endorsed whatever Liberal candidates were standing in their diocese regardless of their shade of politics; but none had even hinted at the desirability of a Whig alliance, and on the other hand several had shown themselves unmistakably friendly to the independent principle. In particular the leaders of the cause could count on the support of the two most influential members of the hierarchy, the Archbishops of Dublin and Tuam. John MacHale, Archbishop of Tuam, had been for thirty years one of the most persistent critics of British administration in Ireland, and his constant appeals to public opinion by speech

[1] Duffy, *League*, p. 372.

and letter had made him one of the most familiar figures in Irish politics. He had been a strong advocate of repeal and on the death of O'Connell he had become perhaps the most prominent spokesman of radical opinion in Ireland. His support was therefore a welcome encouragement to the independent party. Paul Cullen, Archbishop of Dublin, was less well known in the country, because until 1850 he had been living in Rome as Rector of the Irish College; but ecclesiastically he was an even more distinguished figure, for quite apart from the intrinsic importance of his see he held the appointment of Apostolic Delegate, and as such was senior prelate in Ireland. His nomination to Armagh at the end of 1849 had been strongly urged by Dr. MacHale,[1] and since his arrival in Ireland he had shown his sympathy with the ideas of the Archbishop of Tuam in political matters: he had subscribed to the funds of the Tenant League and had presided over the inaugural meeting of the Catholic Defence Association.[2] His translation to Dublin in 1852 appeared as a decided gain to the independent cause, for his predecessor, Archbishop Murray, had been a partisan of the Government, and the diocese of Dublin had hitherto been considered a Whig stronghold. If the rest of the bishops followed the lead of these two prelates, the Independent Opposition would have nothing to fear from the Catholic hierarchy.

No sooner had the Aberdeen Government been formed, however, than signs of opposition to the party began to appear among the bishops. It became apparent that Sadleir and Keogh, on standing for re-election after obtaining office, had secured the support of their local diocesans, for the Bishop of Kildare and Leighlin voted for Sadleir at Carlow,[3] and the Bishop of Elphin allowed Keogh to claim him as a supporter on the hustings at Athlone.[4] The importance of the two prelates' actions should not be exaggerated, for they alone in the hierarchy gave the deserters any countenance, while on the other hand the Archbishop of Tuam and the Bishops of Meath, Killala, Cloyne, and Killaloe publicly

---

[1] B. O'Reilly, *John MacHale*, ii, pp. 220–3.
[2] *F.J.*, 28 Oct. 1851, 20 Aug. 1851.
[3] *F.J.*, 20 Jan. 1853. [4] *F.J.*, 21 Apr. 1853.

condemned the two office-holders for violating their pledges.[1] Moreover, the two bishops did not attempt to impose their own views on their clergy: it was remarked during the Carlow election that the parish priest, who had been Sadleir's most influential supporter at the general election, now remained aloof from him;[2] and, when Sadleir stood for Sligo a little later, he encountered the opposition of a strong section of the local clergy.[3] None the less, it was disquieting that two prelates could be found to condone the action of the two renegades in breaking their solemn engagements, and the moral force of the independent party's appeal to public opinion was thereby weakened.

During 1853 and 1854 there were indications that opposition to the party was spreading in the hierarchy. In the diocese of Ferns, one of the most prominent politicians was the curate of New Ross, Father Doyle, who had been Duffy's right-hand man at the general election; and early in 1853 the bishop showed his disapproval of Father Doyle's activities by transferring him to an inferior rural parish.[4] A year later there was a similar incident in the diocese of Ossory when Father O'Shea, curate of Callan, who was campaigning for the Independent Opposition candidate during a by-election in Louth, was recalled by his bishop and, it was said, narrowly escaped suspension.[5] In both these cases there was, indeed, strong justification for the bishops' action. It was admittedly usual for priests to play a most active part in politics; but there were limits beyond which even in the eighteen-fifties they did not normally go, and those limits had been well passed by both the clergymen concerned. Father Doyle had carried his zeal for Duffy so far as to insult his parish priest, who had supported another candidate, in the columns of the local newspaper;[6] and Father O'Shea was electioneering not in his own district, which would have been normal, but in a county a hundred miles from his parish, which was most exceptional. None the

---

[1] See Archbishop of Tuam's letter to G. H. Moore in *F.J.*, 18 Jan. 1853; letters of Bishops of Meath, Killala, and Cloyne to Meath banquet, *F.J.*, 2 Feb. 1853; and resolutions signed by Bishop of Killaloe in *F.J.*, 12 Apr. 1853.
[2] *F.J.*, 20 Jan. 1853. [3] *F.J.*, 12 July 1853.
[4] *Nation*, 5 Feb. 1853. [5] Duffy, *League*, p. 287.
[6] See p. 74.

less, however unjustifiably, the incidents left a feeling of uneasiness in the minds of many independents.

Far more serious were the signs of a change of attitude in Archbishop Cullen of Dublin, for the Apostolic Delegate was in rank and influence greatly more important than an ordinary diocesan bishop. Rumours of his change of policy can be traced back to the autumn of 1853, for in September of that year the future Cardinal Newman, then Rector of the new Catholic University in Dublin, received news of them from a correspondent:

The archbishop is thick with the Government. Marshall told me as a secret, which he had from the Bishop of Raphoe, that he (the archbishop) had written to sound several of the bishops about presenting a loyal address from the bishops to the Queen, and that he had asked Dr. Slattery to put off his synod on purpose, which Dr. Slattery had resented very much, and snubbed the archbishop in consequence, so that the address fell to the ground. It is the opinion of a party whom Marshall is thick with (not the Tuamites exactly), that the archbishop is getting unpopular in consequence of this and other things such as sending to the right-about his former friends, and surrounding himself with Dr. Murray's people.[1]

By the new year Lucas was writing to Newman in perplexity:

It is impossible to guess, even, at the grounds Dr. Cullen has for the course he takes; but what is clear is, that in almost everything that is in any way open to dispute, he has broken with those bishops with whom he was supposed originally to act, and has approximated to the other side. Everything is touched by this, and unsettled. In politics he has abandoned (apparently) the policy which he himself inaugurated at the Aggregate Meeting . . . and whatever his real opinion is, his influence on men's minds is decidedly against us.[2]

And it was said to be at Dr. Cullen's instigation that the Bishop of Ossory recalled Father O'Shea from the Louth election and threatened him with suspension.[3] To a banquet for Lucas and his colleague in the representation of Meath, held early in 1854, the archbishop sent a letter which was

---

[1] Ambrose St. John to Newman, 19 Sept. 1853: F. McGrath, *Newman's University*, p. 209. Marshall was an English priest then in Dublin; Dr. Slattery was Archbishop of Cashel.
[2] Lucas to Newman, 1 Jan. 1854: McGrath, op. cit., p. 231. The aggregate meeting referred to is the inaugural meeting of the Catholic Defence Association.
[3] Duffy, *League*, p. 287.

cordial enough, indeed, in its personal reference to them but contained a sentence which seemed intended as a rebuke to their politics:

> I fully concur in the propriety of the compliment that the electors of Meath intend paying to Messrs. Corbally and Lucas. Their votes and the services rendered by them in Parliament to our religion and our country give these gentlemen a claim to the esteem and gratitude of all. . . . It should also be my fervent aspiration that we may be able to avoid all dissensions, and that a want of union among ourselves, which has always been so fatal to Ireland, may not leave us an easy prey to our enemies.[1]

A little later he was found praising in a French newspaper 'the liberal spirit of the present ministry'.[2]

It was bad enough for the party to feel they were losing one of their most powerful friends; but the situation was made much worse when they heard that his new views would affect ecclesiastical legislation then under consideration. During 1853 the bishops of all four provinces of Ireland held provincial synods; and in 1854 there was a National Council of the entire hierarchy. It was rumoured that the statutes of two provinces, Armagh and Dublin, and the resolutions of the Council contained clauses limiting the political activity of the clergy.[3] It might be objected that the new rules betrayed no special bias against the independent party, for they were not directed against independent priests alone and would affect friends of the Government just as much as its opponents; but in fact ministerial supporters could do without clerical aid much more easily, for they could call on other assets which were denied to the Independent Opposition: their candidates were often wealthier men, the more aristocratic among them could count on a section of landlord influence, and above all they could dangle before the electors the lure of government patronage. The new legislation might in form be impartial; but in fact it would weight the scales against the Independent Opposition. If the archbishop were able to carry his plan into

[1] *F.J.*, 18 Jan. 1854.
[2] *F.J.*, 18 Mar. 1854, quoting *l'Univers*.
[3] *Tablet*, 21 Oct., 11 Nov. 1854. These are the first published references to the rumours, but it is reasonable to suppose that they had been going round for some time before.

operation, the effect on the independent party might be disastrous.

Dr. Cullen's motives in changing his policy remain, after a hundred years, a matter for conjecture. He has left no published justification of his policy, his private papers are not available for investigation, and we have to be content with stray hints in sources which are often biased against him. But such information as can be obtained on his attitude shows a remarkable concurrence of testimony. The archbishop, it seems, had a fanatical distrust of anything connected with Young Ireland. Lucas reported that Dr. Cullen had described Duffy as 'a wicked man, to act with whom, after his conduct in 1848, was impossible until he had fasted fifty years on bread and water'.[1] Newman recorded that 'Dr. Cullen always compared Young Ireland to Young Italy: and with the most intense expression of words and countenance, assured me they never came right, never—he knew them from his experience of Rome'.[2] Duffy himself found that the archbishop

> regarded me with particular disfavour as an 'Irish Mazzini'—that was his phrase. Whenever I met him, which was rarely, and only at the table of some priest or layman of his diocese, he smiled affably, and I had no sort of notice of his real sentiments. But subterranean murmurs reached me from time to time through friendly ecclesiastics, and at length Lucas assured me that he urged him to separate from so dangerous a connection.[3]

Finally, we have the words of the archbishop himself, in a letter to the Bishop of Kerry:

> I am more & more convinced every day that Duffy deserves no sanction or encouragement from the clergy. It matters not what he is himself while he is put forward & acts as the life & soul of a most dangerous party, the Young Ireland faction, the clerical members of which are likely to fall into the party of Father Gavazzi & the lay members to become disciples of Kossuth & Mazzini who have been so often idolized in the pages of the Nation. As long as Duffy is the leader of such a faction he ought to be looked on with great suspicion. It is most dangerous to do anything tending to give him or his faction an influence

---

[1] E. Lucas, *Life of Frederick Lucas*, ii, p. 123.
[2] F. McGrath, *Newman's University*, p. 362.
[3] Duffy, *League*, p. 174.

in the country which his party would not fail to exercise against Church or state.[1]

Dr. Cullen's suspicions of the Young Irelanders were hardly justified by the facts. He clearly regarded them as being identical in spirit with Young Italy; but in reality the two bodies had quite as much dividing them as they had in common, and to compare a respectable middle-class Catholic like Duffy with an anti-Christian revolutionary like Mazzini was almost ludicrous. Again, the statement that Kossuth and Mazzini had been 'so often idolized in the pages of the Nation' was simply not true: but Lucas reported that when he tried to prove this, the only result was to make the archbishop angry.[2] Dr. Cullen's hatred of Young Ireland seems to have exceeded anything that could be warranted by rational argument, and can be accounted for only by an appeal to psychology. As Rector of the Irish College he had been in Rome during the revolution of 1848, and the best explanation of his subsequent conduct is that the experience had made an impression on him so profound that it coloured his whole political outlook and induced in him a horror of any person or body that could be even suspected of revolutionary tendencies. On this hypothesis, Duffy's connexion with the abortive rebellion of 1848 would have served to turn the archbishop against the whole party with which Duffy acted, and to frighten him into supporting the Government. This theory is not entirely satisfactory as an explanation of Dr. Cullen's conduct, for it leaves unanswered the question of why he should have turned against the movement only in 1853 when Duffy had been prominent in it from the beginning, and one is led to suspect that other factors were influencing the archbishop of which the scanty records show nothing. But whatever the full reasons for the archbishop's change of front, it is beyond question that his obsession with Young Ireland was a major cause of it.

The conflict between the party and those bishops who appeared unfriendly to it was brought finally into the open by an incident in the diocese of Ossory in September 1854. During the session Sergeant Shee, M.P. for County Kil-

[1] Dr. Cullen to Dr. Moriarty, Bishop of Kerry, 20 Jan. 1855: N.L.I. MS. 8319.
[2] E. Lucas, op. cit., p. 124.

kenny, had quarrelled with the other members of the party on a point of tactics, and one of his clerical constituents—Father Keeffe, curate of Callan and a founder of the first tenants' protection society—wrote to reproach him for thus abandoning his colleagues. Shee retaliated by sending this private letter, with his own reply, to the local newspaper,[1] and the next thing that happened was that the Bishop of Ossory, who was a personal friend of Shee's, forbade Father Keeffe to take any further part in politics.[2] This was on quite a different plane from the cases of Father Doyle and Father O'Shea. Father Keeffe had not broken any customary rule of conduct—there had never previously been any objection to clergymen writing private letters to their representatives, and if the letters had reached the papers that was not his fault. It could not even be claimed that he had given just offence to Shee by his tone, for in fact his letter had been temperate and restrained. The bishop's act seemed thoroughly arbitrary. If it was allowed to become a precedent no independent priest could be safe in giving his aid to the party. There was only one way out—one tribunal with authority to override the bishop. The independent leaders decided to appeal to Rome.

This dramatic decision, made public at a League demonstration in Father Keeffe's own town of Callan,[3] naturally had the immediate effect of making the cleavage with the bishops much worse. For once the party had decided to appeal to Rome they were not going to confine themselves to this one case. The mounting resentments of three years now reached the boil and they decided to bring all their grievances, above all the new statutes, before the Holy See. Three different appeals were planned. The curates of Callan —for Father O'Shea as well as Father Keeffe had now been forbidden to take part in politics—were to bring up their own case. A deputation of clergy was to present a memorial detailing the objections to Dr. Cullen's policy from the ecclesiastical point of view. And the Members of Parliament —represented by Lucas and perhaps one other—would present a separate memorial giving the political objections.[4]

---

[1] *F.J.*, 23 Oct. 1854.
[2] *F.J.*, 31 Oct. 1854.
[3] Ibid.
[4] Duffy, *League*, p. 331.

All three appeals met with determined obstruction. The Bishop of Ossory publicly stated that he 'courted appeal';[1] but when it came to the point he flatly refused Father O'Shea permission to visit Rome in person;[2] the Callan curates had to leave their case to be conducted at second hand through Lucas, and in due course the Congregation of Propaganda, then responsible for Irish affairs, found against them.[3] The clerical memorial met difficulties in unexpected quarters. Hundreds of priests were known to sympathize with its objects: in Tipperary, Wexford, and Mayo, priests had even attended public meetings in its favour.[4] But when it came to signing the memorial itself, to directly attacking the Apostolic Delegate in a document to be read at Rome, their enthusiasm suddenly waned. Even in Tuam and Ferns, two dioceses with strong independent leanings, hardly any signatures could be obtained; and in the end all that could be collected were forty-six from Meath, forty-six from Cashel, and not more than twenty-five from all the other dioceses of Ireland.[5] It proved even harder to find anyone to present the memorial in Rome, for when the clergy first selected were approached, they 'pleaded ill-health, urgent local duties, and other excuses'. At last only a curate, Father Dwyer of Doon, County Limerick, could be found prepared to accept the responsibility[6]—and that last hope was dashed when his diocesan, the Archbishop of Cashel, who had not hitherto been considered one of Dr. Cullen's party, refused him leave to go.[7] The memorial had to be left in the hands of Lucas, and it is not clear whether it was ever even presented.

The third appeal, that of the Members of Parliament, was the only one which took place as planned. Lucas himself went to Rome in December 1854 and remained there for five months. His reputation as a Catholic journalist and M.P. stood him in good stead, and he had cordial interviews with Monsignor Barnabo, Secretary of Propaganda, and with the Pope himself. But for all their personal courtesy, they

[1] Letter to *Weekly Telegraph*, 23 Dec. 1854.
[2] *Nation*, 3 Feb. 1855.
[3] The text of the decision is given in *Nation*, 20 Jan. 1856, quoting *Dublin Evening Post*.
[4] Duffy, *League*, p. 348.
[5] Ibid., pp. 349–50.
[6] Ibid., p. 349.
[7] Ibid., p. 351; *Nation*, 24 Feb. 1855.

THE QUARREL WITH THE BISHOPS

showed no sign of accepting Lucas's point of view: on the actual matters at issue between him and the bishops, the Pope showed himself non-committal and Monsignor Barnabo openly unsympathetic.[1] An interview with Dr. Cullen, who was also in Rome, proved still more disappointing, for here even the element of personal cordiality was missing, and Lucas summed up his impressions afterwards by saying

that in the course of it Dr. Cullen did not give one indication of a desire for any amicable settlement; that if any proof had before been wanting, his conversation of Wednesday furnished proof that he wished to get rid of me personally, to break up our party, to discourage opposition to the government, and to put down public opinion in Ireland.[2]

There was only one ray of hope: in the course of an audience the Pope had mentioned to Lucas that he would consider anything put to him in writing;[3] and, seizing this last opportunity to state his case, Lucas set to work on a memorial which would state exhaustively his party's grievances. In May he left Rome, hoping to complete the memorial in a few weeks and present it on his return.

But he was destined never to go back. He had already had one illness in the autumn of 1853;[4] now overwork and worry in an unaccustomed climate shattered his health again, and when he returned home he was seriously ill. In the autumn his condition grew suddenly worse, and on 22 October 1855 he died at Staines, in the house of his friend and parliamentary colleague, Richard Swift. He was forty-three. His memorial was presented after his death, but no official reply seems ever to have been given;[5] and it was in any case a long and diffuse document which was unlikely to impress the Vatican. With the death of Lucas the appeal to Rome had collapsed and Dr. Cullen appeared to have triumphed.

At this point the battered party suffered yet another loss, for Duffy now abandoned it altogether. At the time the

---
[1] E. Lucas, *Life of Frederick Lucas*, ii, pp. 109, 114, 115–19, 130–2; O'Reilly, *John MacHale*, ii, pp. 396–8. [2] E. Lucas, op. cit., p. 122.
[3] Ibid., p. 131. [4] *Tablet*, 1 Dec. 1855.
[5] E. Lucas, op. cit., p. 470.

appeal to Rome was announced he had stated that if the outcome was unfavourable he would resign his seat, and he considered that success was now out of the question. In August 1855, accordingly, he issued a farewell address to his constituents,[1] and in November he sailed in voluntary exile for Australia to seek a new career in a more hopeful land.[2] Now this fact has had an important effect on the historiography of the movement. It has meant that Duffy's history of the party comes to an end at this point; and it has resulted also in his whole account being coloured by the opinions which he held at the time he left Ireland, so that he described as the main cause of the party's failure what was in fact the cause of his own retirement. But his account requires at least to be checked before it is accepted.

It is worth remarking that Duffy seems to have been alone at the time in considering the cause beyond hope. The *Freeman's Journal*, while respecting the sincerity of his farewell address, refused to accept his description of the state of Irish politics as a fair one;[3] while Lucas, in some of the last words he ever published, publicly rejected the contention that the appeal to Rome had failed:

> Without going prematurely into details, I am bound to say that I consider the mission to Rome has been much more satisfactory than we ever had reason to expect; and that the dangers we felt last autumn have been, or are in a fair way to be, in great part removed.[4]

In private he disapproved even more strongly of Duffy's action, for about the same time he wrote to the Archbishop of Tuam:

> I fear you will be annoyed with an announcement of Duffy's which I see in the *Times* of this morning, taken from the *Nation*, to the effect that he leaves Ireland, because those who ought to guide and bless the people's cause have hopelessly deserted it. A more injudicious statement I never read, and as I think it untrue, and the *Times* adds that I am another of the 'disgusted', I think of addressing a short note to that journal to contradict the statement and express opinions. Duffy's real reason is want of means; he sold his paper; but he wants to go off in poetry rather than in prose.[5]

---

[1] *Nation*, 18 Aug. 1855.
[2] *Nation*, 10 Nov. 1855.
[3] *F.J.*, 23 Aug. 1855.
[4] *Tablet*, 11 Aug. 1855.
[5] Lucas to MacHale, 30 July 1855: O'Reilly, *John MacHale*, ii, p. 403.

THE QUARREL WITH THE BISHOPS

The best way to test Duffy's explanation of the party's failure, however, is to carry on the history of the movement past the point at which he left it. If this is done, a curious fact emerges. The bishops who had run foul of the Independent Opposition do not seem to have taken the quarrel any further. One final shot was aimed at the party at the end of 1855, when a letter from Monsignor Barnabo himself arrived forbidding certain named clergymen of the diocese of Meath to attend meetings of the Tenant League without the permission of the bishop (Dr. Cullen) in whose diocese the place of meeting lay.[1] If extended, this policy would have paralysed the League, whose whole strength rested on the support of the local clergy, but in the event it was not extended. The clergy of other dioceses continued to attend League meetings, and within a year the Meath priests themselves were back again.[2] Meanwhile the new statutes which had aroused so much alarm had been promulgated and on inspection they appeared to be not so terrible after all. The decrees of the National Council forbade the clergy to discuss politics inside the churches or to dispute with each other in the press or at public meetings; but far from forbidding the clergy to interfere in politics altogether, they actually enjoined on the clergy the duty of securing the return of suitable representatives. Of the provincial statutes, those of Cashel and Tuam made no mention of politics, and the statutes of Armagh were almost identical with the resolutions of the National Council. Only in Dublin was an additional restriction imposed, for there the clergy were forbidden to attend political meetings at all.[3]

In one way this legislation had a perceptible effect on the conduct of the clergy. It has been noted that in the general election of 1852 clergy were never found acting in isolation, that priests and laity were always associated at political meetings. After the promulgation of the new statutes this was no longer always true. At the Meath by-election in 1855, caused by the death of Lucas, the Liberal candidate

---
[1] *Nation*, 22 Dec. 1855; Rev. J. Dowling to Moore, 17 Dec. 1855: N.L.I. MS. 893, f. 545.
[2] Two are named in report of meeting in *F.J.*, 12 Nov. 1856.
[3] For references see Bibliography, section 4.

was selected by a meeting composed entirely of clergy, and not, as had hitherto been the universal rule, by a mixed meeting of clergy and laity.[1] At the general election of 1857 the same procedure was adopted in Westmeath;[2] and in Mayo and Sligo the sitting members were readopted by exclusively clerical meetings.[3] In Clare a county meeting was held at first, but its decision was later overridden by a conference of the clergy.[4] In Wexford county a preliminary meeting of clergy selected the candidate and the endorsement of the laity at a county meeting was asked for only afterwards.[5] The probable explanation of this new procedure is that the clergy were trying to avoid infringing the directions of the National Council. They were forbidden to show dissension in the presence of the laity; dissension at an adoption meeting was almost inevitable; so the best way out seemed to be to exclude the laity. It is ironic that legislation intended to limit the interference of priests in politics had resulted in their control becoming more exclusive than ever.

But although the new legislation had in some degree altered the methods by which clerical influence was exercised, it does not seem to have affected its extent. True, at Carlow in the general election a new bishop—Sadleir's supporter had died—is reported to have ordered his clergy not to interfere;[6] but this seems to have been a unique case. Generally speaking the clergy at the general election seem to have been as active as ever, and indeed to have been none too meticulous in obeying the provisions of the National Council. At Sligo, the Bishop of Elphin presided at the adoption meeting of the Liberal electors of the borough;[7] and from Dungarvan Maguire was able to report that the clergy had spoken after every mass on his behalf.[8] Dr. Cullen himself, some months before the election, urged his clergy to attend to the registers in the Liberal interest, though he was careful to add his 'disapproval of any manifestation by his clergy at public meetings on political subjects'.[9]

---

[1] *F.J.*, 6 Nov. 1855.
[2] Resolutions printed in *F.J.*, 28 Mar. 1857.
[3] *F.J.*, 26 Mar. and 27 Mar. 1857.
[4] *F.J.*, 28 Mar. and 4 Apr. 1857.   [5] *F.J.*, 26 Mar. 1857.
[6] *D.E.*, 25 Mar. 1857.   [7] *F.J.*, 21 Mar. 1857.
[8] *Cork Examiner*, 30 Mar. 1857.   [9] *Nation*, 6 Dec. 1856.

Nor did the Independent Opposition find themselves handicapped at elections by episcopal opposition. True, some of the hierarchy maintained their Whig views, but they did not attempt to silence clergy who thought differently. The Bishop of Ossory still supported Sergeant Shee, but most of his clergy disagreed with him and used their influence to put the sergeant bottom of the poll in 1857.[1] Only at Waterford did a prelate use his episcopal authority against the party, for there the bishop, who supported a Whig candidate, forbade an independent priest to take any further part in the election.[2] But his displeasure did not prevent the Independent Opposition candidate from being elected.

The quarrel with the bishops had undeniably some most unfortunate results for the party. It helped to kill Lucas, who was the ablest man in the party and could ill be spared. It distracted attention from the task of wresting concessions from the House of Commons—the party was almost a cipher during the session of 1855. It caused some who disliked openly opposing the hierarchy to retreat into neutrality—it is noteworthy that Dr. Gray first separated himself from the other independent leaders at this time, by refusing to declare himself against Dr. Cullen's new policy. But these consequences, important though they were, were not enough in themselves to account for the party's collapse. The party's hopes of recovery depended on regaining seats in Parliament, and that in turn depended on its success in general elections. And by the time of the next general election, in 1857, the supposed danger from the bishops had almost completely disappeared. The party still enjoyed the public support of such prelates as the Archbishop of Tuam and the Bishop of Meath, and if it had lost the friendship of others their attitude scarcely affected the election results. Whatever the reasons for the party's failure, it can hardly be laid at the door of the bishops.

[1] *F.J.*, 6 and 11 Apr. 1857.
[2] J. A. Blake to Moore, 25 Mar. 1857: N.L.I. MS. 894, f. 565.

X

THE FAILURE OF LEADERSHIP

THE two most popular explanations of the party's decline have now been considered, and it is clear that neither of them satisfactorily accounts for its collapse. The defection of Keogh and Sadleir and the quarrel with Archbishop Cullen certainly did not help the party, but equally certainly they did not decide its fate. We must look elsewhere for the real reasons for the débâcle, and that can only be done by giving a full analysis of the party's history. It has seemed best to do this in three stages: to describe the vicissitudes first of the party's leadership, then of the rank and file in Parliament, and finally of its following in the country.

After the loss of Keogh and Sadleir four men stood out among the party's members in Parliament. Roughly in ascending order of importance they were Duffy, Shee, Moore, and Lucas. Duffy's career in the House of Commons was rather a disappointment: it seems fair to say that he was less influential during his three years as a member of the British Parliament than at any other time in his varied political career. His speeches, though polished and well constructed, were perhaps too literary in form for the House of Commons and seem in any case to have made little impact. On one occasion, by accusing the Government of practising upon Irish members corruption equal to 'the worst days of Walpole and the Pelhams', he succeeded in creating a scene and was called upon to explain his words to the House, but it showed no desire to make a martyr of him and the incident was soon forgotten.[1] Ill health, too, handicapped him and in the session of 1854 he did not speak at all. None the less, a man of his connexions and antecedents could never be insignificant: no other member of the House of Commons had the distinction of being a former rebel, and his editorship of the *Nation* meant that he was always a force in the

[1] *Parl. Deb.*, series 3, cxxvi. 1192–1218 and 1236–9 (5 and 6 May 1853).

formation of Irish opinion. Even at his least effective Duffy was still a valuable member of the party.

Sergeant Shee was a leader of the English bar and destined to become the first Catholic since the revolution to reach the English bench. He had a high opinion of his own judgement and was quite capable of asserting that he knew better than the entire Tenant League what was the right course to take. It is perhaps unfair to assess a man's character from his speeches and public writings, but they certainly leave the impression that he was pompous, rather vain, and devoid of a sense of humour. In Parliament, however, he was moderate and level-headed, his speeches were lucid and clearly thought out, and his legal reputation was an asset to the party. It was not surprising that he was given charge of the League's bill when Crawford lost his seat at the general election.

The adherence of G. H. Moore to the party was particularly valuable because he had hitherto been more closely identified with Keogh and Sadleir than with their opponents. He had been openly critical of Lucas's wording of the pledge at the Tenant League conference of September 1852;[1] while he had made Keogh a personal friend, whom he invited to his house and whose advice he sought on private affairs.[2] But having once taken the pledge he stuck to it. Like Keogh and Sadleir he was offered office on the formation of the Aberdeen Government, but unlike them he refused it,[3] and promptly issued a sharp condemnation of their action in accepting.[4] This condemnation helped to prove that the blast of criticism with which they were met was not merely based on personal spite and was not just a continuation of the quarrel which had broken out before the general election: it showed that the grounds for judging them were sufficiently strong to detach from them even one who had hitherto been their friend.

In some ways Moore was one of the most brilliant men in the House of Commons. He had a gift for putting things pithily which was equalled only by Disraeli. His phrases lose

---

[1] See p. 87.
[2] Keogh to Moore, 11 Nov. 1851; Moore to Keogh, 14 June 1852: N.L.I. MS. 892, ff. 341, 364.
[3] According to his own account: see his speech at the Tenant League meeting: *F.J.*, 12 Jan. 1853.   [4] Letter in *F.J.*, 6 Jan. 1853.

half their pungency when divorced from their context, but it is worth quoting some to get the flavour of his style. Take for instance his comment on the Monaghan landlord, already mentioned,[1] who announced to the world that he had penalized a tenant for voting the wrong way at the elections of 1852:

[His letter is] an extraordinary exposition of an ordinary policy. The only difference that exists between Mr. H. de Burgh and the greater part of the landlords in Mayo is, that he has the imbecile manliness to acknowledge what they have the wise cowardice to conceal and disavow.[2]

Or again, take Moore summarizing the suggestion of a colleague in the Tenant League of which he did not approve:

His proposition amounts to this, that in the present state of the tenant cause we are to call upon constituencies that are torpid; call upon representatives that are sold, and to call upon a government that laughs at us to bring in a bill which they are resolved not to carry.[3]

Or, again, there is his description of the consequences of the founding of the Brigade:

I found no Irish party in the House of Commons when I entered it but two miserable bands of despised stipendiaries; I left in it a strong and resolute body of Irish representatives—outwardly feared, and inwardly respected—the arbiters, and not the make weights of party—who have bequeathed to their successors a position more commanding, and a responsibility more honourable, than Irishmen ever possessed in the senate since the Union.[4]

One remembers also his account of how he dealt with an officious police officer during the Mayo election of 1857:

I told the officer I was at a loss to know upon what authority or upon what information he had taken upon himself to act as he had done; that it was the first time in my life that I had ever seen the very respectable body to which he belonged excite terror and alarm in the minds of the peasantry, whom it was their duty to protect; that I should certainly, at a fitting time, make inquiries as to the nature of the scene and the cause of the scene which I had just witnessed; but as I had nothing else to do, and as the people had fled in all directions from me, I would confine my observations to some complimentary

---

[1] See p. 65. [2] *F.J.*, 9 Sept. 1852.
[3] *F.J.*, 17 Oct. 1855.
[4] Election address in *Telegraph* (Castlebar), 14 July 1852.

remarks upon his own personal appearance, in which strain I proceeded for a short period, and he, seeing that the people were gradually coming back, and that all his policemen were in a broad grin, issued some military mandate which I did not understand, and he and his gallant companions in arms took themselves about their business.[1]

Moore's speeches were occasionally long-winded, sometimes not well argued, quite often intemperate; but they were never dull. A man who could talk as he did would always be sure of keeping the attention of his listeners. Indeed there was a magnetism about him which enabled him to hold his own even in the most hostile audience. Perhaps his greatest oratorical triumph occurred not in the House of Commons, but at a meeting called by his political opponents in Dublin.

In the session of 1854 an English back-bencher, Chambers, introduced a bill for the compulsory inspection of convents. A great protest meeting was arranged in Dublin under Whig auspices, and Moore decided to attend the meeting in the hope of turning it into a demonstration in favour of independent opposition. It would need all his debating skill and all his great force of personality to carry out the plan, for the chairman and platform were naturally against him, and when he rose to address the meeting the chairman's first reaction was to refuse him a hearing. But he obtained permission to speak on a point of order, and after winning the audience's goodwill by a few good-humoured comments, he skilfully led on to the question of principle and before the chairman realized what was happening had launched a full-blooded assault on the deserters from the party:

There is another subject upon which I wish to address you, but a subject which I find by advice, to which I bow with submission, I am precluded from entering upon as I should wish to do. I did think that we were here assembled in a council of moral warfare, not to indulge in abstract declamation against this measure or that, but to take counsel together as to the best mode of resisting aggression—(*vehement cheering*)—to take counsel as to the best means of repairing our past errors, of defending our present rights, of establishing and consolidating upon a solid base our future liberties, civil and religious. But I am told

[1] *Mayo elect. pet.*, 1857, p. 461.

that which I thought the most relevant subject that could come before this meeting is the only subject which I am precluded from discussing—that when met here in self-defence we are to be precluded from considering any defensive operations. Now while I bow implicitly to this decision, I hope I may be permitted to say, in vindication of my own opinions, that it is a decision and an advice which my understanding does not enable me to comprehend. Suppose that, instead of this being a moral warfare against convents, it was a real war in which we were engaged; imagine a body of soldiers surrounded, besieged, hemmed in by organised discipline and ruthless enemies—imagine that body of soldiers assembled in a council of war together, and the President of the council thus addressing them: 'Gentlemen, the enemy is about to attack us; they are ruthless, unsparing, determined—they are strong in numbers—they are united in purpose—we are in circumstances of extreme peril—I hope that any gentleman addressing himself to these circumstances will confine himself to protesting with his whole might against the atrocious attacks of the enemy—*(laughter and cheers)*—to declaring that he is prepared to take every measure consistent with his own interests—*(renewed laughter)*—for repelling the aggression; but as to the mode and means of defence which ought to be adopted, that being a subject on which great difference of opinion may exist, it is a subject that ought to be studiously avoided. (*Cheering and laughter*.) But there is one subject to which I would call your special notice: there are some very able officers in our corps who have thought it right and proper to accept commissions from the enemy—*(laughter and cheering)*—and who at the present moment are warmly exerting themselves in their favour. I hope nothing will be said against the feelings of any of these gentlemen, but that, on the contrary, every advice they give us will be received with the most respectful attention.' Would you not believe that any men capable of listening to such admonitions as these were doomed to destruction? (*Cheers*.) Would you not say they deserved their fate?

Having won the audience's favour in the teeth of the platform, he then put and carried, from the floor of the hall, a motion in favour of the independent policy.[1]

Moore, however, had defects as well as qualities. His attendance in Parliament was erratic—in the session of 1855 he hardly appeared at all—and he gave the impression of being unwilling to take trouble over the humdrum details of parliamentary affairs. A far more serious fault was his quarrelsome temper. He was needlessly offensive to Lucas

---

[1] *F.J.*, 16 May 1854; M. G. Moore, *An Irish Gentleman*, pp. 235-9.

THE FAILURE OF LEADERSHIP

on the second day of the Tenant League conference of 1852;[1] and that was not the only occasion on which he appeared to pick quarrels with those who were really his allies. In 1854 he attacked Bowyer, independent member for Dundalk, so sharply that the latter went over to the ministerial benches.[2] In 1856 he wrote to the new editor of the *Tablet*, Wallis, who had ventured to criticize certain phrases in a pamphlet by him, in terms so offensive that for a time the two were not on speaking terms.[3] In 1857 he quarrelled openly with Gray and Cantwell at a meeting of the Tenant League, with the result that they ceased to attend its meetings.[4] In 1859 he even suggested that Maguire, one of the most upright members of the independent party, who happened to disagree with him on a point of policy, was no better than Keogh and Sadleir.[5] His tongue and pen were quite unbridled, and he must have lost his party many friends. Indeed towards the end of his career his enemies were beginning to feel that he might almost be an asset to their cause, and after the meeting at which occurred his rupture with Gray and Cantwell, a Conservative paper cynically remarked:

> Mr. George H. Moore is the best peacemaker after all. He is dispersing the mob. Within the last week two of the noisiest notables of the Tenant League abjured that association rather than take him for their leader. He has only to proceed, still calling upon all Ireland to follow him, and in a very short time he will stand alone in his glory.[6]

The danger of a personality like Moore was that his defects might harm the party more than his undoubted merits assisted it.

Frederick Lucas went into Parliament known to English members, if at all, only as a crank and a fanatic, as the editor of an ultramontane newspaper which published violent editorials against landlords and Protestants, and his chances of being taken seriously seemed remote. Yet his success in Parliament was not merely rapid: it was meteoric. An

---

[1] *F.J.*, 10 Sept. 1852.
[2] *Parl. Deb.*, series 3, cxxxii. 527–34 (6 Apr. 1854); for Bowyer's change of seat see Answers to Correspondents in *Nation*, 24 Feb. 1855.
[3] *Tablet*, 26 Apr., 3 and 17 May 1856.
[4] *F.J.*, 29 Apr. 1857. [5] Letter in *Nation*, 25 Mar. 1859.
[6] *Dublin Evening Mail*, 4 May 1857.

English Catholic paper, by no means wholly in sympathy with him, wrote that he 'achieved a success which was undoubtedly unprecedented among Catholic members, and as far as we can recall, unprecedented for rapidity and decisiveness among any members for the last century'.[1] These are strong terms, but they do not seem to be at all unwarranted by the facts. So remarkable was the manner in which he established a parliamentary position that it is worth describing in detail.

Lucas's first set speech occurred on the second reading of Napier's bills in December 1852. At the outset he stated the point which he intended to prove:

In 1780 Arthur Young estimated the whole rental of Ireland as under £6,000,000 sterling. What was it now? According to the best authorities, it appeared that even after the famine it was near £12,000,000. According to the poor-law valuation of 1850 it was £11,923,459, and the actual rental would of course be greater than these estimates from valuations. Well, whence did this increase of £6,000,000 arise? It must have arisen from improvements on the land effected by somebody. Every one admitted that the landlords had not made them, and there could not be a shadow of doubt, he thought, that they had been made by the tenants.

Now this was a more extreme position than that taken up by previous advocates of the tenants. It was often claimed that they would in future make improvements if they were given security; but Lucas was going further and claiming that they had already made improvements on an enormous scale, that it was not encouragement for the future but recognition for the past that they required. And having taken this strong line, he proceeded to back it up with chapter and verse, a machine-gun fire of well-marshalled examples extending over nine columns of *Hansard*, in which he showed again and again that tenants unassisted in any way by their landlords had made immense improvements only to have all the profit taken away from them by increased rent.[2] Never before, perhaps, had a member shown command of such a wide range of information on the subject, and it is probable that this maiden speech by an untried member was the best

---

[1] *Rambler*, Dec. 1855.
[2] *Parl. Deb.*, series 3, cxxiii. 1545–57 (15 Dec. 1852).

speech on the tenant question that the House had ever heard.

Lucas's second set speech occurred at the beginning of 1853. Two Italian Protestants, Francesco and Rosa Madiai, had been imprisoned by the government of Tuscany on a charge of proselytism; and an evangelical member, Kinnaird, introduced a motion calling on the British Government to intervene on behalf of its oppressed fellow-Protestants. When Lucas rose early in the debate, it must have seemed to onlookers that he had chosen an impossible wicket to bat on: as the known champion of extreme Catholic opinion he could hardly admit the Tuscan government was wrong, and yet he could hardly expect to persuade a Protestant House of Commons that it was right. He began moderately, almost deferentially: he suggested that the framers of the motion were not quite accurate in their facts: the Madiai were being punished, not as a result of any religious persecution, but 'for engaging in a system of proselytism at the bidding and instigation of foreign emissaries and agents'. That at least was the offence for which they had been convicted, and the House in being asked to declare otherwise was in effect being asked to sit as a court of appeal from the courts of Tuscany. However, he was prepared to admit for the sake of argument that the Tuscan decision was mistaken, and he was grateful to the proposers of the motion for raising the question, for 'it opened up a class of considerations he was extremely anxious to submit to the notice of the House'. It seemed to him that the Tuscan government was not unique. The British Government itself had condoned precisely similar behaviour on the part of others—Lord Palmerston had in 1847 supported the expulsion of the Jesuits from Switzerland on grounds almost identical with those on which the Tuscans objected to the Madiai, and a little earlier had approved the expulsion of Catholic missionaries from Tahiti for much the same reason. There were Protestant states such as Sweden and Mecklenburg which maintained in operation laws against proselytism closely similar to those of Tuscany. It could not be admitted that they should protest against persecution in one case and not in the other, and he proposed himself shortly to introduce a resolution in precisely similar terms to that now before them, drawing their attention to other cases of oppression just as much deserving of reprobation as that of the Madiai:

> I propose to begin by requesting the interference of the noble Lord with the cabinet of Sweden; afterwards I propose to go through the Protestant states of Europe—to Mecklenburg next, and then perhaps to Saxony; and he would produce a wonderful change in the social condition of Europe. It cannot be allowed that it is the peculiar duty of the Foreign Office to teach the true principles of toleration to those governments from which they differ in religion; let them first apply their strength to those with which they agree—the Protestant cabinets of Europe—and rebuke the evil spirit out of Protestantism. When they have accomplished that great work, performed that Herculean labour, cleansed that Augean stable, then let them begin with the Catholic states. Sir, I will conclude with repeating, that if this resolution did not contain statements of facts which I believe not to be true, and to be at variance with the papers on the table, it should have my support. As it is, I cannot support it. But I am sure when I have made the motion of which I have given notice, I shall have it seconded by the hon. gentleman opposite.[1]

In strict logic, this speech was not a satisfactory answer, for its argument rested on a *tu quoque* and a *tu quoque* can never decide the point at issue. But as a debating reply it was devastating. It completely altered the tone of the debate, put Lucas's opponents on the defensive, forced them to admit that injustice was not all on one side, and by so doing snatched advantage from an apparently hopeless position. Its effect was well summed up by a contemporary English newspaper:

> Cardinal Wiseman getting elected to the House of Commons, and attempting to secure a hearing, would not have had a more difficult game to play than Mr. Lucas has had; yet, against all the prejudices which met him on the part of the religious members for the violence of the advocacy of his creed, and on the part of the men of business for the political wrong-headedness of his general policy—against a general belief on all sides that he was a fanatic and a fool, who would merely talk fanaticism and folly, and must consequently be summarily put down—this very Catholic, and more Irish than an Irish gentleman, gained on Thursday night a great oratorical success, testified not merely by the chuckling cheers of the delighted 'Brigade' around him, but by

---

[1] *Parl. Deb.*, series 3, cxxiv. 208-21 (17 Feb. 1853).

the encouraging silence, the sign of close attention, of the House generally. . . .

Mr. Lucas has spoken twice since his election—once on tenant-right, and the second time on this Madiai question, and the result is that he is safe of a hearing and of respectful treatment—of a House of Commons position, in fact, for the rest of his sitting life.[1]

From then on Lucas spoke frequently on a wide range of matters of Catholic and Irish interest. The same characteristics that marked his first two speeches continued to be conspicuous—he was exceptionally well informed, always cogent, never ill-tempered, always willing to treat his opponents with courtesy. He soon became accepted as the principal spokesman for Catholic interests in the House and in dealing with these matters was usually replied to by a cabinet minister. In one session he had become the outstanding member in the House of Commons of the Independent Opposition.

Indeed his whole character appeared to be altering for the better. True, the old bitterness of his leading articles, the old recklessness in imputing motives, did not entirely disappear. The memorial which he wrote for the Pope—where above all one might have expected to find restrained and measured statement—contains an astonishing number of sweeping generalizations supported by little or no evidence. He claimed for instance that there was

a regular system of corruption, organized and methodized, by which Whig statesmen have contrived, year after year, to augment the number of Catholic clergy, whom, by the basest and most naked methods, they use as the instruments of their perfidious hostility against the Catholic Church and the Catholic poor.[2]

This statement contains, by implication, an accusation against his own clergy as serious as anything put forward by the most rabid Protestant propagandist, and yet he produced no single instance to support it. But such outbursts, at one time frequent in Lucas's writings, were becoming rarer and rarer: it would be hard, for instance, to find an extreme leading article during the last two years of his editorship of the *Tablet*. And in the last months of his life, when he felt

---
[1] *Leader*, quoted in E. Lucas, *Life of Frederick Lucas*, ii, p. 26.
[2] E. Lucas, op. cit. ii, p. 191.

that he was fighting at Rome the battle of the Church and the poor, his writings take on a new earnestness and a new dignity, as if a fresh side of his nature were being unveiled. It is hard not to feel that when he died he had still not reached his full development and that, as time mellowed his earlier vehemence, he would have become an ever more widely respected figure in the country and in Parliament. It is difficult to say what position he might not have achieved, but he would quite possibly have attained the stature of Cobden or Bright, that of a back-bencher whose name was better known and opinions more widely quoted than those of many cabinet ministers. His early death was perhaps the greatest single blow that the party suffered.

Outside Parliament, the two best-known advocates of the Independent party were Dr. Gray of the *Freeman's Journal* and a Dublin solicitor, John MacNamara Cantwell. Cantwell was a Catholic; he had at one time been joint owner with Dr. Gray of the *Freeman's Journal*, and the two always worked closely together. As a solicitor, he had charge of a case arising out of the Carlow election of 1852 which proved highly damaging to John Sadleir, and refused £750 as his share of a compromise by which the affair might have been hushed up.[1] A little later he spent £1,200 of his own money as Independent Opposition candidate at a by-election in Louth, where his supporters were unable to raise an election fund from their own resources.[2] There was probably no member of the party who had made greater sacrifices for its cause, and though he never succeeded in entering Parliament his services made him a prominent figure in the movement.

These, then, were the men with whom the direction of the party rested. It has already been shown what happened to two of them: how Lucas died in October 1855 and Duffy left the country in November. It remains to be seen what happened to the others.

Lucas and Duffy were not in fact the first casualties. Before death had carried off one and exile the other, Sergeant Shee had broken with the party. The causes of the quarrel

---

[1] Lucas to Moore, 3 Jan. 1854: N.L.I. MS. 892, f. 434.
[2] See his speech at Tenant League meeting: *F.J.*, 29 Apr. 1857.

can be traced back to the session of 1853. The events of that session left the friends of the tenants in a dilemma, for Crawford's bill was defeated in committee, but on the other hand Napier's Tenants' Compensation Bill was actually strengthened in favour of the tenant and was to be considered by the Lords in the following session.[1] The question arose of what the party was to do next—should it stand by its original demands, or should it accept Napier's improved bill as a basis and try to bring it into line with the League's by amendments? Lucas was for the former course, Shee for the latter. The annual conference of the League in October 1853 decided in favour of Lucas, but it allowed control of the party's measure in Parliament to remain in the hands of Shee, and when the new session began Shee brought in, not the League's bill, but a new and more moderate measure of his own.[2]

His action made little difference to the progress of the cause in Parliament, for no bill would be allowed to pass the Commons till the Lords had pronounced upon Napier's bill; and when the Lords did give their verdict—by rejecting the bill altogether[3]—it was too late in the session for any other measure to be proceeded with. But by directly contravening the directions of the Tenant League Shee had made his own continuance as a leader of the party impossible. He declined to attend the next conference of the League,[4] was in effect censured by it for not carrying out his instructions,[5] and henceforward played a lone hand, still sitting on the opposition benches but no longer acting with the independent party.[6] It was at this time that he published the letters which led to the punishment of Father Keeffe and the appeal to Rome.

In itself the loss of the sergeant was not a serious blow. He was not a commanding figure and by the time the rupture occurred could easily be replaced as manager of the tenants'

---

[1] What actually happened was that the committee rejected the first clause of Shee's bill, which would legalize the Ulster Custom, and the League members thereupon abandoned it: Shee, *Papers etc. on the Irish Land Question*, p. 201.
[2] Shee, op. cit., p. 204.
[3] *Parl. Deb.*, series 3, cxxxiii. 517 (18 May 1854).
[4] Shee, op. cit., p. 205. [5] *F.J.*, 27 Sept. 1854.
[6] *Nation*, 5 July 1856.

bill. But the subsequent conduct of the League was such as to render his defection considerably more damaging than it might otherwise have been. In the session of 1855 its leaders were so preoccupied with the appeal to Rome that they introduced no bill of their own; Shee was able once again to act as parliamentary champion of the cause and introduced another unsuccessful bill even more moderate than his previous one.[1] In the session of 1856 the League at last put the management of its cause into reliable hands and requested G. H. Moore to reintroduce the original bill of 1852;[2] but he was so discouraged by the unfavourable reception it received that he did not carry it beyond its second reading.[3] Then, in the session of 1857, realizing that intransigence would not pay, the League altered course completely and brought forward a bill even more moderate than Shee's abortive measures of 1854 and 1855.[4] What he had been driven from the organization for doing in 1854 had become its policy in 1857. The cases were not really parallel —for the complaint against Shee was not that he modified the bill so much as that he modified it without authorization—but the reversal of policy could be construed as a tacit admission that he had been right after all. The Tenant League had not enhanced its reputation for consistency or wisdom.

No sooner had Shee been eliminated than Gray and Cantwell began to follow a line of their own. The divergence first appeared at the time of the appeal to Rome, for Gray refused to join in an attack on members of the Catholic hierarchy, and while the *Nation* and the *Tablet* were openly criticizing the Archbishop of Dublin, the *Freeman's Journal* remained inscrutably silent. Then, towards the end of 1856, dissension broke out in quite a new field. Gray and Cantwell persuaded the Council of the Tenant League to adopt a plan of their invention for strengthening its influence, by which Members of Parliament were to be placed on a roster and not less than three were to attend each monthly meeting of the Council.[5] After the vacillations and inconsistencies of

---

[1] Shee, op. cit., p. 206.   [2] *F.J.*, 12 Dec. 1855.
[3] *Parl. Deb.*, series 3, cxliii. 530–2 (9 July 1856).
[4] *F.J.*, 29 Jan. 1857.   [5] *F.J.*, 30 Nov. 1855.

the past two years the League certainly required some programme to restore its prestige, and this plan, by which the people's representatives would be concerned more closely with its work, seemed a sincere attempt to meet the need. But it had two drawbacks: it involved giving orders to M.P.s; and, as so few M.P.s were still steadfast adherents of the Independent Opposition, it meant sending invitations to some who had abandoned the party, as well as to those who remained loyal, if enough members were to be available to make the scheme work. The consequence was that the plan aroused so much hostility among the parliamentary representatives that it had to be abandoned. Maguire complained of the 'painful and irritating' tone used in addressing them;[1] Moore, Swift, and Magan expressed their resentment at being asked to co-operate with deserters from the cause;[2] and Shee, who had also been invited, declined once again to recognize the authority of the League.[3] There was as yet no complete break between the authors of the plan and the rest of the party. But Gray and Cantwell henceforth almost ceased to attend League meetings, and the line taken by the *Freeman's Journal* on several by-elections in this period shows that they were moving away from the rest of the party.

The smouldering disagreement finally came to a head during the general election of 1857, when Cantwell stood for Dundalk in opposition to Bowyer. Bowyer, elected as an independent member, had drifted away from the hard core of the party, and was on bad terms with Moore personally; but his integrity was unquestioned, he had never become a supporter of the ministry, and it seemed that an Independent Opposition candidate in search of a seat might well have found a more suitable opponent to assail. The Council of the Tenant League, on Moore's instigation, refused to endorse Cantwell's action, Moore and Gray clashed openly at the meeting, and Gray and Cantwell resigned from the Council the same week.[4] Henceforth they were openly critical of the Independent Opposition in general and of Moore in particular.

---

[1] *F.J.*, 12 Dec. 1855.   [2] Letters published in *F.J.*, 18 and 19 Dec. 1855.
[3] Letter published in *F.J.*, 19 Dec. 1855.
[4] *F.J.*, 29 Apr., 1 and 2 May 1857.

Their loss made no difference to the party's parliamentary strength, for neither of them had a seat in the House of Commons; but it must have made some difference to its following in the country. By now only a minority of the Liberal press supported the Independent Opposition and the defection of the *Freeman's Journal*—the one Liberal daily in Ireland and hence an exceptionally influential newspaper—was bound to weaken the party's influence still further.

This left Moore, and Moore alone of the original leaders, still in the service of the party. He rose to the challenge and was never more active than during the sessions of 1856 and 1857 when the conduct of its cause in Parliament rested almost solely with him. He made an excellent speech in introducing the League's bill in 1856, temperate in tone but cogent in construction.[1] He broke the party's tradition of concentrating on Irish and Catholic affairs by invading the field of foreign policy, and moved a resolution critical of the ministry's attitude to the United States.[2] He wrote a devastating pamphlet which demolished the argument of a Whig priest who had criticized the appeal to Rome.[3] He took to electioneering for his colleagues and in the Tipperary by-election of 1857 his caustic speeches were among the high-lights of the campaign. When the general election began shortly afterwards he became almost ubiquitous, speaking for his supporters in half a dozen different constituencies before returning to conduct a whirlwind tour in his own county of Mayo. For all his faults, he at least was a leader who really led. The party had a firmer direction now than at any other period—for the first time it was headed not by a duumvirate, triumvirate, or even quadrumvirate, but by one man who knew his own mind and was more than capable of expressing it. It is possible that had Moore remained in control of the party he might have held it together during the difficult years ahead.

But Moore was destined to be eliminated as so many of

---

[1] *Parl. Deb.*, series 3, cxlii. 922–38 (4 June 1856).
[2] Ibid., cxliii. 109 ff. (30 June 1856).
[3] Letter to the Rev. James Maher, published in *Nation*, 19 Apr. 1856; summarized in M. G. Moore, *An Irish Gentleman*, pp. 250–2.

his colleagues had been. During the general election the clergy of Mayo put forward the most intense efforts on his behalf, and his defeated opponent, Ouseley Higgins, presented an election petition alleging clerical intimidation. Witnesses before the election committee stated that priests had preached sermons against Higgins in the chapels; that they had threatened that the curse of God would fall on his supporters; that they had promised to denounce refractory voters from the altar; and that they had incited mobs to violence. Witnesses came forward for the defence who denied that any such things had occurred; but the committee found for the petitioner and Moore was unseated.[1] By the provisions of the Corrupt Practices Act of 1854 he could not sit again for the same constituency in that Parliament, and as no other seat was available he had to retire from parliamentary life. The party had disintegrated before he had an opportunity to fight an election again, and as events turned out he did not return to the House of Commons until 1868.

The Independent Opposition was not left entirely without a head when Moore was unseated, for during the preceding years some of its other members had been building up a reputation for themselves. M'Mahon, member for County Wexford, was a ready speaker with knowledge of a wide assortment of subjects from fisheries to the Encumbered Estates Court. Bowyer, who after some years of pursuing a line of his own had returned to the fold, was particularly articulate in defence of Catholic interests in every sphere from the law of divorce to the temporal power of the Pope. The O'Donohoe, who entered Parliament for Tipperary in 1857, made the most of the asset of possessing an ancient Irish title and proved a superb popular orator.

The outstanding member of the party, however, after the unseating of Moore, was John Francis Maguire, M.P. for Dungarvan. After several undistinguished sessions he seemed suddenly to have found his feet, and his political friends were able to point with pride to his rapid growth in reputation during 1856 and 1857.[2] When Moore was

---

[1] *Mayo elect. pet.*, 1857.
[2] e.g. *Nation*, 5 July 1856; *F.J.*, 7 Apr. 1857.

unseated he was entrusted by the Tenant League with its bill for the session of 1858, and his speech on introducing it was probably the best the House had heard on the subject since Lucas's maiden oration.[1] As a public figure he had many admirable qualities. He was a good man of business, as he proved by the way in which he made the paper which he had founded, the *Cork Examiner*, the most interesting and most attractively produced of all the Irish provincial papers. He was an energetic Lord Mayor of Cork, long remembered for his campaigns against beggars and against the unhygienic customs of his poorer fellow-citizens.[2] In his public conduct he was meticulously honourable: he was said in later life to have refused offers of office from both parties,[3] and in 1858 he declined even to be named a justice of the peace on the ground that his independence might seem to be compromised.[4] He was deeply religious, with a special loyalty to the head of his Church, and his book *Rome, its Ruler and its Institutions* was the standard apologia in English for the temporal power of the Pope. Though he took part in more than his fair share of political disputes in the course of his life, he always managed to keep the argument above the level of personalities, and he seems to have been the only leader of the Independent Opposition who went through his political career without making an enemy. Taken all round, he was the most attractive of all the personalities brought to the fore by the movement.

But, for all his virtues, Maguire was not a leader in the same sense as Moore. No one ever suggested his being appointed formal head of the party, as was frequently suggested for Moore.[5] His very qualities may have militated against him, for he was perhaps too good-natured to impose his will on others. And one may also suspect that the factor of social status would have been against him in an intensely class-conscious age. Moore, a man of good family and owner of an estate worth £3,000 or £4,000 a year,[6] could hold his own socially with anyone in Ireland; but one may wonder

---

[1] *Parl. Deb.*, series 3, cxlix. 1046–65 (14 Apr. 1858).
[2] See his obituary in *Cork Examiner*, 4 Nov. 1872.
[3] See article in *Dictionary of National Biography*.
[4] *Cork Examiner*, 7 June 1858.
[5] See p. 156. [6] *Mayo elect. pet.*, 1857, p. 448.

what a man like the O'Donohoe would have thought about serving under a merchant's son like Maguire.

At the zenith of its career the party had been directed by a very respectable array of talent: Lucas and Moore, with the support of Shee and Duffy inside Parliament and Gray and Cantwell outside, formed a team fully capable of gaining it a respectful hearing. Indeed they compared in ability with their predecessors and successors among Irish parliamentary parties, for the Repealers had retained the allegiance of no important House of Commons figure apart from O'Connell himself, and the early Home Rulers were not much better off under Butt. But step by step this early talent had been eliminated. To a great extent the fault rested with the individuals concerned: if Shee had been less certain he was always right, if Gray and Cantwell had been more tactful, if Duffy had been less ready to despair, they might all have remained to give their services to the party. But the two most important losses were due to circumstances quite outside the party's control. No one could have foreseen that Lucas would be carried off by sickness in the prime of life, or that Moore would be unseated by a parliamentary committee just when his services were most required. These two strokes of ill fortune must be placed high on the list when the time comes to assess the reasons for the party's failure.

XI
THE DISINTEGRATION OF THE PARLIAMENTARY PARTY

EVIDENCE for the numerical strength of the Independent Opposition at different periods of its existence is less ample than could be desired. There are no surviving records of party meetings from the minutes of which its membership could be reconstructed. Contemporary estimates of its strength provide a useful substitute, but there is no security against carelessness or bias in their compilation, and in any case only three such estimates can be found. Two of them refer to the session of 1853, and form a check on each other because they come from sources politically opposed, the Tenant League on the one hand, and Sadleir's paper, the *Weekly Telegraph*, on the other.[1] The third is an analysis in the Moore papers, dated December 1855, from the pen of Richard Swift, M.P. for Sligo county.[2] These contemporary lists can be supplemented from *Hansard*, for by studying the division lists on the occasions when the Independent Opposition went into one lobby and the rest of the Irish Liberals into the other, it is possible to see who was voting with the party at any particular time; but once again the results are not wholly reliable, for some members appeared in Parliament so rarely that their political attitude cannot be ascertained with accuracy, and party boundaries are in any case confused by members who voted with the Independent Opposition intermittently but not consistently. None the less, if the figures obtained from these various sources are collated a fair idea can be obtained of the rate and extent of the party's decline:[3]

---

[1] *F.J.*, 5 Oct. 1853; *Weekly Telegraph*, 14 Jan. 1854.
[2] Swift to Moore, 24 Dec. 1855: N.L.I. MS. 893, f. 485. A list of deserters is printed in Duffy, *League*, p. 322, which the author claims was 'strictly accurate', but it includes the names of some who had never belonged to the party, excludes others who had undoubtedly left it, and in general conflicts so sharply with all the other available evidence that it must be considered valueless.
[3] For details of individual M.P.s see Appendix B.

THE DISINTEGRATION OF THE PARTY

		Numerical strength	
Session	Source	Ind. Opp.	Marginal
1852 (Nov.–Dec.)	see p. 91	48	
1853	estimate of Tenant League	26	3
	estimate of *W. Telegraph*	24	3
	division lists	23	9
1854	division lists	19	9
1855	Swift's estimate[1]	12	11
	division lists	13	6
1856	division lists	11	4
1857 (Feb.–Mar.)	division lists	12	2
1857 (May–Aug.)[2]		?	?
1858	division lists	12	2
1859 (Feb.–Apr.)		break-up of the party	

It has seemed best to discuss the causes of the party's decline in two stages—to deal first with its fortunes under the administrations of Lord Aberdeen and Lord Palmerston (December 1852–February 1858); and then with its fate under the second administration of Lord Derby (February 1858–June 1859).

The period of the Aberdeen and Palmerston governments was not a propitious time for the discussion of Irish grievances in Parliament. A series of great events drew the attention of members overseas, and left them with little inclination to concentrate on what seemed in comparison the parish-pump politics of Ireland. The Crimean War broke out in 1854 and lasted until 1856; and it had not long come to an end when the mutiny broke out in India. Palmerston's policy towards China provoked a general election in 1857; and his attitude towards France caused a change of government in 1858. Irish members must have looked back with some regret to the days of the Russell administration, when, whatever the merits of the Government's policies, it had at least made Irish affairs the centre of parliamentary attention, and measures directly or indirectly affecting Ireland had formed a major part of the business of every single session.

[1] Swift put question marks opposite two of the members whom he classified as independent; and he subdivided the marginal members into doubtful no. 1 (4 names) and doubtful no. 2 (7 names).
[2] No divisions took place in this session on which an estimate can be founded.

Possibly because of this preoccupation of English members with other matters, the Independent Opposition tacitly abandoned some of its aims, at least for the time being, and concentrated its efforts on a limited range of subjects. The question of repealing the Ecclesiastical Titles Act, of which so much had been heard during the election, was never once raised in Parliament. The case for disendowing the Established Church was put forward on only three occasions: in 1853 by Moore, in 1854 by Shee, and in 1856 by an English Liberal, Miall, who was unconnected with the independent Irish members. The main efforts of the party went into the land question and, as we have seen, a land bill of some kind was before the Commons in every year down to 1858, even though the measure was not always in reliable hands. Apart from this, individual members of the party brought up other matters of Catholic or Irish interest: Lucas, for instance, secured in 1853 the appointment of paid Catholic prison chaplains,[1] and the following year he pressed for the appointment of permanent Catholic chaplains in the forces.[2] Maguire drew attention to the sufferings of Irish-born paupers under the English law of settlement;[3] and M'Mahon urged the claim of Irish fisheries for government aid in their development.[4] Moore, characteristically, preferred to attack personalities, and in 1854 secured a committee of inquiry into the appointment to a colonial judgeship of a man who had been found guilty of bribery in an Irish election. The committee found that Moore's wilder allegations of corrupt influence within the Government were quite untrue, but it did discover that the Colonial Secretary had been culpably careless in checking the qualifications of applicants for official positions.[5]

In its attitude to the general policy of the Government, the independent party did not take the line that it was bound by its pledges to oppose every measure which the adminis-

---

[1] *Parl. Deb.*, series 3, cxxix. 1568–70 (9 Aug. 1853). A vote of the House in the following session rescinded this concession: *Parl. Deb.*, series 3, cxxxiii. 1419 (12 June 1854). The question was not finally settled till the passing of the Prison Ministers Act of 1863. [2] Ibid. cxxxi. 314–27 (3 Mar. 1854).
[3] Ibid. cxxx. 1256–62 (24 Feb. 1854).
[4] Ibid. cxxxvii. 1544–5 (18 Apr. 1855).
[5] *Report from the select committee on Henry Stonor*: H.C. 1854 (278), viii.

tration supported. Lucas had made clear at the time the pledge was adopted that no factious obstruction was intended: and he was the best authority possible on its interpretation, for he had selected the form of words himself.[1] On the contrary, the party was prepared to support measures introduced by ministers when the measures seemed good in themselves, and in practice this frequently occurred. The independent members supported, for instance, the acts extending self-government in the Australian colonies; the Corrupt Practices Act of 1854; and that hardy annual the bill for the relief of Jewish disabilities.

Indeed, apart from the Irish land question, there were only three groups of subjects on which the party at all frequently found itself in opposition to the Government. First, there were proposals coming from the English Radicals which the Government resisted, such as Berkeley's annual motions in favour of the ballot. Secondly, there were matters of foreign and military policy: the party, for instance, voted for the successive motions of censure on the conduct of the Crimean War in the sessions of 1855 and 1856; and in 1857 it supported Cobden's motion condemning the Government's high-handed treatment of China, on which the administration was defeated. Thirdly, the party sometimes, though not always, opposed the administration's financial policy. It voted, for instance, against Gladstone's great budget of 1853 because the chancellor proposed to extend the income-tax to Ireland; and in 1857 it voted with the Conservatives against Cornewall Lewis's budget, which Disraeli attacked on the ground that it did not hold out sufficient hope that the income-tax would soon be abolished. But these three classes of question occupied only a portion of the time of Parliament, and it is probable that in most sessions the party voted with the Government quite as often as it voted against it. The main distinction, indeed, between the Independent Opposition and other Irish Liberals was not how it voted but where it sat, for the independent members remained on the opposition side of the House, and the proof that a member had abandoned the party normally came when he crossed to the ministerial benches.

[1] *Tablet*, 18 Sept. 1852.

Before discussing the causes of the party's decline at this period, we can clear away one misconception at once. The popular legend is that the weak link in the independent opposition movement was the Brigade, and that if it had not been for the dishonest members who were introduced through the Brigade into the parliamentary party, the movement might have had a much more fortunate issue. This view is a generalization from the regrettable careers of Sadleir and Keogh, and it is certainly not fair to the Brigade as a whole. Of the 48 M.P.s who can be classified as independent after the general election of 1852, 14 were former Brigadiers and no fewer than 34 were new recruits. Of the 14 M.P.s still belonging to, or on the margin of, the party in 1857, 6 were ex-Brigadiers and only 6 remained of the other members elected in 1852. It is clear that former members of the Brigade, far from being the unreliable element in the party, tended to remain loyal to it much longer than its other members.

But though it is easy to demolish a legend it is not so easy to ascertain the true reasons for the party's decline. All depends on interpretation of the motives of ordinary M.P.s, and the evidence available is disappointingly meagre when contrasted with the abundant material on the personalities of the leading members of the party. Nor can much be achieved by the kind of statistical analysis which Mr. Conor Cruise O'Brien has applied with such interesting results to the party of Parnell. Investigation does not show any particular social or religious group as being more loyal to the party than any other. Catholics and Protestants, landowners, merchants, and professional men, all tended to leave the party or to remain faithful to it in about the same proportions. None the less, from what material is available it may be inferred that three main motives led members in this period to fall away from the party.

The first of these motives was ambition. As long as the party remained in opposition to the Government, it had no claim to the rewards which governments had to dispense, and some of its members were simply not prepared to abandon their personal interests in this way. Keogh and Sadleir were the obvious examples, but they were by no means the only ones. R. M. Fox, M.P. for Longford, had promised his constituents in 1852 that he would remain independent of all governments until the League's bill was won and the Titles Act repealed;[1] and yet two years later he wrote to the Chief Secretary seeking office and pointed as a recommendation to his consistent support of the administration.[2] Ouseley Higgins, M.P. for Mayo, had been present at the Tenant League conference and had subscribed to the pledge to remain 'independent of and in opposition to' all governments hostile to Crawford's bill; but in 1854 he was described by the Chief Secretary himself as 'a steady friend . . . always on the alert on our side',[3] and two years later he demanded and obtained reward in the form of a militia colonelcy.[4] J. D. Fitzgerald, M.P. for Ennis, and John Ball, M.P. for Carlow county, had also been present at the League conference in 1852; but they both accepted office in Lord Palmerston's government, the former as Solicitor-General for Ireland and the latter as Under-Secretary for the Colonies.

The second motive for abandoning the party was a doubt whether its methods were the best way of obtaining the reforms that its members desired. The theory of independent opposition made sense only on the assumption that the two main parties were more or less equally indifferent to Irish demands, and that either might be induced to yield to them if it needed Irish votes badly enough. But it was rash to suppose that the Conservative party, the party of the Church and the landlords, would be as ready to concede the Irish claims as the Liberals, who were by tradition the party of reform. On the contrary, the Liberals seemed decidedly more likely to be sympathetic, and in that case the best policy for Irish members might be to win their friendship by a firm alliance. It is difficult to know how far such reasoning actually influenced Irish members. Sergeant Murphy,

---

[1] Report of adoption meeting in *F.J.*, 24 Apr. 1852.
[2] Fox to Young, 10 Jan. 1854: B.M. Add. MS. 43197, f. 48.
[3] Young to Duke of Newcastle, 12 Jan. 1854: B.M. Add. MS. 43197, f. 45.
[4] For the details of this transaction see G. H. Moore's letter to the people of Mayo in *Tablet*, 9 Jan. 1858. Moore was bitterly hostile to Higgins, but his account is circumstantial and letters in the Moore papers show that Higgins did not deny the essential facts: Lord Lucan to Higgins, 21 Mar. 1857; Higgins to Lord Lucan, 12 Apr. 1857: N.L.I. MS. 894, ff. 563, 572.

indeed, roundly declared that the Government should be supported as against the Opposition;[1] but that his motives were mixed is suggested by the fact that he shortly afterwards received a lucrative legal appointment.[2] Several of those who had taken the pledge of independence, however, had Whig antecedents, and it would not be surprising if they listened favourably to an argument which tended to justify their previous political course.

The third reason for abandoning the party was disagreement with its members over the interpretation of the pledge. The opposition of the party was, as we have seen, largely confined to questions of foreign and financial policy, and on other issues it frequently voted with the Government. But, it might be argued, why should the line be drawn there? Why should it be legitimate to support the Government on, say, the Jewish disabilities bill, but illegitimate to support it on Gladstone's budget? Many Liberal members claimed that they conscientiously believed that Gladstone's budget was on balance beneficial to Ireland, and in that case could they not vote for it without in any way sacrificing their claim to be considered independent members? The fact was that the terms of the pledge were not precise. Members who had attended the Tenant League and Religious Equality conferences were committed to remaining 'independent of and in opposition to' all governments which did not concede their claims, but no agreed definition existed of what the terms meant.

This was a genuine difficulty and one which the leaders of the party made great efforts to meet. Indeed their articles and speeches during the years after the formulation of the pledge are studded with attempts to make it more precise: to establish a criterion by which members could know when they were expected to oppose the Government and when they need not. Lucas in 1853 explained that the pledge meant 'not to give the minister any unnecessary support'.[3] Shee, a few months later, was a little more ample:

We don't ask you on any occasion to vote against your own conscience:

---

[1] *Parl. Deb.*, series 3, cxxvi. 956 (2 May 1853).
[2] He was appointed Commissioner of Insolvent Debtors.
[3] *Tablet*, 26 Mar. 1853.

be perfectly free to vote as you think right, but we trust you will understand the distinction, and that you will not vote to keep a government in power which won't do justice to this country.[1]

Moore, in 1857, tried to be more clear-cut:

It means that, while on the one hand, the members of the opposition are prepared to assist the executive in maintaining the honour, and conducting the public business of the country; on the other hand—believing that the minister of the day is governing the country on false principles—they will watch his conduct with jealousy; they will show no indulgence to his errors; but, on the contrary, take every legitimate occasion to put him out of power.[2]

But these explanations hardly met the difficulty. Though they became steadily longer, they became scarcely freer from ambiguity. The actual acceptance of office was clearly enough a violation of the pledge, for by no amount of verbal jugglery could it be proved that to hold office under a government was the same thing as to remain independent of and in opposition to it; but with that exception, almost any course could be justified by quoting the words of the independent leaders themselves. Lucas said that the Government should not be given support that was unnecessary; then, by implication, some support for it was necessary. Moore stated that the Government should be turned out on any 'legitimate occasion'; then presumably there were occasions which were not legitimate, and when independent members would be justified in upholding it. Shee left the door wide open to disagreement by conceding that a member should not vote against his conscience or surrender his individual judgement, for a member could justify almost any amount of support of the Government on that ground, while still claiming to be perfectly independent. The small group of members who continued to act together as the Independent Opposition could not claim that theirs was the only legitimate interpretation of the pledge, for the words of their own leaders left room for others.

This was a fact of which backsliders from the party took the fullest advantage. It is noteworthy how few of the M.P.s who had ceased to act with the Independent Opposition ever acknowledged that their opinions had changed: nearly

[1] *F.J.*, 5 Jan. 1854.   [2] Letter in *F.J.*, 26 Mar. 1857.

always, when challenged to explain their course of action, they replied that they were as independent as they had ever been. James Sadleir, for instance, told his Tipperary constituents that he was 'neither the adherent, nor the follower, nor the partisan' of the Aberdeen Government;[1] and Vincent Scully, who nearly always voted with ministers, told his constituents in County Cork that 'he had never voted with the Government except when he believed them to be in the right, and the Government had never ranked him as one of their supporters, nor could they ever tell what vote he would give'.[2] Ouseley Higgins, whom the Government itself considered a steady supporter, used a similar argument in Mayo: 'I separated myself from all parties and, looking to measures, not men, I voted for the Government when I thought they were right, and I voted against them whenever I believed them to be wrong.'[3] William Fagan, M.P. for Cork city, who had pretty generally voted with the administration, told his constituents that he had stood for entire independence of all governments;[4] and Colonel Greville, who had abandoned the party by 1855, said much the same thing on the hustings at Longford when he stood for re-election.[5] No doubt many of the members who used such arguments were simply looking for excuses to abandon the party; but there is no reason to assume that this was always the case. Some of the members who justified themselves in this way were figures of the highest respectability, who cannot easily be suspected of insincerity. Fagan, for instance, had the reputation of being honourable to the point of scrupulosity;[6] and Greville was a large landowner whom Duffy described as 'a man of good sense and honour'.[7] The phrasing of the independent opposition pledge made disagreement over its meaning almost inevitable, and this was perhaps the greatest single

[1] Letter to his constituents in *Tablet*, 23 Apr. 1853, quoting *Tipperary Vindicator*.
[2] *Cork Examiner*, 27 Mar. 1857. Scully had taken no pledges, so there was no question of his having deserted the party: but it is significant that such a man could describe himself as an independent.
[3] *Mayo Constitution*, 4 Apr. 1857.
[4] Speech at nomination: *Cork Examiner*, 30 Mar. 1857.
[5] *Midland Counties Gazette*, 11 Apr. 1857.
[6] See his obituary in *Cork Examiner*, 18 May 1859, a paper politically opposed to him.
[7] Duffy, *League*, p. 228.

factor weakening the party in the years of the Aberdeen and Palmerston administrations.

The defeat of the Palmerston Government on 19 February 1858, and its replacement by a weak Conservative administration under Lord Derby, faced the loyal remnant of the party with a new situation. It found itself in a dilemma which had not arisen under the comparatively strong Governments of Palmerston and Aberdeen.

On the one hand, their pledge would seem to oblige them to treat the new Government in exactly the same way as the old. The resolution of 1852 had never been rescinded; on the contrary, it was introduced and passed anew at each annual conference of the Tenant League. The League's supporters in Parliament were still committed to remaining 'independent of and in opposition to' every government which did not adopt a measure fully equal to Sharman Crawford's bill, and unless the new Government did so—which seemed extremely unlikely—they were bound to oppose it just as they had the last.

But, on the other hand, it could be argued that the wisest course would be to support the new administration. It could hardly prove worse than the old, for Lord Palmerston had shown himself, shortly before he fell, more hostile to the tenants' cause than any minister before, refusing either to support the League's now very moderate bill or to bring in a government measure of his own.[1] On the other hand, the new ministry might even prove sympathetic. Lord Palmerston had been beaten by a chance majority caused by the desertion on a particular issue of many of his normal followers; the Conservatives remained in a decided minority of the House, and were obliged to seek for support wherever they could find it. By bargaining votes in return for concessions, the Irish party might obtain from them some at least of its demands.

The party seems never to have formally decided which policy to adopt, but before the end of the session of 1858 it had drifted into a general support for the Government.[2]

[1] Shee, *Papers etc., on the Irish Land Question*, p. 210.
[2] e.g. it intended to support the Government on Cardwell's motion of censure on its Indian policy, which in the event was never moved: *Cork Examiner*, 17 May 1858.

The 1858 conference of the Tenant League gave a partial endorsement to this course, by deciding to allow the Government four weeks' grace at the beginning of the next session in which to produce a land bill of its own.[1] In the meantime the Government was producing justification for the alliance in the form of a steady trickle of concessions to Irish or Catholic interests. Catholic chaplains in the army were for the first time given permanent rank and salary like those of the Established Churches[2]—an important concession when it is remembered that something like 30 per cent. of the army was Catholic.[3] A contract was negotiated for a mail service direct between Ireland and America, a boon which was expected to bring prosperity to the terminal port of Galway.[4] A government bill on the question of landlord and tenant was known to be in preparation.[5] The Home Secretary showed himself willing to allow Catholic chaplains freer access to their co-religionists in prisons and workhouses.[6] Disraeli gave a friendly reception to a deputation seeking a charter for the Catholic University which would legally empower it to grant degrees.[7] Finally, developments in foreign affairs gave a mainly Catholic party such as the Independent Opposition further reason for wishing to keep the Tories in office. The outbreak of war in Italy endangered the temporal power of the Pope, for revolutionaries were likely to take advantage of the situation to cause a rebellion in the Papal States. The Conservative Government was no friend of the Papacy but at least its foreign policy was aimed at the preservation of peace, while Palmerston and Russell had publicly attacked the Pope's government and were believed capable, if in power, of encouraging revolution if it broke out in his territories. To many Catholics this was a strong motive for keeping them out of office, and Maguire

[1] *F.J.*, 19 Aug. 1858.
[2] *Parl. Deb.*, series 3, cl. 2015 (14 June 1858).
[3] In 1861 the proportion was 28·4 per cent.: *Return stating the numbers and religious denominations of all the soldiers in Her Majesty's land and marine forces* ..., H.C. 1864 (382), xxxv.
[4] *Correspondence etc. relating to postal communication with North America*, H.C. 1859 (1), (230), xvii.
[5] Parliamentary report in *F.J.*, 26 June 1858.
[6] *Cork Examiner*, 6 Oct. 1858, quoting *Tablet*.
[7] *Cork Examiner*, 21 Mar. 1859.

used it later to justify his support of the Tories: 'To save Europe from the horrors of war, Italy from anarchy, and Rome from revolution, I voted against Lord John Russell, and the more dangerous incendiary, Lord Palmerston.'[1]

By the beginning of 1859, however, this curious honeymoon of the Irish and the Conservatives showed signs of coming to an end. The alliance was becoming harder and harder to reconcile with the principle of independent opposition. The four weeks allowed by the League conference for the Government to introduce its Land Bill came and went, and the Government did no more than announce that such a bill would be brought in later.[2] Its main preoccupation at this time was its Reform Bill, on which it knew it would be strongly opposed, and it appeared to be simply playing with the Irish vote to keep its favour until the crucial division was over. The question arose of whether the Independent Opposition would be justified in supporting the ministry any longer.

Maguire and several of his colleagues felt that the arguments in favour of supporting the Conservatives were still sufficient for them to vote for the Reform Bill; but Moore, when he heard of their intention, came out in protest. He felt that their friendship had been extended as long as it possibly could, that any further support for the Government would be inconsistent with their pledge, and in a strong letter to the press he declared: 'I have no hesitation in saying that if those Irish members, who have still the confidence of the Irish people were on any pretence to vote for the second reading of the Reform Bill, they would commit as base and dishonest an act as ever was committed by Keogh and Sadleir.'[3] His views proved to be shared by several of the parliamentary party, and when the fatal vote occurred, on 31 March 1859, the party divided almost exactly in two. Six members voted with the Government for the bill, and five with the Opposition against.[4] The disagreement soon spread to the party's following in the country as prelates, clergy, press, and former members of the parliamentary

---

[1] Address in *Cork Examiner*, 13 Apr. 1859.
[2] *Parl. Deb.*, series 3, clii. 856 (25 Feb. 1859).
[3] *Nation*, 25 Mar. 1859. [4] For names, see Appendix C.

party all lined up on one side or the other. Maguire and those who voted for the Government obtained the approval of Cardinal Wiseman, the clergy of Meath, the *Tablet*, and Richard Swift, formerly M.P. for County Sligo; the O'Donohoe and those who voted against were supported by Archbishop MacHale, the clergy of Tuam, the *Nation*, and of course G. H. Moore, formerly M.P. for Mayo.[1] The issue had split the Independent Opposition from top to bottom.

The division proved to be final. A general election followed the Government's defeat on the Reform Bill; nearly all the members of both sections of the party were re-elected; but on the first vote in the new Parliament the disagreement only reappeared. The party had been through a great many dissensions and schisms already and had still survived as a distinct body of opinion; but the process of fission could not be extended indefinitely: there was bound to come a time when the remaining nucleus became too small to retain its identity. This moment had now come, for there was a mere rump left on either side, and whichever section of the party was considered to be the true descendant of the original movement, it could boast only half a dozen members in Parliament and a handful of committed supporters in the country. The result was that, as a distinct parliamentary body, the party simply collapsed. Individuals professing the principle of independent opposition continued to sit in the Commons, and even to increase in number—the *Nation* counted eighteen after the general election of 1865[2]—but they were just a chance collection of members each interpreting the principle in his own way and having no bond of unity except their label. The Tenant League did not meet again after 1858; and though Maguire probably remained the most prominent single member among the independents he was not looked up to as a leader. Even the issues that most interested them changed. The land question was shelved sometimes for a session at a time; and disestablishment fell for some years into the background. Rather their attention turned to foreign affairs and to demanding changes in the

---

[1] *Nation*, 25 Mar. 1859; *Tablet*, 2 and 9 Apr. 1859; *Cork Examiner*, 2 May 1859.
[2] *Nation*, 29 July 1865.

Irish educational system which would render it more acceptable to Catholics. At the time Moore summed up the result of the division by remarking that 'further separation of the sedimental particles constituting the residuum of the Irish Independent party has ceased to be interesting';[1] and his words, if brutal, proved entirely accurate.

A decisive part in this break-up of the party was played by the pledge. The arguments used on either side paralleled closely those used six years earlier when Keogh and Sadleir deserted the cause. On the one hand it was said that the existing Government was the best they could expect to obtain and should be maintained in office. On the other, it was retorted that this was irrelevant, that their pledge obliged them to oppose the Government if it had not adopted a satisfactory measure of tenant-right. There was one obvious difference between the two cases: Keogh and Sadleir had abandoned their pledges for the sake of personal gain, while Maguire and his colleagues were free from any suspicion of selfish motives, and for this reason the protagonists of 1859 —with the single exception of G. H. Moore who could be relied on to introduce a note of offensiveness into any controversy he undertook—conducted their dispute with far more restraint than those of 1853.[2] But the fact remained that a situation had occurred in which conflicting interpretations arose even in the loyal remnant of the party, and in which it was possible for one half of the party to accuse the other half of breaking its most solemn commitments. Had it not been for the way the original resolution was worded, the dispute might never have arisen at all. The party might still have remained united and continued to exist through the coming years. The pledge had never been an asset to the party—it had never helped to keep the members together. But in its last years it proved a positive handicap, and served only to cause new divisions where none might otherwise have occurred.

This does not mean that no pledge could have been of any

[1] Letter to *Tablet*, 5 Apr. 1859.
[2] The controversy can best be followed in the *Nation* and *Tablet* for April and May 1859.

benefit to the party. If the terms of the commitment had been different, its binding effect might have been greater. This was realized at the time, and in fact two other tests were proposed during the period. One was that the party should be subordinated to a leader. This was frequently suggested during the general election of 1857, by which time G. H. Moore had emerged as the outstanding member of the party, and several candidates at that election explicitly undertook to accept his leadership.[1] But once again the proposed criterion had its disadvantages. Moore was a brilliant man, but his defects of character made him many enemies, and his supremacy would have probably repelled as many potential members as it attracted: if some candidates in 1857 pledged themselves to accept his leadership, others were equally emphatically opposed to it.[2] Again, such a pledge might have led only to another endless dispute on the exact meaning of the term 'leadership'. In any event the unseating of Moore on petition soon caused the idea to be abandoned.

The other proposed test was actually at one time adopted. On 13 December 1852—before the fall of the first Derby Government—thirty-six Irish Liberal members met to consider their future conduct as a party. Those present included Duffy and Lucas, Keogh and most of the Sadleir connexion, and several Whigs, the only important person missing being G. H. Moore. A code of rules was drawn up and accepted with only two dissentients—Duffy and a Whig, Sir Denham Norreys. It was agreed that twenty-one should be a quorum of the party, that the minority should be bound by the decisions of the majority, and that if a member dissented he should leave the party.[3] This seemed a workable system. It did not force any M.P. to vote against his convictions, but it did prevent anyone remaining a member of the party who had repudiated its policy. Thirty years later the Nationalists successfully based their discipline on a somewhat similar pledge: to sit, act, and vote with the party, and to resign

---

[1] e.g. White in Clare, *F.J.*, 28 Mar. 1857; Maley in Roscommon, *F.J.*, 4 Apr. 1857; Corbally and M'Evoy in Meath, *Meath Herald*, 11 Apr. 1857. Cf. *Nation*, 21 Mar. 1857, and *Tablet*, 25 Apr. 1857.

[2] e.g. Conyngham in Clare, *F.J.*, 28 Mar. 1857; resolution of meeting for O'Brien and Bland in King's County, *King's County Chronicle*, 1 Apr. 1857.

[3] *Telegraph*, 15 Dec. 1852.

THE PARLIAMENTARY PARTY

from Parliament if a majority of the party decided that the pledge had not been kept.[1] The terms of 1884 were stricter than those of 1852, for the alternative to obedience was not simply retirement from the party but retirement from Parliament itself, but the principle was the same—that the verdict of the majority was final. What was to work so well for the Nationalists might have proved of some value even in the different circumstances of the 1850's. Even if it did not keep the party together it would at least have provided a criterion by which the loyal could be distinguished from the backsliders.

Unfortunately the arrangements were not adhered to, and the very next meeting of the party under the new rules proved to be its last. On 3 and 5 March 1853 it met to consider its policy towards the new Aberdeen administration. The main question for discussion was whether the party should continue to sit on the opposition benches or should move to the ministerial benches below the gangway, which was the traditional place for an Irish party under a Liberal administration. The debate was long and inconclusive and a decision was not reached until the second day, when a much depleted meeting resolved by thirteen votes to nine that individuals should decide for themselves where they should sit.[2] Lucas, for one, refused to consider the resolution binding;[3] but in any event it had been so phrased that it avoided decision rather than reached it, and all sides seem to have tacitly admitted that so lame a conclusion was evidence that the machinery of consultation had broken down. That was the last that was heard of the scheme. As a bond of unity it had proved even more worthless than the resolutions of the 1852 conferences.

[1] C. C. O'Brien, *Parnell and his Party*, p. 143.
[2] *F.J.*, 5 and 7 Mar. 1853.   [3] *Tablet*, 12 Mar. 1853.

XII

THE PARTY AND THE COUNTRY

So much for the decline of the Independent Opposition in Parliament. It remains only to be shown what happened to it in the country.

In the north, the defection of the party's following was rapid and almost total. The rift first appeared almost immediately after Keogh and Sadleir took office, when the northern leaders, to their colleagues' surprise, took up a different attitude from the rest of the party. Sharman Crawford, in a public letter to Sadleir, condoned his acceptance of office and repudiated for himself the right to judge whether Sadleir had broken his pledges or not.[1] Dr. M'Knight, editor of the *Banner of Ulster*, went further, for at the meeting of the League convened to condemn the deserters, he positively approved their action and asserted that the evil was that twenty men had not got places instead of two.[2] This was a serious matter, for these two men swayed the whole following of the League in the north: Crawford was the doyen of the cause and M'Knight not only ran the leading tenant-right paper but had done more to build up the tenants' organizations in Ulster than any other person.

At first it seemed that the divergence might prove temporary—that, as events made it clear that the deserters had obtained no assurances from the Government, the northerners would admit their mistake and rejoin the fold. But as time passed the division only hardened. The Ulster tenant-righters held a meeting of their own and sent a deputation to London to watch the progress of the land bills through Parliament;[3] and on its arrival it proved more ready to work through the supporters of the ministry than through the independent members.[4] By the next Tenant League conference, in October 1853, the northern representatives were

---

[1] *F.J.*, 11 Jan. 1853. [2] *F.J.*, 12 Jan. 1853.
[3] Letter from M'Knight to Tenant League: *F.J.*, 24 Feb. 1853.
[4] Duffy, *League*, p. 258.

ready to declare that the whole system of imposing pledges on Members of Parliament was mistaken, and before the meeting was over they had withdrawn from further attendance.[1] From this time onwards the Independent Opposition could count on the support in the north of isolated individuals alone, such as William Girdwood, Thomas Neilson Underwood, and Dr. Rentoul.[2]

There were several reasons for this defection in the north. For one thing, Presbyterians had a natural sympathy for the new Government which Catholics could hardly feel, for the Prime Minister and at least one of his cabinet colleagues belonged to the Church of Scotland. For another, some northerners had undoubtedly always disliked being in alliance with the Catholics of the south: tenant-right candidates in 1852 had sometimes found the connexion a liability,[3] and while the *Banner of Ulster* had on the whole been tactful in its handling of religious issues the other tenant-right paper in the north, the *Londonderry Standard*, was quite openly hostile to Catholicism.[4] The main factor, however, seems to have been a personal one. It was hardly possible to have dealings with the Tenant League without coming into contact with Lucas, its most forceful member; and Lucas aroused strong feelings in the north. Crawford found him so unreliable that he eventually declined to speak to him except in the presence of witnesses;[5] and M'Knight's distrust of him dated back to the Ecclesiastical Titles Bill campaign, when the intemperate tone of the *Tablet* articles had dismayed the northern leader.[6] Lucas, however, did not affect most people in the way he did Crawford and M'Knight: it was unfortunate that an incompatibility of temperament should have had such extensive consequences.

The loss of the northerners was bound to damage, to some extent, the party's prestige, for it could no longer claim to speak on behalf of all four provinces of Ireland. But on the other hand the Ulster Leaguers had failed to win a single seat for the party in Parliament; their presence in the movement

---

[1] *F.J.*, 5 and 6 Oct. 1853.   [2] Named in *Nation*, 3 Jan. 1857.
[3] See speeches of the Rev. John Rogers, *F.J.*, 18 June 1852, and of the Rev. Moses Chambers, *Telegraph*, 25 June 1852.
[4] See, e.g., its leading articles of 8 Apr. and 20 May 1852.
[5] Duffy, *League*, p. 277.   [6] Ibid., p. 157 and note.

had brought with it the recurring danger of tension between northern and southern members; and now that they had gone it was possible for the League at a later date to drop the demand for the legalization of the Ulster custom, and so to narrow the front on which they were fighting in Parliament.[1] Lucas may have been ungracious when he suggested that the northerners had been more of a hindrance than a help,[2] but he was not without reason. Certainly their loss went unregretted in the south, except on Duffy's part, and almost unnoticed.

In the three southern provinces the movement of public opinion was more complicated. The party started well when Sadleir stood for re-election at Carlow in January 1853, for its propaganda detached just enough Liberal votes from Sadleir to cause him to be defeated by his Conservative opponent.[3] But this success was followed by a series of disappointments extending over the next three years. Keogh was successful in his re-election for Athlone, and Sadleir shortly afterwards found a seat at Sligo.[4] At a by-election in Tralee, the Independent Opposition candidate was almost swept from the streets by a hostile mob and a Whig retained the seat.[5] Early in 1854 a determined effort was made to defeat Chichester Fortescue, the Whig M.P. for Louth, who was standing for re-election on receiving office; but it was unsuccessful.[6] A little later the party lost a seat at Limerick, where the independent member died and a Whig lawyer was returned unopposed in his place.[7] The only recruit that the Independent Opposition secured during the whole of this period was a new member in Meath, who retained the seat left vacant by Lucas's death; and even here the party majority was heavily reduced.[8] One could easily extend the list of electoral disappointments during these years, but there seems no need to do so; it is enough to say that of the twenty-three by-elections which occurred in Ireland between

---

[1] *F.J.*, 29 Jan. 1857.
[2] *Tablet*, 1 Oct. 1853.
[3] *F.J.*, 20 and 21 Jan. 1853.
[4] *F.J.*, 23 Apr. and 8 July 1853.
[5] *Nation*, 2 July 1853.
[6] *F.J.*, 23 Feb. 1854.
[7] *Tablet*, 4 Nov. 1854.
[8] *F.J.*, 14 Dec. 1855. The figures were: M'Evoy 1,639, Meredyth (Whig) 899. In 1852 they had been: Lucas 2,004, Corbally 1,968, Grattan 565.

the beginning of 1853 and the end of 1855 there was not one, apart from Carlow, where the result could be considered encouraging for the independent party.

Yet too much should not be made of these by-election defeats. The most disappointing results had been in small boroughs—Athlone, Sligo, Tralee—where the electorate was exceptionally open to bribery and government influence and was therefore not properly representative of Irish opinion as a whole. In Louth, though the independent candidate had been defeated, the polling figures indicated very little change in the sentiments of the county.[1] At a by-election in Cork county in 1855 the Liberal adoption meeting had shown where its preferences lay by passing a resolution in favour of independent opposition, and had adopted a ministerialist only when no candidate would come forward distinctly pledged to the independent policy.[2] And in general it may be remarked that nineteenth-century by-elections would always include a deceptively high proportion of ministerial successes, for a large percentage of them were ministerial re-elections, and the Government was unlikely to risk appointing anyone to office who did not have a safe seat. The apparently imposing chain of Government successes can largely be accounted for by the intervention of chance factors on the ministerial side, and down to the end of 1855 the Independent Opposition does not seem to have declined so greatly in popularity as election results would indicate.

Then, at the beginning of 1856, a macabre event occurred which seems to have turned the tide of opinion positively in favour of the party. On 17 February 1856 John Sadleir was found dead on Hampstead Heath, poisoned by his own hand. The news was received at first with astonishment. His political career had indeed received a serious blow two years previously, when a court case had shown that he had procured the wrongful imprisonment of a political opponent during the general election of 1852, and he had been obliged to resign his office;[3] but his private affairs, so far as the world

---

[1] Fortescue (Whig) obtained 53·7 per cent. of the Liberal vote in 1852 and 54·4 per cent. in 1854.   [2] *Tablet*, 14 Apr. 1855, quoting *Cork Examiner*.
[3] Sadleir to Aberdeen, 4 Jan. 1854: B.M. Add. MS. 43251, f. 322.

knew, had continued to prosper. The evidence that came out at the inquest, however, proved that the reality had been far otherwise. He had speculated on an enormous scale, had run into difficulties, had met them by forging securities on which he had raised fresh sums, and when detection seemed imminent had carried out a carefully-planned suicide to avoid facing exposure. The jury brought in a verdict of *felo de se*, and if this had been all he would have done quite enough to damage the reputation of the party with which he had acted. But in his own ruin he brought down others. The Tipperary Joint-Stock Bank, which he had founded and which had become highly popular in the south of Ireland, crashed, and hundreds of small depositors lost their savings, while of the shareholders some went bankrupt and others retreated to America to escape the creditors.[1] His brother James Sadleir, who was manager of the bank, fled the country to avoid a criminal trial and was in due course expelled from the House of Commons.[2] And it was recalled that another associate of the Sadleir group had met a similar fate: the Aberdeen Government had appointed as a Commissioner of Income Tax one Edmond O'Flaherty, brother of the Brigade member for Galway city, but only a year after his appointment he had disappeared, leaving behind evidence of his qualifications for financial employment in the form of numerous forged bills of exchange.[3] The one original intimate of Sadleir's whose fortunes seemed undimmed by these disasters was William Keogh. He had been promoted Attorney-General in 1855; and now, just after the death of Sadleir, he was made a judge.[4]

All this played straight into the hands of the Independent Opposition. They had always claimed that Sadleir and his associates were rogues; and now they had been proved right with a completeness that even they had probably not bargained for. The effect on public opinion was quite unmistakable. Sharman Crawford, for instance, who had been keeping up a running fire of criticism against the party ever

[1] *Annual Register*, 1856, pp. 32–37.
[2] *Parl. Deb.*, series 3, cxliv. 721 (16 Feb. 1857).
[3] Sir William Gregory, *An Autobiography*, pp. 142–3.
[4] *F.J.*, 3 Apr. 1856.

since its condemnation of Keogh and Sadleir in 1853, at last conceded that not all the blame was on one side and that, as he put it, 'there were individual members elected in 1852 who deserve the highest reprobation'.[1] More gratifyingly, by-election results began to take a turn for the better. Of the twelve by-elections that took place between the beginning of 1856 and the dissolution in 1857, not one could be considered a real setback to the Independent Opposition, while several proved decidedly encouraging. At Sligo, vacated by the death of John Sadleir, a section of the Liberals refused to support a ministerial candidate again, twenty-four Catholics voted for the Conservatives, thirty-one abstained, and a Conservative was elected.[2] At Athlone, vacated by the elevation of Keogh to the bench, the same thing happened and the Conservative candidate was elected with the assistance of thirty-six Catholic votes.[3] At New Ross, where the independents claimed to be roughly equal in strength to the other two parties, they decided in the absence of a candidate of their own to coalesce with the Tories against the Whigs and once again a Conservative was successful.[4] It is true that it was the Conservatives who reaped the immediate benefit of these results; but the election of their candidates by the aid of the independent vote showed a new self-confidence and a new cohesion on the part of the independent following; and when it is remembered that two of these constituencies were Sligo and Athlone, the old refuges of Sadleir and Keogh, the results become more remarkable still. It would be hard to find any two places in Ireland where a Government defeat had seemed less probable.

The other by-elections of 1856 proved less disconcerting to the Government, but the continuing strength of the independent following is shown by the fact that in that session —when their strength in Parliament was at its lowest—they received in support of the Tenant League's bill 500 petitions with a quarter of a million signatures.[5] Then, in February 1857, just before the dissolution, they gained their greatest

---

[1] *F.J.*, 27 Jan. 1857.   [2] *F.J.*, 11 Mar. 1856.
[3] *F.J.*, 11 Apr. 1856.
[4] *F.J.*, 15 Mar. 1856; *Nation*, 22 Mar. 1856.
[5] Report of Council of Tenant League: *F.J.*, 12 Nov. 1856.

success since the new parliament began. Tipperary was left open by the expulsion of James Sadleir, and it was significant of feeling in the constituency that both the candidates who came forward—Waldron and the O'Donohoe—claimed to be thoroughly independent and totally free of government connexions.[1] Waldron was a Tipperary man and probably the stronger candidate personally; but the O'Donohoe's professions were slightly the more wholehearted, and he was elected by 3,394 to 2,474.[2] G. H. Moore, who was campaigning for the O'Donohoe, was so delighted with the result that he compared it with the contest of 1828 which had led to Catholic emancipation, and wrote to Archbishop MacHale: 'This election is the turning point of Irish history—and may, if well used, achieve a greater practical purpose than even that of Clare.'[3] It almost seemed as if the tide had turned and a new lease of life for the party was about to begin.

The results of the general election of 1857 seemed at first to justify Moore's optimism, for on most calculations the party had increased its numbers,[4] and it was only after the new parliament had been sitting for some time that it became clear that the party was no stronger than before the dissolution. Indeed the very fact that there was this confusion over the results shows that the independent policy was still popular in the country, for it arose because a number of M.P.s had made insincere professions of support for the party, realizing that to do so was a vote-winning move. Captain Magan in Westmeath, for instance, proclaimed in his election address with all the emphasis of capital letters that he stood for INDEPENDENT OPPOSITION,[5] though once re-elected he proved a fairly firm supporter of the Palmerston administration. The members for King's County, Bland and Patrick O'Brien, were quite as definite in their promises, though they equally promptly forgot them when re-elected.[6]

---

[1] Addresses in *F.J.*, 17 and 18 Feb. 1857.
[2] *Tipperary Free Press*, 17 Mar. 1857.
[3] Moore to MacHale, 14 Mar. 1857: N.L.I. MS. 893, f. 554.
[4] *Nation*, 18 Apr. 1857, gave the party 18 members; *Tablet*, 18 Apr., 16; *Dublin Evening Post*, 21 Apr., 14; *F.J.*, 18 Apr., more than 12. *Dublin Evening Mail*, 22 Apr., gave it 12.   [5] *F.J.*, 24 Mar. 1857.
[6] Speeches in *King's County Chronicle*, 1 Apr. 1857.

All told, it can be shown that twenty-seven of the Liberal M.P.s elected in 1857 gave some kind of pledge to remain independent of all English parties, though in many cases, probably, no one took their protestations very seriously. The existence of so many dubious independents proves, perhaps almost as clearly as the existence of genuine ones would, how strong the feeling for the independent policy still was in the country.

Indeed the Independent Opposition never did lose its popularity outside Parliament. The final collapse of the movement was the result, not of anything that happened in the country, but, as has been shown, of a division within the parliamentary party. Even after the party had disintegrated its survivors continued to receive the support of their constituents, and by-election results such as Calcutt's recapture of Clare in 1860 or Myles O'Reilly's defeat of a junior minister in the traditionally rather Whiggish county of Longford in 1862 showed that the independent spirit lived on in the country. The failure of the independent policy cannot be explained by postulating a drying up of its support in the country.

This, however, does not solve the problem of the party's electoral failure: it only alters the nature of the problem to be solved. For the fact remains that, extensive though the party's following may have been, it did not do well in elections. The question that now arises is why it was unable to make its full weight felt.

One probable reason is that, even if this following remained extensive, it had almost certainly declined in ardour. The grievances from which the party had gained so much advantage in 1852 were receding steadily into the past. The Ecclesiastical Titles Act had seemed like a piece of ruthless bigotry at the time it was passed, but as the years went by and not a single prosecution was instituted under it, the original indignation against it began to lose point. The proclamation and the Stockport riots had raised excitement to fever heat in 1852, but they were soon forgotten and neither English party was foolish enough to offer such provocation again. True, on the eve of the general election of 1857 Lord Derby was ill-advised enough to describe Catholicism as 'religiously corrupt and politically dangerous',[1] but this was a poor substitute for Stockport and efforts to whip up indignation against him provoked little response. And the greatest grievance of all at the beginning of the decade—the terrible condition of the tenantry—seemed to be far less acute than it had been. The figures for evictions fell with a rush from 104,000 in 1850 to 68,000 in 1851, 43,000 in 1852, 25,000 in 1853, and 11,000 in 1854; and thereafter they never again reached five figures until the depression of 1880.[2] The harvests of 1852, 1853, and 1854 were excellent; those of the following four years were good;[3] and if rents remained high the farmers at least had the money to pay them and even to leave something over for themselves. Savings nearly doubled during the fifties, and yet this figure does less than justice to the recovery of the country, for such disasters as the collapse of the Tipperary Bank discouraged the people from investing as much as they could have done.[4] The grievance of insecurity of tenure still remained, but it had rather altered its force, for the danger was no longer that tenants might be turned out to starve, but rather that they were not given sufficient incentive to improve as much as possible. Even the figures for emigration, which were the darkest blot on the economic landscape, declined to some extent, and fell below 100,000 per annum in 1855 for the first time since the famine.[5] The independent Irish party had been formed to protect the tenant from ruin and the Catholic faith from insult, and now both the ruin and the insult were becoming memories of the past. It would not be surprising if even those who supported the party considered its cause less urgent than previously, and if they proved more easily influenced by other factors.

The emergence of such factors can in fact be traced in the years after 1852. One of them was the revival of interest in issues which, from the independent point of view, were

---

[1] *Parl. Deb.*, series 3, cxliv. 2332 (16 Mar. 1857).
[2] *Return . . . of cases of evictions which have come to the knowledge of the constabulary in each of the years from 1849 to 1880*, H.C. 1881 (185), lxxvii.
[3] For agricultural statistics see Hancock, *Report on the Supposed Progressive Decline of Irish Prosperity*, pp. 18–43.
[4] Ibid., p. 53. [5] Ibid., p. 10.

irrelevant. Candidates appear, in particular, to have found it increasingly advisable to attend to local interests. 28 per cent. of Liberal candidates in 1852 had mentioned local interests in their election addresses, 8 per cent. naming specific issues; in 1857 the figures had risen to 40 per cent. and 16 per cent. respectively. If the trend continued it seemed only a matter of time before some elections would be decided mainly on local questions, without reference to the great national causes. And in fact such a case did occur before the Independent Opposition had ceased to exist, at the Galway city by-election of February 1859. The successful candidate was adopted with acclamation; he did not even go through the formality of issuing an address; his only opponent withdrew gracefully in his favour and he was elected in a frenzy of enthusiasm rarely equalled in the period covered by this book. It might be expected that the candidate who gained this unusual triumph would have been someone who had done great service for Ireland—of the stature of Moore or Lucas, say, if not of O'Connell himself. But in fact he was an English businessman, John Orrell Lever, who had been unknown in Ireland a short while before; and the reason for his popularity was that he had made the town the terminus of a transatlantic shipping line.[1] If voters were going to allow elections to be decided by considerations such as this, there was not much use in their showing a theoretical approval of the principle of independent opposition.

Nor did the independent cause suffer only from the competition of other issues. It suffered increasingly from the influence of factors unconnected with the merits of any issue at all. The prevalence of bribery, naturally, is not a factor open to assessment statistically, but certainly more is heard of it in 1857 than at the preceding general election. The Liberal candidate at Carlow complained that electors had asked him for bribes;[2] it was estimated at Drogheda that seventy or eighty electors were open to corruption;[3] and at Galway Anthony O'Flaherty bribed the electors so systematically that he was unseated and many of them were

---

[1] *F.J.*, 5 and 12 Feb. 1859.
[2] *Carlow Sentinel*, 4 Apr. 1857.
[3] *Drogheda elect. pet.*, p. 184.

threatened with disfranchisement.[1] Another member, Major Gavin, was unseated for the same offence after a by-election at Limerick in 1858.[2] This renewed interest of the electors in money was bound to react against the Independent Opposition, for, quite apart from the question of principle, they were the poorest of the three parties and could least afford to use corrupt means.

The pull of government patronage seems also to have been increasingly influential in elections. Independent Opposition members, naturally, were debarred by their principles from asking for patronage and in any case were not likely to receive it. In the excitement of 1852 this attitude of renunciation had coincided with the mood of the country, and so far as can be seen no constituency in that election deliberately selected a place-seeking candidate in preference to an independent one. But as time went on and passions cooled, the advantages of having a member with a claim on the Government for places began to seem more alluring. This was not a factor which could affect Irish politics for much longer, for entrance to the civil service by competitive examination had already been introduced and was steadily spreading, thus correspondingly limiting the power over patronage of M.P.s, but while it lasted its effect was noticeable. It seems, for instance, that the demand for patronage was the decisive factor in the Limerick city election of 1854 —the one by-election in the whole period at which the independents actually lost a seat to the Government. The deceased member, Robert Potter, was one of the staunchest supporters of the Independent Opposition, but precisely because of his independence he had lost popularity with his constituents, and Lucas wrote of him:

> He was pledged not to ask for places. Not the less he was pressed by his constituents to get places! and to the present writer Mr. Potter hardly ever spoke upon public affairs without complaints, half comic and half serious, but always genuine and sometimes detailed and specific, of the pressure put on him by his constituents, and the difficulty he had in meeting that pressure.[3]

---

[1] A Galway Freemen Disfranchisement Bill was introduced but not passed.
[2] *Munster News*, 12 May 1858. The evidence before the election committee was not printed.   [3] *Tablet*, 28 Oct. 1854.

Another consequence of the lowering of the political temperature was that candidates who had been too unpopular to stand a chance in 1852 were beginning to re-emerge. This benefited the Whigs in particular, for they possessed some prominent personalities who in normal times would, because of their local influence, have been strong candidates, but who had in 1852 been driven from the constituencies because of their connexion with the authors of the Ecclesiastical Titles Act. But as one of them put it in 1857, five years of exile from Parliament ought to be sufficient to atone for one error however serious,[1] and as quieter times returned some of them felt able to come forward again. A sign of the times was the appearance of H. G. Hughes, Russell's Solicitor-General for Ireland, as Liberal candidate for Cavan in 1855,[2] and although he was not then successful, he found a seat in Longford the following year. R. M. Bellew, who had been one of Russell's Lords of the Treasury, stood again for Louth in 1857, and although he was unsuccessful he split the Liberal vote and a Conservative replaced the Independent Opposition sitting member. In Queen's County there were even to be found Catholic clergy willing to support J. W. Fitzpatrick, who had not only supported the Russell Government in general but had voted for the Titles Act itself.[3]

At the same time, the balance of influence between clergy and landlords was shifting in favour of the latter. The landlords were still as strong as ever; indeed the cooling of political passions probably increased their influence, as there was less incentive for an elector to go against his landlord's wishes. There are few reports of the use of intimidation in 1857, but there are as many as ever of landlords canvassing the voters, organizing transport, and bringing them up to the poll. Out of a considerable amount of evidence one may quote the testimony of Sir William Gregory, who in his old age remembered with gratitude the help he received from the landlords of County Galway:

In the western baronies, James Martin, of Ross, and George Burke,

---

[1] Address of R. M. Bellew, *F.J.*, 25 Mar. 1857.
[2] Address in *F.J.*, 10 Mar. 1855.
[3] See requisition in *Dublin Evening Post*, 26 Mar. 1857.

of Danesfield, took the lead in bringing up the voters. My dear old friend Tom Joyce took charge of the district about Craughwell, Andrew Comyn of that of Ballinasloe, while, at Eyrecourt, John Eyre worked the baronies of Longford and Leitrim with unflagging zeal and energy, and brought carriages and cars full of voters to Loughrea, amid much noise, cheering and enthusiasm.[1]

One might note also the enterprise shown by the agent of Sir Nugent Humble at Dungarvan, who actually retrieved three paupers from the workhouse to vote for the Conservative candidate; although his initiative failed to meet its reward, for, having nothing to lose, they voted for the independent instead.[2]

The influence of the clergy, on the other hand, appears to have suffered a sharp decline. This was not because they were less active: as has already been shown, they were as prominent as ever in the general election of 1857 and the legislation of Dr. Cullen seems to have made very little difference.[3] It was because they were divided. In 1852, at least after the news of Stockport, there had been hardly a constituency where the clergy were openly at issue with each other. Even in a county like Louth, where some supported a thorough-going Whig like Fortescue and others an equally thorough-going independent like Kennedy, they had at least been able to unite in their common antipathy to the Tories. But since the fall of the Derby government all this had been changed. For in the eyes of some Liberals the Tories remained the main enemy; while in the eyes of others the Whigs were a more serious danger and the Tories might even be used as allies against them. The two views could not be reconciled. The first clash between the clergy appears to have occurred at the Sligo election of 1853, where some priests were for Sadleir and others were violently opposed to him.[4] A similar division occurred in the Louth election of 1854, at New Ross in 1856, and quite sharply in the Tipperary by-election of February 1857, where priests were bringing up their parishioners to the same polling-booths in support of opposing candidates.[5]

[1] Sir William Gregory, *An Autobiography*, p. 163.
[2] *Cork Examiner*, 3 Apr. 1857.   [3] See pp. 122–3.
[4] *F.J.*, 5, 7, and 12 July 1853.
[5] Duffy, *League*, p. 287; *F.J.*, 12 Mar. 1856; *Tipperary Free Press*, 13 Mar. 1857.

At the general election of 1857 the division was widespread, and priest opposed priest in at least a dozen different constituencies. True, in some places the disagreement was patched up before it came to a head: in Longford and Clare, for instance, conferences resolved the difficulties before nomination day;[1] and in Westmeath a clash at the polls was avoided by the retirement of one of the candidates[2]—but elsewhere the electors were treated to the spectacle of priests openly at issue with each other. In Mayo the Archdeacon of Tuam nominated G. H. Moore, and the Dean nominated his bitter opponent, Ouseley Higgins.[3] At Athlone the bishop personally nominated Ennis at the hustings, only to have one of his parish priests asking the candidate 'inconvenient questions about tenant-right'.[4]

These dissensions among the clergy played into the hands of the Conservatives. For wherever they occurred, it would probably mean that no Liberal candidate had a complete network of local assistants, that their potential supporters in some areas would be left uncanvassed and unpolled where the clergy adhered to another candidate, and that in consequence none of them could put forward his full strength. Again and again in these years Conservatives captured seats which had long been held by Liberals. Indeed this decade was to be the most encouraging they ever had in the Irish electoral field. Between 1852 and 1857 they made a net gain of three seats at by-elections,[5] at the general election of 1857 they gained three more, and at the general election of 1859 they reached a strength, according to an estimate from a Liberal source,[6] of fifty-seven—a clear majority of the representation of Ireland and the highest figure they reached at any time after the great Reform Act.

This shift in the balance between clergy and landlord damaged the other wing of the Liberal party as well as the

---

[1] *F.J.*, 4 and 11 Apr. 1857.
[2] Urquhart, though rejected by the clerical adoption meeting, was nominated at the hustings by a priest, but he retired before polling: *Westmeath Guardian*, 9 Apr. 1857.
[3] *F.J.*, 6 Apr. 1857.   [4] *D.E.*, 1 Apr. 1857.
[5] Though this was offset by the defection to the Liberals of three Conservatives already in the Commons: see Appendix B.
[6] *Weekly F.J.*, 21 May 1859.

Independent Opposition, for the Conservatives in 1857 gained seats from each. But it was natural to expect it would damage the ministerial Liberals less, for they had always had more command of resources other than clerical support. Moreover, there is evidence to suggest that in some constituencies there was emerging a third interest, distinct from both the clergy and the great proprietors, which was throwing its influence on the side of the Whigs. The *Nation* believed it had found traces of this in the Louth by-election of 1854 and even earlier:

> This is a contest, not of the aristocracy, but of the middle classes against the people. I have nowhere seen so perfect an illustration of the formation of a regular bourgeoisie in Ireland... there is a very strong, and a very sordid and pretentious class, intervening between the landlords and the people; I speak of it as a class, for of many of its individuals the present writer would be long sorry to say an unkind word; a class that has been forming throughout Ireland since Emancipation, I suppose, but here has thoroughly solidified and stratified. It is selvaged at one end by the *shoneen* and at the other by the *bodagh*, and really coheres wonderfully, considering its motley materials. This is the first time they have declared war directly against the people; and the animosity is terrific. Fortescue was *their* candidate at the last election, as Grattan was the chosen of a precisely similar class in Meath, but in Fortescue's case they managed to engage a very considerable popular sympathy. Now they have taken their stand apart from and against the people. The landlords were never, in any Tory contest within man's memory, so odious.[1]

In Westmeath during the elections of 1857 there was a curious and possibly significant event, a meeting of the 'independent gentry' in support of the sitting ministerialist members, convened by a former president of the independent club who may have been piqued at the decision of the clergy to take the selection of Liberal candidates into their own hands.[2] The new interest emerges most clearly in the far west, where it consisted chiefly of the Catholic proprietors who seem to have been making a concerted attempt to throw off the political supremacy of Archbishop MacHale. In County Galway they supported Gregory, who was elected;

---

[1] *Nation*, 25 Feb. 1854. A *bodagh* is a rich farmer; a *shoneen* is best defined as a would-be gentleman.
[2] *Westmeath Guardian*, 2 Apr. 1857.

but as he also enjoyed the support of two of the four Catholic bishops and three of the four greatest landowners in the county this could hardly be counted as their victory.[1] Their performance was much more remarkable in Mayo. There were three candidates—Palmer,[2] Conservative, supported by nearly all the great landlords; Moore, Independent Opposition, supported by nearly all the priests; and Higgins, ministerialist, depending mainly on the Catholic gentry.[3] The Conservative and the independent were in alliance[4] and their supporters used their influence to the full: the zeal of Moore's supporters, indeed, as has already been shown, led to his unseating. With the two great interests arrayed against him Higgins ought not to have stood a chance, but in fact he gave his opponents an extremely stiff fight, and the final figures were:

>Palmer 1,225
>Moore 1,150
>Higgins 1,037[5]

As most of those who voted for Palmer also voted for Moore, this shows that the Catholic gentry had proved themselves not much weaker than the other two interests combined.

It would be mere conjecture to assess the extent of this third interest or even the degree to which it existed as a consciously distinct force. But it does seem legitimate to suggest that as time went on it would become stronger. Natural migration in the social scale appears to have been leading to a gradual increase in the proportion of Catholics among the landed gentry, as the artificial supremacy once guaranteed to the Protestants by the penal laws receded into the past; and this process may have been hastened by the sale of so many old estates in the Encumbered Estates Court. One comes across striking individual cases of Catholics rising to landed wealth: John Sadleir had bought £230,000 worth of land in the court before his fall;[6] and Charles Bianconi, who came to Ireland a penniless pedlar, lived to

---

[1] Sir William Gregory, *An Autobiography*, pp. 161-3.
[2] Son of the evicting landlord mentioned on p. 67.
[3] *Mayo elect. pet.*, 1857, pp. 42, 192.
[4] Ibid., p. 256.   [5] Ibid., p. 1.
[6] *Returns of the several purchases made in the Incumbered Estates Court by the late John Sadleir*, H.C. 1856 (187), liii.

spend £70,000 in building up an estate in Tipperary.[1] In the years to come Irish history took another turn and the political influence of Catholic and Protestant gentry alike was destined to be swept away. But so long as it remained, the influence of the wealthier Catholics seemed likely to provide a constant and indeed growing obstacle to the rise of any Irish party with extreme views.

Yet another difficulty facing the Independent Opposition was the shortage of reliable candidates. In the general election of 1857 the Cavan County Liberal Club resolved for an Independent Opposition candidate but none ever appeared.[2] The Liberals of King's County were by no means anxious to return their sitting members again, but nobody else came forward, and after both had given strong assurances about their conduct for the future they were readopted.[3] In Westmeath, the clergy wanted to oust both the sitting members, but were able to find only one candidate, Sir Richard Levinge,[4] and even he was far from ideal. He had been the Conservative contestant for the county in 1852, had asked the Aberdeen government for a peerage in 1854 on the ground, among other reasons, that he had always been a Peelite, and now by standing as an independent had practically boxed the political compass.[5] In Tipperary the Independent Opposition started a partner for the O'Donohoe in the person of Major Massy, but a dispute broke out between the two candidates about the division of election expenses, and Massy retired in dudgeon.[6] In County Cork the party appeared to have a strong candidate in Denis Shine Lawlor, but only a week before nomination day he suddenly withdrew on the ground that he had given a private undertaking to another candidate not to oppose him.[7] The party was left frantically seeking a substitute, and how desperate

---

[1] Mrs. M. J. O'Connell, *Charles Bianconi*, p. 266.
[2] *Anglo-Celt* (Cavan), 19 Mar. 1857.
[3] *King's County Chronicle*, 1 Apr. 1857.
[4] *F.J.*, 28 Mar. 1857.
[5] *D.E.*, 15 June 1852; Newcastle to Aberdeen, 9 Apr. 1854: B.M. Add. MS. 43197, f. 57.
[6] *Limerick Reporter*, 10 Apr. 1857.
[7] *Cork Examiner*, 30 Mar. 1857.

they were is shown by the fact that some of them rallied to none other than Vincent Scully, cousin of John Sadleir and one of the most consistent supporters of the Government, on the grounds that he had given them assurances about his future conduct.[1]

Even where the Independent Opposition found a candidate, he might well prove unsatisfactory for personal reasons. Captain Bellew, sitting member for County Galway, was disliked as a man even by those who approved his politics, and was so tepidly backed by his supporters that he was defeated at the polls.[2] Difficulties with his own supporters seem also to have led to the defeat of Richard Swift, M.P. for County Sligo.[3] Maley in Roscommon and Colonel French at Galway both lived in England, were apparently unknown in their constituencies, and came forward late in the campaign when the other candidates had probably completed their canvasses and made sure of their majorities.[4]

Enough evidence has been offered to show that the Independent Opposition lost several seats largely or even mainly through a shortage of suitable candidates. Seats in Cork, Galway, King's County, Sligo, and Tipperary might well have been won had better men come forward. The impression left by the elections is that where a genuine independent came forward who was not entirely unacceptable on personal grounds, the constituencies would nearly always elect him. It does seem that shortage of candidates was one of the most important factors limiting the party's success.

Preceding chapters have revealed a variety of reasons for the collapse of the Independent Opposition. The defection of Keogh and Sadleir drew off a portion of the party's strength, though not enough by itself to make much difference to the movement's fortunes. The change of attitude on the part of Archbishop Cullen had important temporary consequences, though in the long run it made little difference to the party's electoral strength. More decisive was the

---

[1] See speech of McCarthy Downing, *Cork Examiner*, 6 Apr. 1857.
[2] Sir William Gregory, *An Autobiography*, p. 160.
[3] *Dublin Evening Post*, 11 Apr. 1857; *F.J.*, 9 Apr. 1857.
[4] *F.J.*, 2 and 4 Apr. 1857; *Galway elect. comm.*, pp. xi, 89.

number of casualties among the parliamentary leaders, which in the end deprived the party of that unified direction which was essential for success or even for survival. Equally important was the failure to find a formula sufficiently definite to unite the party in a single course of action, for it was the difficulty of interpreting the pledge actually adopted which led to the final disintegration of the party.

But it may be suggested that if one set of causes was more fundamental than another, it was that discussed in this chapter. The other misfortunes which befell the party were largely accidental, and it is quite possible to conceive circumstances in which they would not have arisen. But even if that had been so—even supposing that Lucas had lived, that Moore had kept his seat, that the party had adopted a pledge which was free from ambiguity—the probabilities are that the final outcome would not have been very different. In the long run there was only one kind of success which could keep the party in existence, and that was success in winning elections: no amount of triumphs elsewhere would avail the party if it failed to recruit its strength in the House of Commons. Now victory in elections largely depended on the factors discussed in this chapter, and it will have been noted how the influence of these factors was almost entirely unfavourable to the Independent Opposition. The disposal of government patronage, for instance, was a weapon which could often be used against it but never in its favour, and the same was true in a hardly lesser degree of bribery. The influence of the landlords was consistently hostile, while that of the clergy, on whom the independents so greatly depended, was a varying factor affected by many influences outside the party's control. The problem of obtaining candidates was one which the independents would inevitably find far more serious than the Whigs or Tories did, so long as candidates were normally drawn from classes prejudiced in favour of the two traditional parties. In a period of exceptional excitement, as in 1852, these difficulties might be overcome and an Irish party could be carried on a wave of enthusiasm to a spectacular victory at the polls. But the obstacles were masked, not destroyed, and as quieter times returned would only re-emerge. This was exactly what happened in the years from 1853 onward, and the ill-success of the independents in the general election of 1857 reflected the process. So long as these factors remained influential the cards were stacked against an independent Irish party, and their combined effect was to make a strong party almost impossible. It has been said that a series of fortunate accidents led to the striking success of the movement in 1852: it cannot be said that a series of particularly unfortunate accidents led to its collapse, for, although luck was certainly against it, in the electoral field conditions were merely reverting to normal. The structure of Irish politics was all along unfavourable to the existence of an independent Irish party, and in spite of initial successes it was doomed to a short life.

APPENDIX A

IRISH LIBERAL M.P.S 1851–2

THE following table is designed to illustrate the growth of the Irish Brigade. Columns (1) to (4) show the voting on the four questions of confidence in the session of 1851 in which the Brigadiers sided with the Conservatives;[1] column (5) distinguishes those members who walked out of the House on the Thesiger amendments from those who voted with the Government,[2] and column (6) gives the division on the motion censuring Lord Clarendon debated early in 1852.[3] Column (7) shows those known to have been present at party meetings of the Brigade in the session of 1852: three such meetings are recorded, in the *Telegraph* for 4 February, 6 February, and 12 May 1852.

Column (8) summarizes the results of the previous ones and classifies the members as they stood at the dissolution. One case perhaps requires a word of explanation: it may seem surprising that Sir Henry Winston Barron has been classified as a Whig when he twice voted against the Government on issues of confidence; but he appears to have voted as he did, not out of sympathy with the Brigadiers, but because he stood politically on the right wing of the Whig party and was in some respects closer to the Protectionists.

The final column shows, as a matter of interest, the religion of each M.P. It is based on the list given in the *Tablet* for 27 June 1857 and has been checked where possible by other sources.

W = Whig; B = Brigadier; ? = marginal or uncertain; RC = Roman Catholic; P = a member of the Established Church.

Name	Constituency	(1)	(2)	(3)	(4)	(5)	(6)	(7)	(8)	(9)
Anstey, C.	Youghal	W	W	W	W	W	W	..	W	RC
Armstrong, Sir A.	King's Co.	W	W	W	W	W	W	..	W	P
Barron, Sir H. W.	Waterford city	..	B	B	..	..	..	..	W	RC
Bellew, R. M.	Louth	W	W	W	W	..	W	..	W	RC
Blackall, Major S. W.	Longford	W	colonial governor			..	..	..	..	P
Blake, M. J.	Galway borough	W	B	B	B	B	B	B	B	RC
Burke, Sir T.	Galway co.	..	W	W	W	..	W	..	W	RC
Butler, P. S.	Kilkenny co.	..	..	..	W	B	W	..	W	P
Caulfeild, Lt.-Col. J. M.	Armagh co.	W	W	W	W	..	W	..	W	P
Clements, S. C.	Leitrim	W	..	..	W	..	W	..	W	P
Corbally, M. E.	Meath	..	B	B	B	B	B	B	B	RC
Dawson, T. V.	Monaghan	W	W	W	W	W	..	..	W	P
Devereux, J. T.	Wexford borough	B	B	B	B	B	..	B	B	RC
Fagan, J.	Wexford co.	B	B	B	B	..	..	..	B	RC
Fagan, W.	Cork city	W	resigned			..	..	..	..	RC
Ferguson, Sir R.	Derry borough	W	W	W	W	..	W	..	W	P
Fitzpatrick, J. W.	Queen's Co.	..	W	W	W	W	W	..	W	P
Fortescue, C. S.	Louth	W	W	W	W	W	W	..	W	P
Fox, R. M.	Longford	W	..	..	W	..	W	..	W	P
French, Col. F.	Roscommon	..	W	..	W	W	..	..	W	P

[1] Names in *F.J.*, 17 Feb., 10 Apr., 14 Apr., 2 June 1851. See also p. 22.
[2] Names in *F.J.*, 1 July 1851. See also p. 23.
[3] Names in *F.J.*, 21 Feb. 1852. See also p. 34.

APPENDIX A

Name	Constituency	(1)	(2)	(3)	(4)	(5)	(6)	(7)	(8)	(9)
Goold, W.	Limerick co.	B	B	B	..	B	B	..	B	P
Grace, O. D. J.	Roscommon	B	B	B	B	B	B	B	B	RC
Grattan, H.	Meath	B	B	B	B	B	B	B	B	P
Greene, J.	Kilkenny co.	W	B	B	B	..	B	B	B	P
Hawes, B.	Kinsale	W	W	W	W	W	resigned		..	P
Higgins, G. G. O.	Mayo	W	B	B	B	B	B	B	B	RC
Howard, Sir R.	Wicklow	..	..	..	W	..	W	..	W	P
Keating, R.	Waterford co.	B	B	B	B	..	B	B	B	RC
Keogh, W.	Athlone	B	B	B	B	B	B	B	B	RC
Kildare, Marquess of	Kildare	W	W	..	W	..	W	..	W	P
Lawless, C.	Clonmel	B	B	B	B	B	B	B	B	P
M'Cullagh, W. T.	Dundalk	B	B	..	W	B	..	..	B	P
M'Namara, W. N.	Clare	..	..	..	..	..	..	..	W	P
Magan, W. H.	Westmeath	W	B	B	B	..	..	..	B	P
Maher, N. V.	Tipperary	..	B	B	B	..	..	..	B	RC
Meagher, T.	Waterford city	B	B	B	B	B	B	B	B	RC
Milton, Viscount	Wicklow	..	W	..	..	..	W	..	W	P
Monsell, W.	Limerick co.	B	B	..	B	B	B	..	B	RC
Moore, G. H.	Mayo	B	B	B	B	B	B	B	B	RC
Morgan, H. K. Grogan	Wexford co.	..	..	..	..	..	W	..	W	P
Norreys, Sir D.	Mallow	W	W	W	W	..	W	..	B	P
Nugent, Sir P.	Westmeath	..	B	B	B	..	..	..	B	RC
O'Brien, Sir T.	Cashel	B	B	B	B	B	B	B	B	RC
O'Brien, John	Limerick city	..	B	B	B	..	..	B	B	RC
O'Connell, J.	Limerick city	..	B	..	B	B	resigned		..	RC
O'Connell, M.	Tralee	W	..	..	..	..	W	..	W	RC
O'Connell, M. J.	Kerry	W	W	W	W	W	..	..	W	RC
O'Flaherty, A.	Galway borough	B	B	B	B	B	B	B	B	RC
O'Gorman Mahon, The	Ennis	W	..	W	W	W	W	..	W	RC
Power, Dr. M.	Cork co.	W	B	..	B	..	W colonial governor		W	RC
Power, N.	Waterford co.	B	W	..	..	..	W	..	W	RC
Rawdon, J. D.	Armagh borough	W	W	W	W	W	..	..	W	P
Reynolds, J.	Dublin city	B	B	B	B	B	B	B	B	RC
Roche, E. B.	Cork co.	B	..	..	B	B	W	..	W	P
Sadleir, John	Carlow borough	B	B	B	..	..	B	B	B	RC
Scully, F.	Tipperary	B	B	B	B	B	B	B	B	RC
Sheil, R. L.	Dungarvan	minister to Tuscany					..	..	..	RC
Somers, J. P.	Sligo borough	W	W	W	W	..	W	..	W	RC
Somerville, Sir W.	Drogheda	W	W	W	W	W	W	..	W	P
Sullivan, M.	Kilkenny borough	B	B	B	B	B	B	B	B	RC
Talbot, J. H.	New Ross	..	..	..	W	B	..	..	W	RC
Tenison, E. K.	Leitrim	W	W	W	W	..	..	..	W	P
Tennent, R. J.	Belfast	..	..	..	W	..	..	..	W	P
Westenra, J.	King's Co.	..	..	..	..	..	..	..	W	P

Returned at by-elections 1851–2

Name	Constituency	(1)	(2)	(3)	(4)	(5)	(6)	(7)	(8)	(9)
Ponsonby, C. F. A.	Dungarvan, 22.3.51	..	W	W	W	..	W	..	W	P
O'Ferrall, R. More	Longford, 21.4.51	..	..	..	W	B	B	..	B	RC
Murphy, Sgt. F. S.	Cork city, 23.4.51	..	..	..	W	W	..	..	W	RC
Arundel, Earl of	Limerick city, 1.8.51	..	..	..	B	..	..	..	W	RC
Heard, J. I.	Kinsale, 12.2.52	..	..	..	..	..	..	..	W	P
Cogan, W. H. F.	Kildare, 13.3.52	..	..	..	..	..	..	..	?	RC
Scully, V.	Cork co., 22.3.52	..	..	..	..	..	..	B	B	RC

APPENDIX B

IRISH LIBERAL M.P.S 1852–7

THIS table is intended to show how the Independent Opposition disintegrated in the years after 1852. Column (1) shows how far each Liberal M.P. was committed to the policy of independence when the new parliament met. The letter A means that he pledged himself to this policy in his election address; an M means that he is known to have done so at his adoption meeting. The letter T means that he accepted the resolution on independence at the Tenant League conference of September 1852, and an R that he accepted the similar resolution at the Religious Equality conference in October.

Two contemporary estimates of the party's strength in the session of 1853 are given in columns (2) and (3). The former shows the classification given at the Tenant League conference in October of that year, and the latter shows that published in the *Weekly Telegraph* of 14 January 1854.[1]

In columns (4), (5), (6), (8), and (9), the letter I is used to indicate those members who, in each of the sessions 1853 to 1857, were, on the evidence of the division lists, still faithful to the independent party. Marginal members are shown by a question-mark.

Column (7) gives Richard Swift's estimate of the party's strength in December 1855.[1] He classified members in three groups—Independent, Doubtful No. 1, and Doubtful No. 2—which are shown in the table as I, ?1, and ?2. He also marked two of the Independents with question-marks and they are indicated accordingly.

The final column shows the religion of each M.P. As far as members returned at the general election are concerned, it is based on the lists given in the *Telegraph* for 30 July and 4 August 1852, which have proved reliable when they could be checked against other evidence. Information on the members returned at by-elections comes mainly from a list in the *Tablet* for 26 July 1857.

Name	Constituency	(1) '52	(2) '53	(3) '53	(4) '53	(5) '54	(6) '55	(7) '55	(8) '56	(9) '57	(10)
Ball, J.	Carlow co.	T	..	..	..	..	..	..	..	..	RC
Bellew, T. A.	Galway co.	MTR	?	..	?	I	?	..	I	I	RC
Blake, M. J.	Galway borough	TR	I	I	I	I	I	I	I	I	RC
Bland, L.	King's Co.	..	I	..	?	..	..	..	..	..	P
Bowyer, G.	Dundalk	A	I	I	?	?	?	?1	I	I	RC
Brady, Dr. J	Leitrim	MT	I	I	I	I	?	I?	?	..	RC
Browne, V.	Kerry	..	..	..	..	..	..	..	..	..	RC
Burke, Sir T.	Galway co.	T	?	I	?	I	..	?2	..	..	RC
Caulfeild, Lt.-Col. J. M.	Armagh co.	..	..	..	..	..	..	..	..	..	P
Cogan, W. H. F.	Kildare	TR	..	..	..	I	..	..	..	..	RC

[1] See p. 142.

APPENDIX B

Name	Constituency	(1) '52	(2) '53	(3) '53	(4) '53	(5) '54	(6) '55	(7) '55	(8) '56	(9) '57	(10)
Corbally, M. E.	Meath	AM	1	?	1	1	1	1	1	1	RC
Devereux, J. T.	Wexford borough	TR	1	1	1	1	1	1	?	..	RC
Duffy, C. G.	New Ross	A TR	1	1	1	1	1	resigned	..	..	RC
Dunne, M.	Queen's Co.	TR	1	?	?	1	?	?2	..	..	RC
Esmonde, J.	Waterford co.	T	..	..	?	1	..	..	..	..	RC
Fagan, W.	Cork city	T	..	..	..	..	..	..	..	..	RC
Ferguson, Sir R.	Derry borough		..	..	..	..	..	..	..	..	P
Fitzgerald, Sir J.	Clare		..	..	..	..	..	..	..	..	P
Fitzgerald, J. D.	Ennis	A T	..	..	..	..	..	..	..	..	RC
Fortescue, C. S.	Louth		..	..	..	..	..	..	..	..	P
Fox, R. M.	Longford	M	..	..	..	..	..	..	..	dead	P
French, Col. F.	Roscommon	T	1	1	1	?	1	?2	..	..	P
Goold, W.	Limerick co.		..	..	..	..	dead	..	..	..	P
Grace, O. D. J.	Roscommon	A TR	..	..	..	?	..	..	..	..	RC
Greene, J.	Kilkenny co.	A TR	1	1	1	?	?	?1	?	?	P
Greville, Col. F. S.	Longford	MT	1	1	1	?	..	?2	..	..	P
Heard, J. I.	Kinsale		..	..	..	..	..	..	..	..	P
Henchy, D. O'C.	Kildare	A TR	1	1	1	..	..	?1	..	..	RC
Higgins, G. G. O.	Mayo	A T	..	..	..	..	..	..	..	..	RC
Keating, R.	Waterford co.	A	..	..	?	?	..	..	..	..	RC
Kennedy, T.	Louth	MTR	1	1	1	1	1	1	1	1	P
Keogh, W.	Athlone	TR	..	..	..	..	..	..	..	judge	RC
Kirk, W.	Newry		..	..	..	..	..	..	..	..	Presb.
Lawless, C.	Clonmel	A T	..	..	..	dead	..	..	..	..	P
Lucas, F.	Meath	A TR	1	1	1	1	1 dead	..	..	..	RC
M'Cann, J.	Drogheda	R	1	1	1	?	..	?2	..	..	RC
M'Mahon, P.	Wexford co.	A T	1	1	1	1	1	1?	1	1	RC
Magan, W. H.	Westmeath	A TR	1	1	1	?	?	?1	..	..	P
Maguire, J. F.	Dungarvan	A TR	1	1	1	1	1	1	1	1	RC
Meagher, T.	Waterford city	TR	1	1	1	1	1	1	1	1	RC
Milton, Viscount	Wicklow		..	..	..	..	..	..	..	..	P
Monsell, W	Limerick co.		..	..	..	..	..	..	..	..	RC
Moore, G. H.	Mayo	A TR	1	1	1	1	1	1	1	1	RC
Murphy, Sgt. F. S.	Cork city	T	..	..	..	commissioner for debtors					RC
Norreys, Sir D.	Mallow		..	..	..	..	..	..	..	..	P
O'Brien, C.	Clare	MT	..	..	..	..	..	..	..	..	P
O'Brien, P.	King's Co.	A TR	1	1	1	..	?	?2	..	..	RC
O'Brien, Sir T.	Cashel	A TR	1	1	1	..	..	?2	..	..	RC
O'Connell, M.	Tralee		..	..	..	dead	..	..	..	..	RC
O'Flaherty, A.	Galway borough	TR	..	..	..	..	..	..	..	..	RC
Potter, R.	Limerick city	AMTR	1	1	1	1	dead	..	..	..	RC
Power, N.	Waterford co.	R	..	?	?	..	..	..	..	..	RC
Roche, E. B.	Cork co.		..	..	..	..	..	..	peer	..	P
Russell, F. W.	Limerick city		..	..	..	..	..	..	..	..	P
Sadleir, James	Tipperary	A TR	..	..	..	..	..	..	..	expelled	RC
Sadleir, John	Carlow borough[1]	T	..	..	..	..	..	..	dead	..	RC
Scully, F.	Tipperary	A TR	..	..	..	..	..	..	..	..	RC
Scully, V.	Cork co.		..	..	..	..	..	..	..	..	RC
Shee, Sgt. W.	Kilkenny co.	TR	1	1	1	1	..	..	..	..	RC
Sullivan, M.	Kilkenny borough	T	1	1	1	?	1	1	?	?	RC
Swift, R.	Sligo co.	A TR	1	1	1	1	1	1	1	1	RC
Towneley, C.	Sligo borough	A	..	..	..	unseated	..	..	..	..	RC
Urquhart, W. P.	Westmeath	T	..	..	..	..	..	..	..	..	P

Members returned at by-elections		Date									
O'Connell, D.	Tralee	4.7.53	..	..	..	..	..	..	..	..	RC
Beamish, F. B.	Cork city	20.8.53	..	?	..	..	..	..	..	..	P
Richardson, J. J.	Lisburn	14.10.53	..	..	..	..	..	..	..	..	Quaker
O'Connell, J.	Clonmel	21.12.53	..	..	..	..	..	..	..	office[2]	RC
O'Brien, Sgt. James	Limerick city	28.10.54	..	..	..	..	..	..	..	..	RC
De Vere, S. E.	Limerick co.	26.12.54	..	..	..	..	..	..	..	..	RC
Deasy, R.	Cork co.	23.4.55	..	..	..	..	..	..	..	..	RC
M'Evoy, E.	Meath	17.12.55	..	..	..	..	..	1	1	1	RC
Hughes, H. G.	Longford	13.5.56	..	..	..	..	..	..	..	..	RC
Ker, R.	Downpatrick	12.2.57	..	..	..	..	..	..	..	..	P
Bagwell, J.	Clonmel	17.2.57	..	..	..	..	..	..	..	..	P
O'Donohoe, The	Tipperary	16.3.57	..	..	..	..	..	..	..	1	RC

Members elected as Conservatives who became Liberals		Approx. date of conversion									
Herbert, H. A.	Kerry	Jan. 1853	..	..	..	..	..	..	..	..	P
Butt, I.	Youghal	Feb. 1857	..	..	..	..	..	..	..	..	P
Ker, D. S.	Down	Feb. 1857	..	..	..	..	..	..	..	..	P

[1] Defeated on standing for re-election, 20.1.53; elected for Sligo borough, 8.7.53.
[2] Appointed clerk of the crown and hanaper in Ireland.

APPENDIX C

IRISH LIBERAL M.P.S 1857-9

This appendix illustrates the final collapse of the Independent Opposition. In column (1) those who gave the Conservative government a general support in 1858-9 are marked with an I, and members whose attitude was uncertain are indicated with a question mark. Column (2) shows how those marked in the previous column voted in the crucial division on the Reform Bill of April 1859 which finally broke up the party—members supporting the Conservatives are marked with a C and those opposing them with an L. M'Mahon, who was absent but paired for the Government,[1] is marked (C). The final column shows, once again, each member's religion. It is based mainly on the list in the *Tablet* for 26 June 1857, supplemented by other information.

Name	Constituency	(1)	(2)	(3)
Bagwell, J.	Clonmel	..	..	P
Beamish, F. B.	Cork city	..	..	P
Blake, J. A.	Waterford city	I	C	RC
Bland, L.	King's Co.	..	..	P
Bowyer, G.	Dundalk	I	C	RC
Brady, Dr. J.	Leitrim	I	C	RC
Burke, Sir T.	Galway co.	..	..	RC
Butt, I.	Youghal	..	..	P
Calcutt, F. M.	Clare	I	L	RC
Castlerosse, Viscount	Kerry	..	..	RC
Cogan, W. H. F.	Kildare	..	..	RC
Conyngham, Lord F.	Clare	?	absent	P
Corbally, M. E.	Meath	I	C	RC
Deasy, R.	Cork co.	..	..	RC
De Vere, S. E.	Limerick co.	..	..	RC
Devereux, J. T.	Wexford borough	..	..	RC
Dunkellin, Lord	Galway borough	..	..	P
Dunne, M.	Queen's Co.	..	..	RC
Ellis, Hon. L. Agar	Kilkenny co.	..	..	P
Ennis, J.	Athlone	I	L	RC
Esmonde, J.	Waterford co.	..	..	RC
Fagan, W.	Cork city	..	..	RC
Ferguson, Sir R.	Derry borough	..	..	P
Fitzgerald, J. D.	Ennis	..	..	RC
Fortescue, C. S.	Louth	..	..	P
French, Col. F.	Roscommon	..	..	P
Grace, O. D. J.	Roscommon	..	..	RC
Greene, J.	Kilkenny co.	I	L	P
Greer, S. M.	Derry co.	..	..	Presb.

[1] *Tablet*, 2 Apr. 1859.

APPENDIX C

Name	Constituency	(1)	(2)	(3)
Gregory, W.	Galway co.	..	..	P
Greville, Col. F. S.	Longford	..	..	P
Hatchell, J.	Wexford co.	..	..	P
Heard, J. I.	Kinsale	..	..	P
Henchy, D. O'C.	Kildare	..	..	RC
Herbert, H. A.	Kerry	..	..	P
Ker, R.	Downpatrick	..	..	P
Kirk, W.	Newry	..	..	Presb.
Levinge, Sir R.	Westmeath	?	L	P
M'Cann, J.	Drogheda	..	..	RC
M'Carthy, A.	Cork co.	..	..	RC
M'Evoy, E.	Meath	I	C	RC
M'Mahon, P.	Wexford co.	I	(C)	RC
Magan, W. H.	Westmeath	..	..	P
Maguire, J. F.	Dungarvan	I	C	RC
Milton, Viscount	Wicklow	peer	..	P
Monsell, W.	Limerick co.	..	..	RC
Moore, G. H.	Mayo	unseated	..	RC
Norreys, Sir D.	Mallow	..	..	P
O'Brien, Sgt. James	Limerick city	judge	..	RC
O'Brien, P.	King's Co.	..	..	RC
O'Brien, Sir T.	Cashel	..	..	RC
O'Connell, D.	Tralee	..	..	RC
O'Donohoe, The	Tipperary	I	L	RC
O'Flaherty, A.	Galway borough	unseated	..	RC
Power, N.	Waterford co.	..	..	RC
Richardson, J. J.	Lisburn	..	..	Quaker
Russell, F. W.	Limerick city	..	..	P
Somers, J. P.	Sligo borough	unseated	..	RC
Sullivan, M.	Kilkenny borough	I	L	RC
Waldron, L.	Tipperary	..	..	RC
White, Col. H.	Longford	..	..	P

Members returned at by-elections   *Date*

Name	Constituency	Date		
Browne, Lord J.	Mayo	30.12.57	..	P
Gavin, Major G.	Limerick city	15.2.58	unseated	RC
Proby, Ld.	Wicklow	25.2.58	..	P
Lever, J. O.	Galway borough	11.2.59	..	P

BIBLIOGRAPHY

1. *Manuscripts*

MANUSCRIPTS proved the least valuable type of material for this book. Most of the collections listed below yielded interesting and even important information, but nearly always its value lay in illustrating a point already known from other sources. Even if all the manuscript evidence had been suppressed, the main conclusions of this book would not have been notably altered.

Bodleian Library, Oxford
  Clarendon papers.

British Museum, London
  Aberdeen papers: Add. MSS. 43039–358.

Public Record Office, London
  Russell papers: P.R.O. 30/22.8 to 30/22.12.

Royal Irish Academy, Dublin
  Duffy papers: 12 P. 16.

National Library of Ireland, Dublin
  Moore papers: MSS. 891, 892, 893. (Easily the most valuable collection for the subject of this book.)
  Duffy papers: MS. 5757.
  Mayo papers: unbound. (Papers of the Earl of Mayo who, as Lord Naas, was Conservative Chief Secretary for Ireland in 1852 and 1858–9.)
  Monsell papers: in boxes—MSS. 8317, 8318, 8319. (Of little value for the subject of this book: they would, however, be useful to any student of Irish and English Catholicism in the fifties and sixties.)

2. *Parliamentary Papers*

The largest group of relevant parliamentary papers is formed by the reports of the trial of election petitions, of which no fewer than fifteen were printed during the period covered by this book. Some of them dealt with purely technical matters such as members' property qualifications; but the more far-ranging covered almost the entire scope of an election campaign, and in particular threw light on just those points on which other sources had least to say: on such unspectacular but important details as the cost of fighting an election, the functioning of party organizations, and the motives of ordinary electors. The most useful reports were those for Clare, Cork city, Mayo, and Sligo borough in 1852 and for Mayo in 1857. With them should be bracketed the report of the Galway Election Commission of 1857, sent down to investigate the three preceding elections for the borough after the trial of an election petition had proved the existence there of gross and systematic bribery.

BIBLIOGRAPHY

Another parliamentary paper that deserves mention is the report of a committee of the House of Commons—known in Ireland as the corruption committee—appointed in 1854 to examine the truth of statements in a *Times* leading article to the effect that Irish M.P.s were trafficking in government patronage. The committee found the allegation unproved, but in the course of its proceedings it heard witnesses of many different shades of opinion and uncovered some interesting facts about the murkier side of Irish politics.

Reports and evidence of the select committee on the poor laws (Ireland), H.C. 1849 (58, 356), xv.
Return of the number of parliamentary electors . . . 1848–49, and 1849–50, H.C. 1850 (345), xlvi.
Registered electors (Ireland), H.C. 1851 (383), l.
Minutes of evidence taken before the select committee on the Athlone election petition; together with the proceedings of the committee, H.C. 1852–3 (383), viii.
Minutes of evidence taken before the select committee on the Clare election petition; together with the proceedings of the committee, H.C. 1852–3 (595), ix.
Minutes of evidence taken before the select committee on the Cork city election petition; together with the proceedings of the committee, H.C. 1852–3 (528), xi.
Minutes of evidence taken before the select committee on the Mayo election petition; together with the proceedings of the committee, H.C. 1852–3 (415), xvi.
Minutes of evidence taken before the select committee on the New Ross election petition; together with the proceedings of the committee, H.C. 1852–3 (463), xvi.
Report from the select committee on the Newry election petition; with the minutes of proceedings, H.C. 1852–3 (346), xvi.
Minutes of evidence taken before the select committee on the Sligo borough election petition; together with the proceedings of the committee, H.C. 1852–3 (600), xviii.
Minutes of evidence taken before the select committee on the Waterford election petition; together with the proceedings of the committee, H.C. 1852–3 (389), xix.
Abstract return of all fees . . . charged by any returning officer or his deputy, or by any sheriff, under sheriff, sheriff clerk or sheriff's officer, clerk of the peace or town clerk, to any person returned to serve in the present parliament . . . or to any candidate; and, return of all sums received, H.C. 1852–3 (311), lxxxiii.
Report from the select committee on complaint (7th February), together with the proceedings of the committee, and the minutes of evidence, H.C. 1854 (314), viii [i.e. the corruption committee].
Report from the select committee on Henry Stonor; together with the proceedings of the committee, minutes of evidence, and appendix, H.C. 1854 (278), viii.
Report from the select committee on the Dungarvan election petition; together

with the proceedings of the committee, minutes of evidence, and index, H.C. 1854 (162), viii.

Report from the select committee on the Sligo borough election petition, together with the proceedings of the committee and minutes of evidence, H.C. 1854 (78), viii.

A return of the number of newspaper stamps at one penny, issued to newspapers in England, Ireland, Scotland, and Wales, for the years 1851, 1852, and 1853, specifying each newspaper by name, and the number of stamps issued in each of the above years to each newspaper, H.C. 1854 (479), xxxix.

Report of Her Majesty's commissioners appointed to enquire into the management and government of the college of Maynooth. Part II—minutes of evidence, and answers to paper K, etc., H.C. 1854–5, [1896–I], xxii.

Report from the select committee on the Sligo borough election petition; together with the proceedings of the committee and minutes of evidence, H.C. 1856 (234), vii.

Returns of the several purchases made in the incumbered estates court by the late John Sadleir, or any one in trust for him, H.C. 1856 (187), liii.

Report from the select committee on the Drogheda election petitions; together with the proceedings of the committee, minutes of evidence, and index, H.C. 1857 (2), (255), vi.

Report from the select committee on the Dublin city election petition; together with the proceedings of the committee, minutes of evidence, and index, H.C. 1857 (2), (293), vi.

Minutes of evidence taken before the select committee on the Mayo county election petition; with the proceedings of the committee and index, H.C. 1857 (2), (182), vii.

Report from the select committee on the Sligo borough election petition; together with the proceedings of the committee and minutes of evidence, H.C. 1857 (2), (206), ix.

Report of the commissioners appointed to investigate into the existence of corrupt practices in elections of members to serve in parliament for the county of the town of Galway, together with the minutes of evidence, H.C. 1857–8, [2291], xxvi.

Correspondence &c. relating to postal communication with North America, H.C. 1859 (1), 230, xvii.

Return stating the numbers and religious denominations of all the soldiers in Her Majesty's land and marine forces . . ., H.C. 1864 (382), xxxv.

Two reports for the Irish government on the history of the landlord and tenant question in Ireland, with suggestions for legislation. First report made in 1859;—second, in 1866. By W. Neilson Hancock, LL.D., H.C. 1868–9, [4204], xxvi. [An admirable exposition of the question.]

Return by provinces and counties (compiled from returns made to the inspector general, Royal Irish Constabulary), of cases of evictions which have come to the knowledge of the Constabulary in each of the years from 1849 to 1880, H.C. 1881 (185), lxxvii.

3. Newspapers

A glance at the footnotes will show that newspapers proved by far the most valuable class of material in the writing of this book. There are several reasons why this should have been so. In the first place, they were the main source of information about electioneering matters. Secondly, the party of the eighteen-fifties was remarkably open in its proceedings, and several of its most important decisions were taken in public conferences reported by the press. Thirdly, many of the principal figures in the party were newspaper editors, which meant that their changes of opinion could be traced most easily in the columns of their leading articles.

Practically every newspaper published in Ireland was examined at one stage or another in the preparation of this book. There seems little point in listing them all, as to do so would only mean duplicating information already available in the British Museum newspaper catalogue. Most of these papers, however, were searched only for information on specific points where the Dublin press was unhelpful—in particular for the election addresses of rural candidates. Normally speaking the Dublin papers were quite as informative on local affairs as the local press itself: they reprinted from the local papers the more interesting items and for important events would send their own correspondents. Only a handful of papers therefore were examined systematically. Those selected were the following:

Paper	Proprietor or editor	Place of publication	Dates for which examined
Freeman's Journal	Dr. Gray	Dublin	1850–9
Nation	to 1855: C. G. Duffy 1855–8: Cashel Hoey 1858 on: A. M. Sullivan	Dublin	1850–62
Tablet	to 1855: F. Lucas 1855 on: J. E. Wallis	Dublin London	1851–8 1858–9
Telegraph	John Sadleir	Dublin	1852
Weekly Telegraph	John Sadleir	Dublin	1853–4
Daily Express	(Conservative)	Dublin	election periods in 1852 and 1857
Cork Examiner	J. F. Maguire	Cork	1852, 1857–61
Banner of Ulster	Dr. M'Knight	Belfast	1850–3

4. Reference Works and Official Publications

Acta et Decreta Concilii Provinciae Casseliensis in Hibernia (Dublin, 1854).
Acta et Decreta Concilii Provincialis Armacani (Dublin, 1855).
Acta et Decreta Conciliorum Provinciae Tuamensis (Dublin, 1859). [This also contains the decrees of the National Council of 1853.]
Annual Register (London).
C. R. Dod, *Electoral Facts* (2nd ed., London, 1853).

C. R. Dod, *Parliamentary Companion* (London, 1850–9).
[Sir Richard Griffith], *General Valuation of Rateable Property in Ireland* (Dublin, 1847–64, 202 parts).
[J. P. Kennedy], *Digest of Evidence taken before Her Majesty's Commissioners of Inquiry into the State of the Law and Practice in respect to the Occupation of Land in Ireland* (Dublin, 1847–8, 2 vols.).
Parliamentary Debates, 3rd series (London).
Synodus Dioecesana Dublinensis . . . una cum Statutis Concilii Provincialis Dublinensis, an. 1853 (Dublin, 1857).

5. Contemporary Books and Pamphlets on the General Election of 1852 in Ireland

The works listed here are based mainly on newspapers and have little independent value; but they are of interest as showing the amount of indignation which the activities of the Catholic clergy aroused among Protestants.

A Barrister, *Observations on Intimidation at Elections in Ireland* (Dublin, 1854).
Eladrius, *Thoughts on the late General Election in Ireland* (Dublin, 1853).
Sir Francis Head, *A Fortnight in Ireland* (London, 1852).
James Lord, *Popery at the Hustings* (London, 1852).

6. Other Contemporary Books, Pamphlets, and Articles

J. N. Carleton, *Compendium of the Practice at Elections . . . in Ireland* (4th ed., Dublin, 1857). [Legal.]
Edinburgh Review, xcviii (Oct. 1853).
T. C. Foster, *Letters on the Condition of the People of Ireland* (London, 1846).
[James Grant], *Impressions of Ireland and the Irish* (London, 1844, 2 vols.).
W. Neilson Hancock, *Report on the Supposed Progressive Decline of Irish Prosperity* (Dublin, 1863).
[William Keogh], *Ireland Imperialised: a Letter to His Excellency the Earl of Clarendon* (Dublin, 1849).
J. G. Kohl, *Ireland, Scotland and England* (London, 1844, 3 vols.).
J. F. Maguire, *Rome, its Ruler, and its Institutions* (2nd ed., London, 1859).
Rev. William Meagher, *Notices of the Life and Character of His Grace Most Rev. Daniel Murray* (Dublin, 1853).
Asenath Nicholson, *Ireland's Welcome to the Stranger* (London, 1847).
S. G. Osborne, *Gleanings in the West of Ireland* (London, 1850).
ed. Henry Reeve, *A Journal of the Reigns of King George IV, King William IV and Queen Victoria by the late Charles C. F. Greville, Esq.* (London, 1888, 8 vols.).
A Roman Catholic, *The Liberal Party in Ireland: its Present Condition and Prospects* (Dublin, 1862).
Nassau William Senior, *Journals, Conversations and Essays relating to Ireland* (London, 1868, 2 vols.).

BIBLIOGRAPHY

WILLIAM SHEE, *The Irish Church: its History and Statistics* (London and Dublin, 1852).
WILLIAM SHEE, *Papers, Letters, and Speeches in the House of Commons, on the Irish Land Question* (London, 1863).
E. A. STOPFORD, *The Income and Requirements of the Irish Church: being a Reply to Sergeant Shee* (Dublin, 1853).
JOHN WIGGINS, *The 'Monster' Misery of Ireland* (London, 1844).

7. Later Works

For an appraisal of the most important of these, see the Preface, pp. vi–viii.

F. E. BALL, *The Judges in Ireland, 1221–1921* (London, 1926, 2 vols.).
H. C. F. BELL, *Lord Palmerston* (London, 1936, 2 vols.).
TERENCE DE VERE WHITE, *The Road of Excess* (Dublin, [1946]). [A life of Isaac Butt.]
Dictionary of National Biography.
SIR CHARLES GAVAN DUFFY, *Four Years of Irish History, 1845–1849* (London, 1883).
SIR CHARLES GAVAN DUFFY, *The League of North and South* (London, 1886).
SIR CHARLES GAVAN DUFFY, *My Life in Two Hemispheres* (London, 1898, 2 vols.).
ed. LADY GREGORY, SIR WILLIAM GREGORY, *An Autobiography* (London, 1894).
PHILIP HUGHES, 'The Uproar of 1850', in *Tablet*, 30 Sept. 1950.
W. W. HUNTER, *A Life of the Earl of Mayo* (London, 1875, 2 vols.).
B. A. KENNEDY, 'The Tenant-Right Agitation in Ulster, 1845–50', in *Bulletin of the Irish Committee of Historical Sciences*, no. 34.
E. LUCAS, *The Life of Frederick Lucas, M.P.* (London and New York, 1886, 2 vols.).
FERGAL MCGRATH, S.J., *Newman's University: Idea and Reality* (Dublin, 1951).
J. L. MONTROSE, 'The Landlord and Tenant Act of 1860', in *Bulletin of the Irish Committee of Historical Sciences*, no. 1.
W. F. MONYPENNY and G. E. BUCKLE, *The Life of Benjamin Disraeli, Earl of Beaconsfield*, vol. iii (London, 1914).
M. G. MOORE, *An Irish Gentleman—George Henry Moore* (London, [1913]).
C. CRUISE O'BRIEN, *Parnell and his Party 1880–90* (Oxford, 1957).
R. BARRY O'BRIEN, *The Parliamentary History of the Irish Land Question* (London, 1880).
MRS. M. J. O'CONNELL, *Charles Bianconi, a Biography* (London, 1878).
T. P. O'CONNOR, *The Parnell Movement* (London, 1886).
RT. REV. BERNARD O'REILLY, *John MacHale, Archbishop of Tuam, his Life Times and Correspondence* (New York and Cincinnati, 1890, 2 vols.).
A Record of Traitorism; or the Political Life and Adventures of Mr. Justice Keogh (Dublin, n.d.).
C. J. RIETHMÜLLER, *Frederick Lucas—a Biography* (London, 1862).

C. H. STUART, 'The Formation of the Coalition Cabinet of 1852', in *Transactions of the Royal Historical Society* (5th series), iv (1954).
A. M. SULLIVAN, *New Ireland* (7th ed., Glasgow and London, 1882).
RT. REV. W. B. ULLATHORNE, *History of the Restoration of the Catholic Hierarchy, in England* (London, 1871).
MGR. BERNARD WARD, *The Sequel to Catholic Emancipation* (London, 1915, 2 vols.).

INDEX

Abbreviations
gen. el.: general election.
by-el.: by-election.

Aberdeen, Earl of, forms government, 97, 125; refuses to appoint Redington, 99; disavows Lord John Russell, 100; views on land question, 102; correspondence with Sadleir, 104–6; attitude of bishops to, 111, 114; independent Irish party during his government, 143–51, 157; Presbyterians favour him, 159; Levinge seeks peerage from, 174.
Anstey, C., M.P., 20 n.
Antrim, county, in gen. el. 1852, 75.
Archdall family, 75.
Armagh, Archbishop of, *see* Cullen, P.
Armagh, borough, in gen. el. 1852, 82.
Armagh, county, in gen. el. 1852, 84.
Armagh, synod of, 114, 121.
Armstrong, Sir A., M.P., 52.
Arundel and Surrey, Earl of, M.P., 51.
Athlone, borough, in gen. el. 1852, 61, 103; in by-el. 1853, 111, 160, 161; in by-el. 1856, 163; in gen. el. 57, 171.

Balbriggan, 71.
Ball, J., M.P., 52, 147.
Ballina, 78.
Ballinasloe, 170.
Ballingarry, 6 n.
Ballyhale, 6.
Baltinglass, 6 n.
Bankers, as parliamentary candidates, 49 and n.; as M.P.s, 90.
Banner of Ulster, 44, 159.
Barnabo, Mgr. A., 118, 119, 121.
Barron, Sir H. W., M.P., 16, 46.
Barton, T. H., 60.
Belfast, city, in gen. el. 1852, 82.
Bellaghy, 78.
Bellew, R. M., M.P. 45, 52, 169 and n.
Bellew, Capt. T. A., M.P., 175.
Belmullet, 70.
Berkeley, F. H. F., M.P., 145.
Bianconi, C., 173.
Blackall, Major S. W., M.P., 16 n., 45.

Blackburne, F., 98.
Blake, M. J., M.P., 29 n., 32 n., 48.
Bland, L., M.P., 89, 99, 164.
Booth, Sir R. Gore, M.P., 69.
Bowyer, G., M.P., 129, 137, 139.
Boyd, Dr. J., M.P., 44 n.
Boyle, 78.
Bribery, 64–65, 72, 167–8, 176.
Brigade, the Irish, origin, 21–22, 126; characteristics, 23; name, 24; leaders, 24–27; rejects obstruction, 24; public support for, 28; controls Catholic Defence Association, 29; agreement with Tenant League, 32; distrusted by Duffy and Lucas, 33; and censure motion on Lord Clarendon, 34, 35; and Kildare by-el., 34, 35; effect on fortunes of independent party, 37, 146; mostly readopted in 1852, 51; mostly re-elected in 1852, 85; and appointment of Blackburne, 98; part stays loyal to independent party, 108, 146; term dies out, 109.
Brooke family, 75.
Browne, G. J., Bishop of Elphin, 78, 111, 122, 171.
Burke, George, of Danesfield, 169.
Burke, Sir T., M.P., 89.
Butt, I., M.P., 82 n., 141.
By-elections in 1851, 31; in 1850–2, 50–51; in 1853–7, 160–4; *see also under* individual constituencies.

Calcutt, F. M., M.P., 165.
Callan, 5, 117.
Callan, curates of, 6, 73, 118; *see also* O'Shea, Rev. T., Keeffe, Rev. M.
Candidates, parliamentary, machinery for selecting Liberal, 40–41; shortage of Liberal, 47–50; Conservative, 57; influence of landlords and clergy on selection, 75–76; Liberal, in gen. el. 1857, 174–5; difficulty of finding, 176.

INDEX

Cantwell, J., Bishop of Meath, 29 n., 111, 123.
Cantwell, J. M., a founder of Tenant League, 12; at Tenant League conference of 1852, 87; quarrels with Moore, 129; services to independent party, 134; breaks away from party, 136-7; tactlessness, 141.
Canvassing, 64, 76-79.
Carlow, borough, in gen. el. 1852, 65, 161; in by-el. 1853, 105, 111, 112, 160, 161; in gen. el. 1857, 122, 167.
Carlow, county, in gen. el. 1852, 52 and n., 61, 67, 69, 82.
Carlton Club, 15, 55.
Carlyle, Thomas, 10.
Carrickfergus, borough, in gen. el. 1852, 75.
Carrickmacross, 69.
Cashel, 6 n.
Cashel, M. Slattery, Archbishop of, 113 and n., 118.
Cashel, clergy of diocese of, 118.
Cashel, synod of, 113, 121.
Castlebaldwin, 78.
Castlebar, 6 n.
Castlecomer, 6 n.
Castlereagh, Viscount, M.P., 15 n., 21 n.
Catholic chaplains, in prisons, workhouses, and armed services, 95, 144 and n., 152.
Catholic clergy, at tenants' conference of 1850, 12; support Liberals, 39, 63; political influence, mentioned, 42, 63, 110, 176; analysed, 68-81; at height of their power, 81, 91; in Ulster, 84; at Tenant League conference of 1852, 86; and appeal to Rome, 117, 118; effect on, of new statutes, 122, 171; influence declines, 170-1.
Catholic Defence Association, founded, 28; controlled by Brigade, 29; aims, 29-30, 31; and Presbyterians, 31; Lucas excluded from office in, 33; permanent secretaryship of, 33, 107; parliamentary committee supports Grattan, 36 n.; guides public opinion, 41, 92; finds candidates, 42; ceases to exist, 88; and Archbishop Cullen, 111, 113.
Catholic ecclesiastical legislation, 114, 121-2, 170.
Catholic hierarchy in England, restoration of, 19.

Catholic hierarchy in Ireland, and Dr. Gray, 10, 136; and university education, 19; during gen. el. 1852, 110-11; some members oppose independent party, 111-17; appeal to Rome against, 117-19; subsequent attitude of, 122-3.
Catholic landowners, becoming a distinct political interest, 172-4.
Catholic M.P.s, 14.
Catholic University, the, 95, 113, 152.
Caulfeild, Lt.-Col. J. M., M.P., 83.
Cavan, county, in by-el. 1855, 169; in gen el. 1857, 174.
Chambers of Commerce, 40.
Chambers, T., M.P., 127.
Charlemont, Earl of, 44.
Chief Secretary for Ireland, see Naas, Lord, M.P., Somerville, Sir W., M.P., Young, Sir J., M.P.
China War, 143, 145.
Church of Ireland, see Established Church.
Clancarty, Earl of, 75.
Clanricarde, Marquess of, 44.
Clare, county, in gen. el. 1852, 61, 67, 69, 70, 76, 78, 82; in gen. el. 1857, 122, 171; in by-el. 1860, 165.
Clarendon, Earl of, 34, 35, 97.
Cloghan, 71.
Clonalvey, 6 n.
Clonbrock, Lord, 75.
Clonmel, borough, in gen. el. 1852, 52 n., 60.
Close, Col. M. C., M.P., 77.
Cloyne, T. Murphy, Bishop of, 111.
Cole family, 75.
Comyn, Andrew, 170.
Conolly, T., M.P., 15 n.
Conservative party, strength in parliament, 14, 91; attitude to land question, 14; Peelites returning to, 15; takes office, 39; a basic division in Irish politics, 39; local organization, 54, 75; finances, 55; unity of party, 55; Irish policy, 56; candidates, 55, 57; landlords support, 39, 55, 63; and gen. el. 1852, 82-83, 93; social composition, 90 and n.; independent party's attitude to, 147; gaining ground 1852-9, 171 and n.; see also Derby, Earl of.
Consolidated annuities, 56.

INDEX

Convents, bill for inspection of, protest meeting, 127.
Corbally, M. E., M.P., 17, 23, 114, 160 n.
Cork, city, in by-el. 1851, 51; in gen. el. 1852, 48, 55, 61, 70, 73, 82; in gen. el. 1857, 150.
Cork, county, 5; in by-el. 1852, 51; in gen. el. 1852, 57, 71; in by-el. 1855, 161; in gen. el. 1857, 150, 174, 175.
Cork, W. Delany, Bishop of, 72.
Cork Examiner, 43, 59 and n., 86, 140.
Corrupt Practices Act of 1854, 139, 145.
Corruption, *see* Bribery.
Craughwell, 170.
Crawford, W. Sharman, M.P., land bill of 1847, 7; negotiations with Tenant League, 32; stands for Down, 84; and Tenant League conference of 1852, 87; attitude to Sadleir and Keogh, 158, 162; dislikes Lucas, 159.
Crawford's bill, origin, 32; adopted by Tenant League conference of 1852, 87, 88; Derby government's attitude to, 94; management confided to Shee, 95; Keogh and Sadleir pledged on, 101; rejected, 135; Tenant League continues to pledge itself to, 151.
Crimean War, 143, 145.
Cullen, P., Archbishop of Armagh, 1850–2, Archbishop of Dublin, 1852–78, and Dr. Gray, 10, 123, 136; and Catholic Defence Association, 29 n., 111; career and influence, 111; subscribes to Tenant League, 111; his change of policy, 113; praises Aberdeen government, 114; motives for change of policy, 115–16; suspicion of Young Ireland, 115–16; appeal to Rome against his policy, 117–20; interview with Lucas, 119; permission required to attend Tenant League meetings, 121; urges clergy to attend to registration, 122; limited effect of his change of policy, 123, 124, 170, 176.

Daily Express, 57, 70, 74.
Daly, R., 60.
De Burgh, H., 65, 126.
Delane, J. T., 96 n.
Delany, W., Bishop of Cork, 72.
Derby, Earl of, forms first government, 39; conciliatory to Ireland, 56; becomes unpopular in Ireland, 58, 59, 60; denounces Shee's bill, 96, 97; government falls, 96; hampered by support of Irish landlords, 98; second government, 143, 151–4; criticizes Catholicism, 166.
Desart, Earl of, 5.
Devereux, J. T., M.P., 32 n.
Devon Commission, 1, 2, 3 n., 4, 7.
Disraeli, B., M.P., motion on agricultural distress, 22; takes office, 39; conciliatory to Ireland, 56, 152; and negotiations with Tenant League, 96 n.; compared with Moore, 125.
Donegal, county, 8; in gen. el. 1852, 66, 82.
Dowling, Very Rev. J., 76.
Down, county, in gen. el. 1852, 40 n., 54, 66, 68, 69, 75, 82, 84.
Downpatrick, borough, in gen. el. 1852, 75.
Downshire, Marquess of, 75, 77.
Doyle, Rev. T., 74, 76, 112, 117.
Drogheda, borough, in gen. el. 1852, 74; in gen. el. 1857, 167.
Dublin, Archbishop of, *see* Murray, D., Cullen, P.
Dublin, city, in gen. el. 1852, 76, 82 and n., 85; Lord Mayor and Town Clerk of, 12.
Dublin, county, 12; in gen. el. 1852, 42, 71.
Dublin, diocese of, 111.
Dublin, synod of, 114, 121.
Dublin Evening Post, 42, 43.
Duffy, C. G., M.P., Young Irelander, 9; personality and ideas, 10–11; a founder of Tenant League, 12; opinion of Keogh, 26; opinion of Brigade, 31, 33, 35; negotiates with Crawford, 32; a Liberal, 40; property qualification, 47; adopted for New Ross, 51; canvassing, 64, 77; attitude of New Ross clergy to, 74, 112; elected, 86; and Tenant League conference of 1852, 93; and Derby government, 95, 97; challenges Keogh, 101 n.; blames bishops for failure of independent party, 110; distrusted by Archbishop Cullen, 115, 116; resigns from Parliament and emigrates, 120, 134; criticized by Lucas, 120; importance in party, 124, 141; career in Parliament, 124; inaccurate list of party

members, 142 n.; description of Greville, 150; at party meeting of 13 Dec. 1852, 156; alone in regretting loss of Ulster support, 160; see also *Nation*.
Dunamaggin, 6 n.
Dundalk, borough, in gen. el. 1852, 76; in gen. el. 1857, 137.
Dungannon, borough, in gen. el. 1852, 75.
Dungannon, Viscount, 68.
Dungarvan, borough, in by-el. 1851, 50; in gen. el. 1852, 86; in gen. el. 1857, 122, 170.
Dunkellin, Lord, M.P., 48.
Dunne, M., M.P., 49 and n.
Durham, Lord John Russell's letter to Bishop of, 20, 58.
Dwyer, Rev. J., 118.

Easky, 77.
Ecclesiastical Titles Act, passage through Parliament, 20–23, 37, 159; Keogh demands repeal, 37; effects, 58, 62, 81, 85, 91, 169; demand for repeal abandoned, 144; indignation at, dies down, 165.
Education, as a political issue, 56, 155.
Elections, *see* By-elections, General elections, *and under* individual constituencies.
Elections, expense of, 47.
Electorate, size of, 63.
Elphin, G. J. Browne, Bishop of, 78, 111, 122, 171.
Emigration, 166.
Encumbered Estates Court, 173.
Ennis, borough, in gen. el. 1852, 52.
Ennis, J., M.P., 171.
Enniscorthy, 6 n.
Enniskillen, borough, in gen. el. 1852, 65, 75.
Enniskillen, Earl of, 75.
Erne, Earl of, 66.
Established Church, M.P.s belonging to, 14; clergy support Conservatives, 39; Conservatives support, 56; as a political grievance, 18, 37, 88, 99, 144, 154.
Evictions, 4, 8, 166.
Eyre, John, 170.

Fagan, J., M.P., 17.
Fagan, W., M.P., 28, 48, 51, 150.

Feeny, T., Bishop of Killala, 78, 111.
Ferguson, Sir R., M.P., 83.
Fermanagh, country, in gen. el. 1852, 75, 84.
Ferns, M. Murphy, Bishop of, 112.
Ferns, clergy of diocese of, 118.
Fitzgerald, J. D., M.P., 83 n., 87, 88, 99, 147.
Fitzpatrick, J. W., M.P., 43 n., 169.
Fitzwilliam, Earl, 44.
Foran, N., Bishop of Waterford, 76.
Fortescue, C. S., M.P., 160, 170, 172.
Fox, R. M., M.P., 52, 83, 147.
Freeman's Journal, owners, 9, 12; advocates an independent party, 42; condemns the proclamation, 58; condemns Keogh and Sadleir, 107; and Duffy's emigration, 120; defection from independent party, 136–8.
French, Col. F., M.P., 89.
French, Lt.-Col. P. T., 175.
Friends of Religious Freedom and Equality, inaugural conference of, 88–89, 101, 106, 109, 148; denounce Keogh and Sadleir, 107.

Galmoy, 6 n.
Galway, city, and transatlantic packet station, 56, 152; in gen. el. 1852, 48, 61, 64, 70; in gen. el. 1857, 167, 175; in by-el. 1859, 167.
Galway, county, in gen. el. 1852, 41, 60, 61, 75, 82; in gen. el. 1857, 169, 172, 175.
Gavin, Major G., M.P., 168.
General Assembly of the Presbyterian Church, 8.
General election of 1852, approaches, 39; and Presbyterians, 44; adoption of Liberal candidates for, 51–53; Conservative campaign, 54–57; landlord and clerical influence in, 63–81; results, 82–86, 91, 159; and Catholic hierarchy, 110; unusual circumstances of, 176; *see also under* individual constituencies.
General election of 1857, Moore's leadership in, 138, 156; results, 164 and n., 171; landlord and clerical influence in, 122, 169–74; Liberal candidates in, 174–5; *see also under* individual constituencies.
General election of 1859, 154, 171.

INDEX

General election of 1865, 154.
Girdwood, William, 159.
Gladstone, W. E., M.P., 97; budget of 1853, 145, 148.
Goold, W., M.P., 50 n., 89.
Gore, Capt. W. R. Ormesby, M.P., 69.
Gormanstown, Viscount, 29 n.
Grace, O. D. J., M.P., 23.
Graham, Sir James, M.P., 97.
Grattan, H., M.P., a Brigadier, 23; in election of 1852, 36 n., 51 n., 172; defeated, 85, 160 n.
Gray, Dr. J., personality, 9–10; age, 11; a founder of Tenant League, 11; and origin of Brigade, 22 and n.; attacks Brigade, 35; a Liberal, 40; adopted for Monaghan, 51; defeated, 84; at Tenant League conference of 1852, 87; quarrels with Moore, 129; defection from independent party, 123, 136–8; mentioned, 134, 141; see also *Freeman's Journal*.
Greer, S. M., M.P., 11.
Gregg, Rev. T., 76.
Gregory, W., M.P., 169, 172.
Greville, C. C. F., 96 n.
Greville, Col. F. S., M.P., 52, 150.
Gurteen, 78.

Hallewell, E. G., 77.
Haly, F., Bishop of Kildare and Leighlin, 111.
Hamilton, Lord Claude, M.P., 15 n.
Hamilton, G. A., M.P., 56 n., 71.
Hayter, W. G., M.P., 105.
Heard, J. I., M.P., 83 and n.
Herbert, H. A., M.P., 21 n.
Herbert, Sidney, M.P., 103, 104.
Hertford, Marquess of, 8, 75.
Higgins, G. G. O., M.P., and Tenant League, 17 and n.; and Brigade, 29 n., 32 n., 33 n.; endorses Keogh's Athlone speech, 37 n.; ally of Sadleir, 108; supports government and is rewarded, 147 and n.; claims to be independent, 150; and gen. el. of 1857, 139, 171, 173.
Holycross, 5.
Holy See, Lucas's appeal to, 117–20, 135, 136.
Home Rule party, 141.
Hughes, H. G., M.P., 52, 169.
Humble, Sir N., 170.

Independent Irish party, development of idea of, and Young Ireland, 10; and Tenant League, 12; and Catholic Defence Association, 29; and Brigade, 36–37; at Tenant League conference of 1852, 88; at conference of Friends of Religious Equality, 89.
Independent Irish party, forces favouring the growth of, 41–43; obstacles to growth of, 43–50; and results of gen. el. 1852, 84–86; numbers, 89, 91, 142–3; social composition, 90, 146; reasons for rise, 91–92; and Villiers's motion, 94; votes against Derby government, 96; desertion by Sadleir and Keogh, 97; adopts term 'Independent Opposition', 109; threatened by ecclesiastical legislation, 114; and appeal to Rome, 117–20, 135, 136; its leadership, 124–41, 156; limits its aims, 144; sits with opposition, 145; why members abandoned it, 146–51; final collapse, 153–5; plan for party meetings fails, 156–7; Ulstermen desert, 158–60; and by-els. 1852–7, 161–4; proved right about Sadleir, 162; and gen. el. 1857, 123, 164–5; reasons for limited success in elections 1853–9, 165–75; summary of its difficulties, 175–7.
'Independent Opposition', origin of term, 88, 89, 109; see also Independent Irish party.
Inniskeen, 6 n.
Intimidation, in gen. el. 1852, 64–71; in gen. el. 1857, 169.
Irish Brigade, the, see Brigade, the Irish.
Irish Tenant League, see Tenant League.

Joyce, Thomas, 170.

Kanturk, 6 n.
Keane, Henry, 67.
Kearney, Very Rev. J., 76.
Keating, R., M.P., 108.
Keeffe, Rev. M., 6, 117, 135; see also Callan, curates of.
Kenmare, Earl of, 44, 54.
Kennedy, Sir E., 60.
Kennedy, T., M.P., 90, 170.
Kenny, William, 71.
Keogh, W., M.P., Peelite background, 15, 23, 104; at tenants' conference of 1850, 17; personality, 26–27; and

Catholic Defence Association, 29 and n.; and Tenant League, 32 n.; and permanent secretaryship of Catholic Defence Association, 33 n.; and Kildare by-election, 34, 35 n.; attacked by Lucas, 36; Athlone speech, 37, 101; and breaking-up of entail, 37 and n.; subscription for his election, 48, 103; re-elected 1852, 85; and Tenant League conference of 1852, 87, 93, 100; and conference of Friends of Religious Equality, 89, 101; encourages Lucas, 93; and Derby government, 94, 97; takes office, 97, 125; judgement on his acceptance of office, 98–107, 146, 155; tenders resignation, 99; Cork speech, 101; date of his change of policy, 107; public reaction to his acceptance of office, 107; reaction in North, 158; limited effect of his defection from independent party, 109, 110, 124, 175; supported by Bishop of Elphin, 111; friend of Moore, 125; at party meeting of 13 Dec. 1852, 156; re-elected for Athlone, 160, 161; Attorney-General and judge, 162; mentioned, 51, 129, 153, 163.

Ker, D. S., M.P., 54 n., 75.
Kerry, county, 4, 54.
Kerry, D. Moriarty, Bishop of, 115.
Kieran, Very Rev. M., 76.
Kildare, county, 6; in by-el. 1852, 34, 35; in gen. el. 1852, 55, 60.
Kildare and Leighlin, Bishop of, *see* Haly, F., Walshe, J.
Kilkenny, county, 12; in gen. el. 1852, 41, 68, 73, 86; in gen. el. 1857, 123.
Killala, T. Feeny, Bishop of, 78, 111.
Killaloe, D. Vaughan, Bishop of, 111.
Kilmactigue, 78.
Kilmore West, 77.
Kilmorey Estate, 77.
Kilrush, 69.
Kiltimagh, 73.
King's County, in gen. el. 1852, 52, 61, 71; in gen. el. 1857, 164, 174, 175.
Kinnaird, A. F., M.P., 131.

Lalor, J. F., 5.
Land bills, *see under* Crawford, W. S.; Land bills, government; Napier, J.; Shee, Sgt. W.; Tenant League.

Land bills, government, of 1845–50, 4, 7, 15, 95.
Land bill, government, of 1859, 152, 153.
Landlords, political influence of, mentioned, 43, 55, 114, 176; analysed, 65–68, 75–81; in Ulster, 84; gains in strength, 169–70, 171.
Landlords, Catholic, becoming a distinct interest, 172–4.
Landowning class, mostly Conservative, 39, 55, 63; some Liberal, 43, 54; hostile to independent party, 49; as parliamentary candidates, 49 and n.; numbers among M.P.s, 90.
Land question, declining in importance, 154, 166.
Land system in Ulster, 3, 6–8.
Land system in southern three provinces, 1–6; condition improving, 166.
Lansdowne, Marquess of, 54.
Lawlor, D. S., 174.
Lawyers, and a political career, 49; as M.P.s, 90 and n.
Leitrim, barony, 170.
Leitrim, county, in gen. el. 1852, 42 n., 82, 83.
Leitrim, Earl of, 44.
Leix, *see* Queen's County.
Lever, J. O., M.P., 167.
Levinge, Sir R., M.P., 174.
Lewis, Sir G. C., M.P., 145.
Liberal party, strength in Parliament, 14, 91, 93; characteristics, 16; and Tenant League, 17; and Established Church, 18; and Ecclesiastical Titles Bill, 20, 21; a basic division in Irish politics, 39; clerical support for, 39, 63, 110; local organization, 40–41, 54, 76; press and, 42; aristocratic families in, 43, 54; attitude of independent party to other Liberals, 147; meeting of Irish Liberals, 13 Dec. 1852, 156; loses ground to Conservatives, 171 and n.; *see also* Brigade, Independent Irish party, Radicals, Whigs.
Limerick, city, 6 n., 70; in by-el. 1851, 51; in gen. el. 1852, 61, 73; in by-el. 1854, 160, 168; in by-el. 1858, 168.
Limerick, county, in by-el. 1850, 50.
Lisburn, borough, in gen. el. 1852, 75.
Local interests, growing importance of, 167.

INDEX

Local organizations, *see* Conservative party, Liberal party, *and under* individual constituencies.
Londonderry, Marquess of, 54 n., 75, 79.
Londonderry Standard, 159.
Longford, barony, 170.
Longford, county, in by-el. 1851, 50; in gen. el. 1852, 52, 147; in by-el. 1856, 169; in gen. el. 1857, 150, 171; in by-el. 1862, 165.
Lorton, Viscount, 68.
Loughrea, 170.
Louth, county 6; in gen. el. 1852, 40, 52, 60, 73, 161 n., 170, 172; in by-el. 1854, 112, 113, 160, 161 and n., 170, 172; in gen. el. 1857, 169.
Lucan, Earl of, 5.
Lucas, F., M.P., personality, 11, 129–34; a founder of Tenant League, 11; negotiates with Crawford, 32; opinion of Brigade, 33, 35, 36; adopted for Meath, 36 n., 51 and n., 85; a Liberal, 40; property qualification, 47; on position of clergy, 80; elected, 86, 160 n.; and Tenant League conference of 1852, 86, 87, 93, 129; tribute to Keogh, 93; and Derby government, 94, 95, 97; and defection of Keogh and Sadleir, 109; and Archbishop Cullen's change of policy, 113; Meath banquet and, 113, 114; reports Cullen's opinion of Duffy, 115; appeals to Rome against Cullen's policy, 117–20, 134; writes memorial for Pope, 119, 133; death, 119, 123, 134; criticizes Duffy, 120; importance in independent party, 124, 141, 176; criticized by Moore, 125; differs from Shee, 135; and Catholic chaplains, 144; his interpretation of party pledge, 145, 148, 149; at party meeting of 13 Dec. 1852, 156; and party meeting of 5 Mar. 1853, 157; distrusted in Ulster, 159; comment on loss of Ulstermen, 160; mentioned, 121, 167, 168; see also *Tablet*.

M'Alpine, Col. J., 61.
M'Clintock, J., M.P., 60.
M'Cullagh, W. T., M.P., 17 and n.
M'Gettigan, P., Bishop of Raphoe, 113.

MacHale, J., Archbishop of Tuam, and Dr. Gray, 10; and Catholic Defence Association, 29 n.; political influence, 73, 110, 172; urges appointment of Archbishop Cullen, 111; condemns Keogh and Sadleir, 111; supports independent party, 123; attitude on final split of party, 154; Catholic landowners hostile to, 172; mentioned, 120, 164.
M'Knight, Dr. J., 12, 158, 159; see also *Banner of Ulster*.
M'Mahon, P., M.P., 90, 139, 144.
Madiai, Francesco and Rosa, 131.
Magan, Capt. W. H., M.P., 32 n., 137, 164.
Maguire, J. F., M.P., contests Dungarvan, 50 and n.; elected, 86; challenges Keogh, 101 n.; attitude of clergy to, 50 and n., 122; Moore compares him to Keogh and Sadleir, 129, 153; disagrees with Gray and Cantwell, 137; personality, 139–41; and law of settlement, 144; supports second Derby government, 153; remains prominent after collapse of party, 154; motives above suspicion, 155; see also *Cork Examiner*.
Maher, N. V., M.P., 32 n., 33 n., 48 n.
Mahon, Major D., 5.
Mahon, the O'Gorman, M.P., 52.
Maley, A. J., 175.
Manufacturers, as parliamentary candidates, 49 and n.; as M.P.s, 90.
Marshall, Rev. H. J., 113 and n.
Martin, James, 169.
Massy, Major H. W., 174.
Mayglass, 6 n.
Maynooth College, government grant to, 56, 57; opinions of professors of, 72, 73.
Mayo, county, 5; in gen. el. 1852, 48, 55, 60, 61, 67, 68, 70, 73, 75, 79; in gen. el. 1857, 122, 126, 138, 139, 150, 171, 173; clergy of, 118.
Mazzini, G., 115, 116.
Meagher, T., M.P., 16, 29 n., 102.
Meath, J. Cantwell, Bishop of, 29 n., 111, 123.
Meath, clergy of diocese of, 118, 121, 154.
Meath, county, 12; in gen. el. 1852, 36 and n., 48, 51, 86, 172; in by-el. 1855,

121, 160 and n.; banquet to Lucas and Corbally, 113, 114.
Meelick, 70.
Merchants, as parliamentary candidates, 49 and n.; as M.P.s, 90.
Miall, E., M.P., 144.
Mill, J. S., 10.
Millstreet, 6 n.
Mob violence, in gen. el. 1852, 68–71.
Monaghan, county, in gen. el. 1852, 51, 55, 65, 69, 82, 84.
Monsell, W., M.P., 89, 97, 99, 100.
Moore, G. H., M.P., and tenants' conference of 1850, 17 n.; and origin of Brigade, 22 and n.; personality, 24–25, 125–9, 155; and Tenant League, 24, 32 n.; advocates obstruction, 24; opinion of Sadleir, 25; relations with Keogh, 27 and n., 102, 125; and Catholic Defence Association, 29 n.; and permanent secretaryship of Catholic Defence Association, 33 n.; and censure motion on Lord Clarendon, 34; and government patronage, 47; and coercion of tenants by landlords, 67, 125; and local clergy, 76; re-elected 1852, 85, 103; and Tenant League conference of 1852, 87, 88, 93, 125, 129; and Friends of Religious Equality, 88, 89; and Disraeli's budget, 97; motion on Established Church, 99, 144; importance in independent party, 124, 141, 176; denounces Keogh and Sadleir, 125; introduces land bill, 136; quarrels with Bowyer, 129, 137; quarrels with Gray and Cantwell, 129, 137; criticizes Maguire, 129, 153; leadership in 1856–7, 138, 156; unseated, 139, 156; proposal that he should be chosen as formal leader of party, 140, 156; wealth, 140; criticizes a government appointment, 144; and interpretation of party pledge, 149; attitude in final split of party, 154, 155; jubilation at Tipperary by-el., 164; and election for Mayo 1857, 171, 173; mentioned, 23, 51, 167.
Moriarty, D., Bishop of Kerry, 115.
Mullinahone, 6 n.
Murphy, Sgt. F. S., M.P., 48, 51, 89, 148 and n.
Murphy, M., Bishop of Ferns, 112.

Murphy, T., Bishop of Cloyne, 111.
Murray, D., Archbishop of Dublin, 27, 111, 113.

Naas, Lord, M.P., Chief Secretary, 34, 56; and Kildare by-el., 34, 35; mentioned, 55, 58, 103.
Napier, J., M.P., and his land bills, 15, 56, 94, 95, 130, 135.
Nation, owner, 10; attitude to Brigade, 31; advocates an independent party, 42; condemns the proclamation, 58; and defection of Keogh and Sadleir, 107, 108; criticizes Archbishop Cullen, 136; attitude on final split of party, 154; traces rise of a new electoral interest, 172.
National Council, of Catholic hierarchy, 114, 121, 122.
Newcastle, Duke of, 45 n., 100.
Newman, Very Rev. J. H., 10, 113, 115.
New Ross, borough, in gen. el. 1852, 42 n., 51, 64, 74, 77, 86, 112; in by-el. 1856, 163, 170.
Newry, borough, in gen. el. 1852, 69, 77, 82, 84.
Newtownards, 84 n.
Newtownbarry, 6 n.
Norreys, Sir D., M.P., 156.
Northland, Viscount, M.P., 15 n.
Nugent, Sir P., M.P., 51 n.

O'Brien, C., M.P., 90.
O'Brien, Conor Cruise, 146.
O'Brien, D., Bishop of Waterford, 123.
O'Brien, P., M.P., 164.
O'Brien, Sir T., M.P., 32 n., 33 n.
Obstruction, rejected by Brigade, 24.
O'Connell, Daniel, 9, 108, 111, 141, 167.
O'Connell, John, M.P., 9, 12, 28.
O'Connell, Maurice, M.P., 28, 83.
O'Connell, Morgan John, M.P., 47.
O'Connor, T. P., 26.
O'Donohoe, the, M.P., 139, 154, 164, 174.
O'Ferrall, R. More, M.P., 51.
O'Flaherty, A., M.P., and Brigade, 29 n., 32 n., 33 n., 35 n.; ally of Sadleir, 108; brother absconds, 162; guilty of bribery, 167.
O'Flaherty, E., 162.
Offaly, *see* King's County.
O'Neill, Lord, 75.
O'Reilly, M., M.P., 165.

INDEX

O'Shea, Rev. T., 6, 112, 113, 117, 118; see also Callan, curates of,
Ossory, E. Walsh, Bishop of, 112, 113, 117, 118, 123.

Pakington, Sir J., M.P., 101 n.
Palmer, Sir R., 67, 68, 173 n.
Palmer, W. H. R., M.P., 173.
Palmerston, Viscount, M.P., saves Derby government, 94; in Aberdeen government, 97; criticized by Lucas, 131; Prime Minister, 143; independent party during his government, 143–51; defeated, 151; hostility to land reform, 151; Italian policy, 152–3.
'Papal aggression', the, 19, 23, 35.
Parnell, C. S., 24, 108, 146.
Patronage, government, 45–47, 114, 146–7, 168, 176.
Peel, Sir R., 18.
Peelite party, numbers in Parliament, 14, 15, 90, 91, 93; attitude to tenants, 15; and Ecclesiastical Titles Bill, 21, 98; splinter-group of Conservatives, 40; and Derby government, 94, 96; support appointment of Blackburne, 98; Keogh and, 104; Levinge and, 174.
Pius IX, 118, 119.
Pledges, and Young Ireland, 10; and Tenant League, 13; and Catholic Defence Association, 30; imposed by adoption meetings, gen. el. 1852, 51; resolution adopted by Tenant League conference of 1852, 88; resolution adopted by Friends of Religious Equality, 89; interpretation of, 94, 96, 144, 148–55; broken by Keogh and Sadleir, 100–7; help to break up party, 155, 176; possible alternatives, 156–7; Ulstermen condemn, 159; in gen. el. 1857, 165.
'Pope's Brass Band', the, 24.
Portarlington, borough, in gen. el. 1852, 75.
Portarlington, Marquess of, 75.
Potter, R., M.P., 168.
Power, Dr. M., M.P., 17, 45.
Power, N., M.P., 89.
Presbyterian M.P.s, 14, 44 and n.; demand for, 44, 85.
Presbyterian ministers, 8, 12, 84.
Presbyterians, and Catholic Defence Association, 31; and gen. el. 1852, 44, 84; and Tenant League conference of 1852, 86; and defection of Keogh and Sadleir, 107, 158; favour Aberdeen government, 159; and Catholics, 159.
Proclamation, the royal, of June 1852, 57; its effects, 58–59, 81, 165.
Professions, the, and parliamentary candidates, 49 and n.; and M.P.s, 90 and n.
Propaganda, Congregation of, 118.
Property qualification, for M.P.s, 47.
Protestants, see Established Church, Presbyterians.
Provincial synods, 114, 121.

Quaid, Rev. P., 76.
Queen's colleges, 18, 50 n.
Queen's County, in gen. el. 1857, 169.

Radicals, 14, 21, 96.
Railways, government aid for, 56.
Ranfurly, Earl of, 75.
Raphoe, P. M'Gettigan, Bishop of, 113.
Redington, Sir T., 74, 99.
Reform Act, Irish, of 1850, 50, 63.
Reform Bill of 1859, 153.
Reform Club, 15.
Religious Freedom and Equality, Friends of, see Friends of Religious Freedom and Equality.
Rentoul, Rev. A., 159.
Rents, 4, 8, 166.
Repeal of the Union, movement for, 8–9, 10, 40, 81, 111.
Repeal party, 10, 16, 23, 141.
Reynolds, J., M.P., personality, 25; and Catholic Defence Association, 29 and n.; and Tenant League, 32 n.; and policy of independence, 36; loses seat, 85.
Roche, E. B., M.P., 87, 88.
Roden, Earl of, 96.
Rome, Lucas's appeal to, 117–20, 135, 136.
Roscommon, county, 5; in gen. el. 1852, 68; in gen. el. 1857, 175.
Royal proclamation, see Proclamation, the royal.
Russell, Lord John, M.P., Prime Minister, 14; suspects Irish clergy, 19 n.; Durham letter, 20; resigns 1851, 22; resigns 1852, 39; unpopularity in Ireland, 51, 58, 98; in Aberdeen government, 97; in conflict with Irish

INDEX

members of government, 99; disavows Sadleir's alleged statement, 103; his government attentive to Ireland, 143; Italian policy, 152–3; mentioned, 18, 35, 36, 47.

Sadleir, James, M.P., 108, 150, 162, 164.
Sadleir, John, M.P., personality, 25–26; and Catholic Defence Association, 29 and n.; and Tenant League, 32 n.; founds *Telegraph*, 33; attacked by Lucas, 36; and policy of independence, 36; and breaking-up of entail, 37 n.; re-elected in gen. el. 1852, 85; and Tenant League conference of 1852, 93, 100, 106; and Disraeli's budget, 97; takes office, 97, 125; judgement on his acceptance of office, 98–107, 146, 155; tenders resignation, 99; stands for re-election 1853, 105, 111, 112, 160; and conference of Friends of Religious Equality, 106; public reaction to his acceptance of office, 107, 162; in Ulster, 158; personal following in Parliament, 108; limited effect of his desertion, 109, 110, 124, 175; attitude of clergy to, 111, 112, 170; resignation, 161; suicide, 161; effect on public opinion, 162–3; wealth, 173; mentioned, 64 n., 90, 129, 153; see also *Telegraph*.
Scully, F., M.P., 17 n., 29 n., 32 n., 33 n., 108.
Scully, V., M.P., 51, 89, 108, 150 and n., 175.
Seymour, Sir H., M.P., 15 n.
Shee, Sgt. W., M.P., offered Longford seat, 50; elected in gen. el. 1852, 86; and Tenant League conference of 1852, 87, 93; and Derby government, 95, 97; and land bills, 95, 96, 103, 125, 135 and n., 136; quarrels with independent party, 116, 134–6; supported by Bishop of Ossory, 117, 123; importance in party, 124, 141; personality, 125, 141; and motion on Established Church, 144; and interpretation of party pledge, 148, 149; mentioned, 51, 68 n.
Sheil, R. L., M.P., 45.
Shirley, E. P., 8.
Sixmilebridge, 69, 70.
Skreen, 77.

Slattery, M., Archbishop of Cashel, 113 and n., 118.
Sligo, borough, in gen. el. 1852, 46, 48, 64, 70, 71, 73; in by-el. 1853, 112, 160, 161, 170; in by-el. 1856, 163; in gen. el. 1857, 122.
Sligo, county, in gen. el. 1852, 52 n., 61, 68, 69, 70, 77–78, 80 n., 82; in gen. el. 1857, 122, 175.
Sligo, Marquess of, 75.
Somers, J. P., M.P., 46, 71, 73.
Somerville, Sir W., M.P., 27, 45.
Statutes, ecclesiastical, 114, 121.
Stockport riots, 59; their effects in Ireland, 59–62, 71, 81, 85, 91, 165.
Stonor, H., 144 and n.
Sullivan, A. M., 26.
Sullivan, M., M.P., 16.
Swift, R., M.P., in gen. el. 1852, 69, 77–78; and Lucas's death, 119; disagrees with Gray and Cantwell, 137; estimate of independent party's strength, 142, 143 and n.; attitude in final split of party, 154; loses seat, 175.
Swinford, 70.
Synods, Catholic provincial, 114, 121.

Tablet, owner, 11; violent tone, 11, 159; undercut by *Telegraph*, 33; advocates an independent party, 42; condemns the proclamation, 58; blames Derby government for Stockport riots, 59; condemns Sadleir and Keogh, 107; mellows in tone, 133; criticizes Archbishop Cullen, 136; attitude in final split of party, 154.
Taylor, Lt.-Col. T. E., M.P., 71.
Telegraph, founded, 33; replies to attacks on Brigade, 35; condemns the proclamation, 58; condemns landlord intimidation, 63; defends Keogh and Sadleir, 103, 107.
Telegraph, Weekly, 42, 142, 143.
Tenant League, founded, 12; decision to contest elections, 13, 14, 31; and parties in 1850, 14–17; county demonstrations, 17; comparison with Catholic Defence Association, 30; support for, declining, 31, 38, 85; agreement with Brigade, 32; suspicions of Brigade among, 33; influence on building up of an independent party, 37; guides public opinion, 41, 92; finds

INDEX

candidates, 42; contests by-els., 50; conference of 1852, 86–88, 92, 100, 101, 106, 109, 125, 129, 147, 148; land bills, 95, 96, 135–6, 140, 144; censures Keogh and Sadleir, 107; conference of 1853, 109, 135, 158; Archbishop Cullen subscribes to, 111; demonstration at Callan, 117; restriction on Meath clergy attending meetings, 121; Moore quarrels with Gray and Cantwell at meeting of, 129; conference of 1854, 135; Gray and Cantwell's plan for improving, 136–7; they resign, 137; estimates strength of independent party, 142, 143; continues to pledge itself to Crawford's bill, 151; and second Derby government, 152, 153; last meeting, 154; Ulster members abandon, 159; petitions in support of, 163.

Tenant protection societies, 6, 11, 36 n., 117.

Tenant-right associations, 8, 11, 40 n., 84.

Tenantry, the, grievances of, 1–8, 91; mostly Liberal, 39, 42; do not produce M.P.s, 49; their condition improving, 166.

Tenants' conference of 1850, 12.

Tenants' societies in 1847, 5 and n.

Thurles, synod of, 19, 20.

Tipperary, county, 6, 174; in gen. el. 1852, 48, 52 n., 57, 61, 71; in by-el. 1857, 138, 164, 170; in gen. el. 1857, 174, 175; clergy of, 118.

Tipperary Joint-Stock Bank, 162, 166.

Towneley, C., M.P., 48, 72.

Tralee, borough, in gen. el. 1852, 40 n.; in by-el. 1853, 160, 161.

Tuam, 6 n.

Tuam, Archbishop of, see MacHale, J.

Tuam, clergy of diocese of, 36, 118, 154, 171.

Tuam, synod, 121.

Tubbercurry, 78.

Tyrone, county, in gen. el. 1852, 41, 84.

Ullathorne, W. B., Bishop of Birmingham, 19.

Ulster, land system in, 3, 6–8; results of gen. el. 1852 in, 84, 159; collapse of support for independent party in, 158–60; see also Presbyterians.

Ulster custom, 7, 160.

Underwood, T. N., 44 n., 159.

University education, as a religious issue, 18, 50 n., 95.

Urquhart, W. P., M.P., 51 n.

Vaughan, D., Bishop of Killaloe, 111.

Villiers, C. P., M.P., 93.

Waldron, L., M.P., 164.

Wallis, J. E., 129.

Walpole, S. H., M.P., 57, 59, 60, 95 and n.

Walsh, Rev. J., 74.

Walsh, E., Bishop of Ossory, 112, 113, 117, 118, 123.

Walshe, J., Bishop of Kildare and Leighlin, 122.

Waterford, Bishop of, see Foran, N., O'Brien, D.

Waterford, city, in gen. el. 1852, 52 and n., 76; in gen. el. 1857, 123.

Waterford, county, in gen. el. 1852, 61.

Weekly Telegraph, 42, 142, 143; see also *Telegraph*.

Westmeath, county, in gen. el. 1852, 40, 71, 76; in gen. el. 1857, 122, 164, 171, 172, 174.

Wexford, county, 4, 6, 12; in gen. el. 1852, 41 n., 48, 82, 83; in gen. el. 1857, 122; clergy of, 118.

Whigs, of British Isles in general, 14, 94, 96.

Whigs, Irish, characteristics, 16, 43–44; leanings towards, among nominal independents, 49, 148; Liberal constituency organizations hostile to, 52, 53; strong in Kerry, 54; and results of gen. el. 1852, 83, 90 and n., 91; attend Liberal meeting, 13 Dec. 1852, 156; re-emerging after 1852, 169, 172.

Whips, government, 47.

Wicklow, county, in gen. el. 1852, 82.

Wilberforce, H. W., 33, 34.

Windgap, 6 n.

Wiseman, N., Cardinal Archbishop of Westminster, 20, 132, 154.

Youghal, borough, in gen. el. 1852, 82 and n.

Young, Sir J., M.P., 15 and n., 21 n., 97, 102, 147.

Young Ireland, 9, 10, 11, 115, 116.

PRINTED IN
GREAT BRITAIN
AT THE
UNIVERSITY PRESS
OXFORD
BY
CHARLES BATEY
PRINTER
TO THE
UNIVERSITY